The Poetical Works

of

William Henry Drummond

With an Introduction by

Louis Fréchette

And an Appreciation by

Neil Munro

G. P. Putnam's Sons
New York and London
The Knickerbocker Press

In Memory of William Henry Drummond

BY S. WEIR MITCHELL, M.D., LL.D.

PEACE to his poet soul.   Full well he knew
    To sing for those who know not how to
praise
The woodsman's life, the farmer's patient toil,
The peaceful drama of laborious days.

He made his own the thoughts of simple men,
And with the touch that makes the world akin
A welcome guest of lonely cabin homes,
Found, too, no heart he could not enter in.

The toilworn doctor, women, children, men,
The humble heroes of the lumber drives,
Love, laugh, or weep along his peopled verse,
Blithe 'mid the pathos of their meagre lives.

While thus the poet-love interpreted,
He left us pictures no one may forget—
Courteau, Batiste, Camille mon frère and best,
The good brave curé, he of Calumette.

IN MEMORIAM

With nature as with man at home, he loved
The silent forest and the birches' flight
Down the white peril of the rapids' rush,
And the cold glamour of your Northern night.

Some mystery of genius haunts his page.
Some wonder secret of the poet's spell
Died with this master of the peasant thought.
Peace to your Northland singer, and farewell!

William Henry Drummond

THE name of Canada to me, as to many of
my race and age, has a romantic charm
that does not rise from any great historical as-
sociations, but survives from early youth, the
true period of natural magic, of unquestioning
illusions, when great men and great deeds have
less power to stir the imaginative faculty than
a hint, in some trumpery fiction, of wild, free
spaces of the unspoiled world. Not to pre-
natal glory does the memory of youth go back,
as Wordsworth thought; not to some Platonic
Eden where, in a previous incarnation we were
as angels in a sinless garden; but to the early,
primitive, and essentially mundane valleys,
plains, and hills that knew the toils and wander-
ings of our ancestors. It is the unfenced, un-
inhabited, and tractless areas our subliminal
memory recalls; the lonely morning forest, the
shouting cataract with no name, lakes undis-
covered, hunts perilously followed, evening fires
with their ashes deep below the mould of cen-
turies. No savage tribe with rude camp equi-
page set forth at dawn from the sheltering edge

of pines, pursuing the windings of the river through the mist, without, in some sensitive heart, a pang of wonder and surmise which we in our blood inherit. We have all come from the tribes, trailing no clouds of glory, but still with rags of zest in things adventurous, still capable of a thrill at the thought of phantoms and of dangers now no longer waiting us on our morning march along the clean-swept pavements of a thousand cities.

It was natural that Canada should evoke the visionary romance of our youth in Scotland, for yet the more favoured of us saw surviving scraps of that ancient unpossessed, uncultivated, and untamed world whereof Scotland and Canada alike were parts. In both lands Nature wore much the same aspect; clothing the bluffs with pine, the plains with northern wild-flowers, spilling her streams down precipices, filling the mountain crevices with snow or mist, or the creeks and bays with the same Atlantic Ocean. The very cold of Canada in winter helped to render her familiar—were our happiest hours not those when the North wind whistled and our lakes were ice? We knew that, with the frost, to men came grandeurs of endurance and reserves of zest incommunicable to the offspring of the South.

Then, too, only a tiny period, as time goes in

History—less than two hundred years—separated us in our Highland life from many of the customs of the Indian. We had still—though hung upon the wall—the weapons of our forefathers, and our fireside tales were yet of native war-trails, forays, feuds, old passions, and alarms. Little wonder that the Red River settlers from Sutherlandshire found the aboriginals less strange and inimical than the whites, or that the great North-West should prove so hospitable to the Gaelic winterers from Hudson's Bay! And one last feature especially, of the New World rendered it more alluring to our youth—our folk were there! They had blazed trails and builded flourishing communities, they occupied the outmost forts and knew the land from sea to sea; they had given their names to the mightiest rivers.

I have been through Canada at a time when the early affections for things unseen and enterprises unexperienced are usually worn rather thin; when the "radiance that was once so bright" is replaced by

> ——a sober colouring from an eye
> That hath kept watch o'er man's mortality,

and though the views which I had previously formed of the country and its life had necessarily to undergo some process of readjustment, I am happy to say it yet retains an infinite glamour and romance. For the preservation of this fond illusion—as the realist may consider it—I owe much to the good fortune of knowing one man who, after living nearly all his life in Canada, had not discarded a single jot of his youthful vision of her as a land magnificent and romantic; a man for whom the Redskin or the half-breed still was a being not to be despised; for whom the woodman, the trapper, and the pioneer were glorified by all the antique circumstances of their lives. The forest for William Henry Drummond, as for me, had not relinquished any of its early power to rouse half-awed expectancy, to challenge, to allure. A Celt in every artery of his being, it was not for him, as it never was for me, by fauns and fairies that the thickets, glades, or verges of the solitary lakes were inhabited, but by the creatures of his boyish worship, by Leather-Stocking rather than the dryads.

No alien could doubt the persistance of romance in Canada, who saw the joy of Drummond in it, his delight in the very things that thrilled in the books of youth; in guides and *voyageurs*, in camps, and portages, and canoes. He was himself a sportsman, and the woods and rivers, therefore, had a fascination for another portion of his nature, but rightly or wrongly, I fancy his love of the wilds and his sense of kinship with the courageous, hardy, and enduring men he found in sporting camps, were more often the attraction of the Laurentian lakes and woods than the fishing and the shooting to be got there.

It was not in Montreal where he practised medicine that he found the inspiration of his written work; poems associated with the life of towns and cities are almost wholly absent from his books, for his most impressionable years had been spent elsewhere—in Bord-à-Plouffe, on the banks of the Rivière des Prairies, at Marbleton, and Stornoway near Lake Megantic. From Ireland, his direct heredity, he probably took no more than a childish memory which gave a tinge of Celtic pensiveness to his later years. He was born near Mohill, County Leitrim, on April 13, 1854, and taken by his parents to the Dominion while yet a boy. At Bord-à-Plouffe, where he worked for a while in the telegraph service, he was in a great centre of the lumber trade and came for the first time in contact with the *habitant* and the *voyageur*, a class of men for whom his destiny was to be expositor. Their *chansons* gave to his first literary essays the mould and spirit which were to distinguish the greater part of his poetical work. Later, he returned to study in the High School, passing thence to McGill College and on to Bishop's Medical College, where he graduated in 1884. If academic prizes went for athletic feats, the Irishman would have achieved the highest distinctions in his college years, but in truth he won no medals save on the college campus. Of such are good doctors made, and often poets also! His first medical appointment was that of House Surgeon at the Montreal Western Hospital, but at an early date he established a physician's practice at Stornoway, and later at Knowlton, where the mountains, glens, woods, and lakes of Brome ministered to every aspect of his love for nature. What was the character of his duties there may be gathered from his pictures of "The Canadian Country Doctor" and "Ole Docteur Fiset." At the end of four years, he returned to practise in Montreal, and, in 1894, he married Miss May Harvey, a lady with whom he became acquainted while she and her father were on a visit from the West Indies to the Dominion.

On his marriage with one who shared his own romantic and poetic nature, and was, further, dowered with the finest literary sensibilities, Drummond's muse, aforetime somewhat shy and fugitive, assumed more confidence and zeal. He was already known in Canada and throughout the United States as the author of "The Wreck of the 'Julie Plante,'" a poem at no time greatly valued by himself, but holding some essential charm for the very class of men it pictured, no indecisive proof that a poet has a definite call. He had written other poems in the dialect of the French-Canadian *habitant*, hitherto the medium of buffoonery in verse, but dignified by him to graver purposes, and his own recitation of these poems at occasional public gatherings earned for him the name of "Poet of the *Habitant*" before he had published a single book.

In an old house in Mountain Street, Montreal, which had sheltered Jefferson Davis during the first years after the American war, the poems for Drummond's first book were written rather for domestic entertainment than for the world, and at the solicitation of his wife and brothers, the manuscript of "The Habitant" was sent to the publishers of New York. Its merits were discerned by the Putnams, and the book, beautifully illustrated by Frederick Simpson Coburn, whose drawings marvellously caught the atmosphere and spirit of the poems, immediately proved successful. Drummond's place in the highest rank of North American bards was assured. He was hailed by the Poet Laureate of Canada, Louis Fréchette, as a new "pathfinder in the land of song," and the credentials of such a French-Canadian dispelled all fears that the fidelity to the dialect, portraiture, and foibles of the *habitant* might prove unpleasant to the race and class delineated.

In truth, the work had no fonder admiration than with the *habitants* themselves. They found in it not only a scrupulous representation of their racial life, customs, and character, but the attitude of a sympathetic and admiring friend. A man of the tenderest sentiment, of the finest tact, devoid of any cankering notion of superiority, he never wrote a line but in affection, and the humour, wit, and pathos of his verses carried the irresistible conviction of a great and generous soul. Of ridicule he was temperamentally incapable; on the human weaknesses of his characters he held his judgment in suspense; he gave to Anglo-Saxon Canadians a new respect for their French compatriots. Till then, French-Canadian minstrelsy, for the outside world, was represented so far as the *habitant* and the *voyageur* were concerned, by academic English renderings of the old *chansons;* it was Drummond's· place to make the living *habitant* and *voyageur* articulate in the patois which distinguished them, and yet the naïveté and the natural magic of the old régime, of "À La Claire Fontaine" and "En Roulant ma Boulé" are reproduced, transfigured strangely, in the language of the modern *Canayen* of lumberers and peasants of to-day as Drummond gave them voice in "Johnnie Courteau" or "The Curé of Calumette."

Drummond's increasing reputation as a man

of letters in no way affected the conscientious discharge of his professional work; his practice was not permitted to lose his unremitting attention, however far his imagination might wander or however briskly his pen might run in his scanty leisure hours as a physician. Rich and poor alike among his patients shared his consideration, and it is related of him that on one occasion, when two calls came simultaneously, one from a wealthy man, and the other from a poor carter from whom a fee might scarcely be expected, he chose to attend the latter first, saying "The rich can get any number of doctors, but poor Pat has only me." Mrs. Drummond, in the touching biographical sketch she prefixes to his posthumous book *The Great Fight*, says:

"Many of his patients declared that just to see Doctor Drummond did them good, and grumbled at the scarcity of his visits, but he, never dreaming that he had anything other than a prescription to bestow, said: 'What 's the use of paying professional visits to people for whom I can do nothing more? I might just as well steal the money out of their pockets.' On the other hand, if the case was a serious one, it absorbed him, and his attention to it was unremitting. At such times he was with difficulty persuaded to take proper rest or food, and would often leave the dinner-table to search his book-shelves for yet another authority on the disease he was fighting; then he would return with the book to the table, and if it contained what he sought, his plate would be pushed aside, and, in spite of remonstrances from the rest of us, he was off and away to his 'case' once more."

For several years he occupied the chair of Medical Jurisprudence in his Alma Mater, in which position he earned and kept the affection and confidence of students and professors alike. In 1901 appeared his second volume of poems, *Johnnie Courteau*, and in the following year the University of Toronto conferred on him the degree of LL.D. He was subsequently elected Fellow of the Royal Society of Literature of England, and, later, one of the Royal Society of Canada. These honours, with the degree of D.C.L., of Bishop's College, Lennoxville, sat so lightly on him that I confess I was unaware of them till his death. In England he was simply "*Habitant* Drummond."

It was in the year last-mentioned that I met · him. He was paying his first visit to the mother-land since he had left it as a child, and Scotland was included in his itinerary. A man, it seemed to me, less physically suggestive of a poet, it was difficult to conceive. There was nothing fragile about the build of William Henry Drummond—

a massive yet athletic figure seemingly endowed with the health and sinews of a wrestler, emanating airs of active life and the open country; the last man to suspect of literary vigils and of enervating dalliance with the sisters of the sacred well. And yet I would not for the world have had him otherwise. The poetry of Canada, particularly the poetry of the *voyageur*, should not, in common decency, be made by delicate and myopic men; to such, indeed, the heart and mystery of the child of nature, reticent and shy, are rarely to be revealed. If I had had doubts— the usual journalistic doubts—of the poet's likelihood to express the lowly life of Eastern Canadian country places with authority, they would have been immediately dispelled, for here was unmistakably a plain man's man with whom it would be joyous to go fishing. I put him to the test with young folk at that period full of the book romance of Canada, and apt to think the most heroic qualities were requisite in every man with his badge the Maple Leaf, and my visitor came grandly up to the most fastidious standard. For them he clinched the matter—Canada was genuine; the moose, and the wapiti, and the bear were not mere beasts of myth like the dragons on our coinage; the trapper was still in Ungava, and the red canoe was yet upon the waters. To a child his unsophistication and trustworthiness

were instantly apparent; he was himself an unspoiled and eternal boy!

I incline to think Drummond was never a
bookish man; at all events, like Wordsworth, he
was certainly no bookworm; and his conversation
having rapturously dealt with three or four
modern poets who were at the time his deities,
tangentially escaped as soon as possible into
affairs of prose; of nature, dogs, and angling;
children, weather, travel, politics, and nation-
ality. He was plainly the kind of man to be
fascinated by any novel phase of the wild and
vagabondish in mankind; his eye was ever alert
for racial idiosyncrasy. I went with him on a
flying visit to my native Highlands of Argyll;
the woods of Inveraray roused his admiration,
—I see him still, the good physician Melampus,
walk under the hoary oaks of Easachosain,—
but it was, I think, by gipsy pipers, shaggy, wild
rogues and ragged, that he was most permanently
impressed.

It was, however, especially to revisit Ireland
he had come across the sea, and after some days
in Scotland he set out for the scenes of childhood.
He got as far as Dublin, and here, as I have
written elsewhere, something came to him—an
apprehension possibly of the fact that the actual
Ireland was not the Ireland of his warm imagination, that the "first, fine, careless rapture" of his

childhood in Leitrim could never be recaptured—
the saddest of discoveries for middle age. He
came back to Glasgow and went home to Canada
without accomplishing the purpose that had
brought him three thousand miles.

In the following year, I brought a long tour
in Canada to a termination with a week in the
society of Dr. and Mrs. Drummond, in the at-
tractive homes of his brothers George and
Thomas, on the lake-bespangled property of St.
Bruno, and later at the sporting camp of the
Laurentian Club on Lac La Péche. With the men
and women of that holiday community among
primeval woods, it was obvious that the poet was
the supreme inspiring friend and favourite, high
priest of revels, councillor and high grand con-
sultant upon all projects and contemplated
exploits. Not even the old "Commodore,"
Director Parker, had more potent sway with the
Laurentians. The French-Canadian guides and
boatmen were on the most affectionate and even
playful terms with "the Doctor"; it was always
he who could most easily induce them to indulge
the expectant tenderfoot with song or dance.
It was then I found that though full of the
lore of the hunter, Drummond had long since
lost his love of the gun. He preferred to see
the creatures of the wood inviolate, and I shall
not readily forget his indignation and contempt

for anything savouring of unsportsmanlike slaughter.

In 1905, Drummond joined his brothers in the exploitation of new mines at Cobalt, northern Ontario, and, released from his medical work in Montreal, he took up the active personal superintendence of operations which were by no means uncongenial to him, since they were pursued in a region new to him, of magnificent lakes and forests. The fall of the year saw the publication of his last completed work, *The Voyageur*, which met with the same great vogue and high eulogium that attended its predecessors. It looked as if in worldly prospects and in literary fame the best of his life was still before him, but in truth life smiled but to deceive, and the end came as narrated in the memoir of his widow:

"It had been his intention to spend Easter Day of 1907 with us in Montreal, but hearing that smallpox had broken out in the camp at Cobalt, he hurried away a week earlier. The night of his departure from Montreal he seemed possessed by a strange and overwhelming reluctance to go. 'I don't know why I hate to go away so much this time,' he said, and I, thinking that his health was not as good as usual, would have persuaded him to stay at home, but no, his duty lay there with the sick of the little camp, and bidding us an unusually solemn good-bye, he left the home he was never more to enter. It was just a week from this time that he was stricken with cerebral hemorrhage, and on the morning of April 6th, after five unconscious days, passed to the beyond.''

Drummond's grave on the side of Mount Royal has upon its stone a phrase of Moira O'Neill's that has the secret of his wide appeal and his endearment to the readers of the English-speaking world:

> Youth 's for an hour
> Beauty 's a flower,
> But love is the jewel that wins the world.

Among the poets of the British Empire, he holds a place unique. The poetry and romance of the North American continent have found, in one form or another, expression in the works of innumerable modern writers, struck, like him, by the natural grandeur of their country, the picturesque side of the struggle by which men subdue it to the purposes of civilisation, and the gallantry and devotion of humble lives. But the laureates of camp-fire, shack, and mine, too generally indulge a strident, even brutal, note which is never found in the poems of Drummond as collected in the present definitive edition.

WILLIAM HENRY DRUMMOND.

Melampus dwelt upon men: physician and sage,
  He served them, loving them, healing them, sick or
    maimed,
Or them that frenzied in some delirious rage
  Outran the measure, his juice of the woods reclaimed.
He played on men, as his master, Phœbus, on strings
  Melodious: as the God did he strive and check,
Through love exceeding a simple love of the things
  That glide in the grasses and rubble of woody wreck.

NEIL MUNRO.

Introduction

ON me demande, pour ce charmant volume,
un mot de préface en français; le voici:
Quand, en 1863, je publiai mon premier recueil
de poésies—écrites au collège, pour la plupart,
—le grand poète américain Longfellow eut la
flatteuse bienveillance de m'appeler *The pathfinder of a new land of song.*

Avec mille fois plus de raison puis-je aujourd'-
hui passer le compliment à mon sympathique
confrère et ami, l'auteur de ce livre; car, si
jamais quelqu'un, chez nous, a mérité le titre de
pathfinder of a new land of song, c'est assurément
lui.

Non seulement il a découvert le champ, la
clairière, la vallée fertile et encore inexplorée;
il en a fait l'exploitation à sa manière, avec des
outils et des moyens de son invention; et, fier
de sa conquête, il laisse, de son épaule robuste,
tomber à nos pieds le fruit de son travail, la
gerbe plantureuse aux ors vierges, à l'arome
sauvage, aux savoureuses promesses, toute
fraîche et toute crissante dans sa rusticité saine.

N'est-elle pas, en effet, d'une originalité peu

commune, l'idée de prendre un pauvre illettré, de le présenter comme un type national à part, de lui mettre aux lèvres une langue qui n'est pas la sienne et qu'il ne connaît qu' à demi; d'en faire en même temps un personnage bon, doux, aimable, honnête, intelligent et droit, l'esprit en éveil, le cœur plein d'une poésie native stimulant son patriotisme, jetant un rayon lumineux dans son modeste intérieur, berçant ses heures rêveuses de souvenirs lointains et mélancoliques?

Et cela sans que jamais, dans ce portrait d'un nouveau genre, le plus subtil des critiques puisse surprendre nulle part le coup de crayon de la caricature!

Dans ses inimitables contes villageois, George Sand a peint les paysans du Berry sous des dehors très intéressants. Elle nous les montre même d'un sentiment très affiné dans leur simplicité naïve et leur cordiale bonhomie. En somme, elle en fait des natures, des tempéraments, quelque chose de typique, en même temps qu' harmonieux de teinte et de forme.

Mais George Sand faisait parler ses personnages dans la langue du pays, dans la langue de la chaumière, dans leur propre dialecte, enfin. Elle n'avait, pour ainsi dire, qu' à faire pénétrer le souffle de son talent sous le réseau de la phrase, pour animer celle-ci d'un reflet de lyrisme ou d'une vibration attendrie.

La tâche abordée par M. Drummond présentait un caractère beaucoup plus difficile.

Ici, le poète avait bien, il est vrai, le milieu à saisir, placé, droit en face de son objectif. Il était assez familier avec ses acteurs pour les grouper avantageusement, en ménageant les effets d'ombres et de lumière. Il est naturellement assez artiste pour ne rien négliger de ce qui ajoute du pittoresque à la pose; surtout, il connaissait à fond le type à reproduire, ses mœurs, ses passions, ses sentiments, ses penchants, ses superstitions et ses faiblesses.

Mais comment, sans tomber dans la charge ou la bouffonnerie, faire parler systématiquement à ses personnages une langue étrangère, forcément incorrecte dans la bouche de quelqu'un qui l'a apprise par oreille, sans savoir lire même dans sa propre langue?

La tentative était hardie; mais on sait que le succès a un faible pour les audacieux.

Dans son étude des Canadiens-français, M. Drummond a trouvé le moyen d'éviter un écueil qui aurait semblé inévitable pour tout autre que pour lui. Il est resté vrai, sans tomber dans la vulgarité, et piquant sans verser dans le grotesque.

Qu'il mette en scène le gros fermier fier de son bien ou de ses filles à marier, le vieux médecin de campagne ne comptant plus ses états de service, le jeune amoureux qui rêve au clair de la lune, le vieillard qui repasse en sa mémoire la longue suite des jours révolus, le conteur de légendes, l'aventurier des "pays d'en haut," et même le Canadien exilé—le *Canadien errant*, comme dit la chanson populaire—qui croit toujours entendre résonner à son oreille le vague tintement des cloches de son village; que le récit soit plaisant ou pathétique, jamais la note ne sonne faux, jamais la bizarrerie ne dégénère en puérilité burlesque.

C'est là un tour de force comme il ne s'en fait pas souvent, et c'est avec enthousiasme que je tends la main à M. Drummond pour le féliciter de l'avon accompli.

Il a véritablement fait là œuvre de poète et d'artiste.

J'ajouterai qu'il a fait aussi œuvre de bon citoyen. Car le jour sous lequel il présente mes compatriotes illettrés ne peut manquer de valoir à ceux-ci—et partant à tout le reste de la nationalité—un accroissement désirable dans l'estime de nos compatriotes de langue anglaise, qui n'ont pas été à même de les étudier d'aussi près que M. Drummond.

La peinture qu'en fait le poète **est** on ne peut plus sympathique et juste; et de semblables procédés ne peuvent que cimenter l'union de cœur et n'esprit qui doit exister entre toutes

les fractions qui composent la grande famille
canadienne appelée à vivre et à prospérer sous
la même loi et le même drapeau.

En lisant les vers de M. Drummond, le Ca-
nadien-français sent que c'est là l'expression
d'une âme amie; et, à ce compte, je dois à
l'auteur plus que mes bravos, je lui dois en
même temps un chaleureux merci.

LOUIS FRÉCHETTE.

MONTRÉAL, 13 octobre 1897.

Preface

IN presenting to the public "The Habitant, and other French-Canadian Poems," I feel that my friends who are already, more or less, familiar with the work, understand that I have not written the verses as examples of a dialect, or with any thought of ridicule.

Having lived, practically, all my life, side by side with the French-Canadian people, I have grown to admire and love them, and I have felt that while many of the English-speaking public know perhaps as well as myself the French-Canadian of the cities, yet they have had little opportunity of becoming acquainted with the habitant, therefore I have endeavored to paint a few types, and in doing this, it has seemed to me that I could best attain the object in view by having my friends tell their own tales in their own way, as they would relate them to English-speaking auditors not conversant with the French tongue.

My good friend, Dr. Louis Fréchette, Poet Laureate, has, as a French-Canadian, kindly written an "Introductory" in his own graceful language, and I have to thank him above all for his recognition of the spirit which has actuated me in writing "dialect" verse.

WILLIAM HENRY DRUMMOND.

MONTREAL, September, 1897.

Contents

CONTENTS

CONTENTS

CONTENTS

CONTENTS

Remember when these tales you read
Of rude but honest "Canayen,"
That Joliet, La Verandrye,
La Salle, Marquette, and Hennepin
Were all true "Canayen" themselves—
And in their veins the same red stream:
The conquering blood of Normandie
Flowed strong, and gave America
Coureurs de bois and voyageurs
Whose trail extends from sea to sea!

The Habitant

D^E place I get born, me, is up on de reever
   Near foot of de rapide dat 's call Cheval
      Blanc
Beeg mountain behin' it, so high you can't
      climb it
   An' whole place she 's mebbe two honder
      arpent.

De fader of me, he was habitant farmer,
   Ma gran' fader too, an' hees fader also,
Dey don't mak' no monee, but dat is n't
      fonny
   For it 's not easy get ev'ryt'ing, you mus'
      know—

All de sam' dere is somet'ing dey got ev'ry-
      boddy,
   Dat 's plaintee good healt', wat de monee
      can't geev,
So I 'm workin' away dere, an' happy for stay
      dere
   On farm by de reever, so long I was leev.

O! dat was de place w'en de spring tam she 's
    comin',
  W'en snow go away, an' de sky is all blue—
W'en ice lef' de water, an' sun is get hotter
    An' back on de medder is sing de gou-
      glou—

W'en small sheep is firs' comin' out on de
    pasture,
  Deir nice leetle tail stickin' up on deir back,
Dey ronne wit' deir moder, an' play wit' each
    oder
    An' jomp all de tam jus' de sam' dey was
      crack—

An' ole cow also, she 's glad winter is over,
  So she kick herse'f up, an' start off on de
    race
Wit' de two-year-ole heifer, dat 's purty soon
    lef' her,
  W'y ev'ryt'ing 's crazee all over de place!

An' down on de reever de wil' duck is quackin'
  Along by de shore leetle san' piper ronne—
De bullfrog he 's gr-rompin' an' doré is jompin'
  Dey all got deir own way for mak' it de
    fonne.

But spring 's in beeg hurry, an' don't stay long
    wit' us
  An' firs' t'ing we know, she go off till nex'
    year,
Den bee commence hummin', for summer is
    comin'
  An' purty soon corn 's gettin' ripe on de ear.

Dat 's very nice tam for wake up on de
    morning
  An' lissen de rossignol sing ev'ry place,
Feel sout' win' a-blowin', see clover a-growin',
  An' all de worl' laughin' itself on de face.

Mos' ev'ry day raf' it is pass on de rapide
  De voyageurs singin' some ole chanson
'Bout girl down de reever—too bad dey mus'
    leave her,
But comin' back soon' wit' beaucoup d'argent.

An' den w'en de fall an' de winter come roun
    us
  An' bird of de summer is all fly away,
W'en mebbe she 's snowin' an' nort' win' is
    blowin'
An' night is mos' t'ree tam so long as de
    day.

You t'ink it was bodder de habitant farmer?
  Not at all—he is happy an' feel satisfy,
An' cole may las' good w'ile, so long as de wood-
      pile
  Is ready for burn on de stove by an' bye.

W'en I got plaintee hay put away on de stable
  So de sheep an' de cow, dey got no chance to
      freeze,
An' de hen all togedder—I don't min' de
      wedder—
  De nort' win' may blow jus' so moche as she
      please.

An' some cole winter night how I wish you can
      see us,
  W'en I smoke on de pipe, an' de ole woman
      sew
By de stove of T'ree Reever—ma wife's fader
      geev her
  On day we get marry, dat 's long tam ago—

De boy an' de girl, dey was readin' it's lesson,
  De cat on de corner she 's bite heem de pup,
Ole "Carleau" he 's snorin' an' beeg stove is
      roarin'
  So loud dat I 'm scare purty soon she bus' up.

4

Philomene—dat 's de oldes'—is sit on de winder
   An' kip jus' so quiet lak wan leetle mouse,
She say de more finer moon never was shiner—
   Very fonny, for moon is n't dat side de house.

But purty soon den, we hear foot on de outside,
   An' some wan is place it hees han' on de latch,
Dat 's Isidore Goulay, las' fall on de Brulé
   He 's tak' it firs' prize on de grand ploughin'
      match.

Ha! ha! Philomene!—dat was smart trick you
      play us
   Come help de young feller tak' snow from
      hees neck,
Dere 's not'ing for hinder you come off de winder
   W'en moon you was look for is come, I
      expec'—

Isidore, he is tole us de news on de parish
   'Bout hees Lajeunesse Colt—travel two forty,
      sure,
'Bout Jeremie Choquette, come back from
      Woonsocket
   An' t'ree new leetle twin on Madame Vail
      lancour'.

But nine o'clock strike, an' de chil'ren is sleepy,
   Mese'f an' ole woman can't stay up no more

So alone by de fire—'cos dey say dey ain't tire—
  We lef' Philomene an' de young Isidore.

I s'pose dey be talkin' beeg lot on de kitchen
  'Bout all de nice moon dey was see on de sky,
For Philomene 's takin' long tam get awaken
  Nex' day, she 's so sleepy on bote of de eye.

Dat 's wan of dem ting's, ev'ry tam on de
      fashion,
  An' 'bout nices' t'ing dat was never be seen.
Got not'ing for say me—I spark it sam' way
      me
  W'en I go see de moder ma girl Philomene.

We leev very quiet 'way back on de contree
  Don't put on sam style lak de big village,
W'en we don't get de monee you t'ink dat is
      fonny
  An' mak' plaintee sport on de Bottes Sau-
      vages.

But I tole you—dat 's true—I don't go on de
      city
  If you geev de fine house an' beaucoup
      d'argent—
I rader be stay me, an' spen' de las' day me
  On farm by de rapide dat 's call Cheval
      Blanc.

The Wreck of the "Julie Plante"—A Legend of Lac St. Pierre

ON wan dark night on Lac St. Pierre,
    De win' she blow, blow, blow,
An' de crew of de wood scow "Julie Plante"
    Got scar't an' run below—
For de win' she blow lak hurricane
    Bimeby she blow some more,
An' de scow bus' up on Lac St. Pierre
    Wan arpent from de shore.

De captinne walk on de fronte deck,
    An' walk de hin' deck too—
He call de crew from up de hole
    He call de cook also.
De cook she's name was Rosie,
    She come from Montreal,
Was chambre maid on lumber barge,
    On de Grande Lachine Canal.

De win' she blow from nor'-eas'-wes',—
    De sout' win' she blow too,
W'en Rosie cry "Mon cher captinne,
    Mon cher, w'at I shall do?"
Den de Captinne t'row de big ankerre,
    But still the scow she dreef,
De crew he can't pass on de shore,
    Becos' he los' hees skeef.

7

De night was dark lak' wan black cat,
  De wave run high an' fas',
W'en de captinne tak' de Rosie girl
  An' tie her to de mas'.
Den he also tak' de life preserve,
  An' jomp off on de lak',
An' say, "Good-bye, ma Rosie dear,
  I go drown for your sak'."

Nex' morning very early
  'Bout ha'f-pas' two—t'ree—four—
De captinne—scow—an' de poor Rosie
  Was corpses on de shore,
For de win' she blow lak' hurricane
  Bimeby she blow some more,
An' de scow bus' up on Lac St. Pierre,
  Wan arpent from de shore.

MORAL

Now all good wood scow sailor man
  Tak' warning by dat storm
An' go an' marry some nice French girl
  An' leev on wan beeg farm.
De win' can blow lak' hurricane
  An' s'pose she blow some more,
You can't get drown on Lac St. Pierre
  So long you stay on shore.

Le Vieux Temps

VENEZ ici, mon cher ami, an' sit down by
    me—so
An' I will tole you story of old tam long ago—
W'en ev'ryt'ing is happy—w'en all de bird is
    sing
An' me!—I 'm young an' strong lak moose an'
    not afraid no t'ing.

I close my eye jus' so, an' see de place w'ere
    I am born—
I close my ear an' lissen to musique of de horn,
Dat 's horn ma dear ole moder blow—an only
    t'ing she play
Is "viens donc vite Napoléon—'peche toi
    pour votre souper."—

An' w'en he 's hear dat nice musique—ma
    leetle dog "Carleau"
Is place hees tail upon hees back—an' den
    he 's let heem go—
He 's jomp on fence—he 's swimmin' crik—
    he 's ronne two forty gait,
He say "dat 's somet'ing good for eat—Car-
    leau mus' not be late."

9

O dem was pleasure day for sure, dem day of
    long ago
W'en I was play wit' all de boy, an' all de girl
    also;
An' many tam w'en I 'm alone an' t'ink of day
    gone by
An' pull latire an' spark de girl, I cry upon my
    eye.

Ma fader an' ma moder too, got nice, nice
    familee,
Dat 's ten garçon an' t'orteen girl, was mak' it
    twenty t'ree
But fonny t'ing de Gouvernement don't geev
    de firs' prize den
Lak w'at dey say dey geev it now, for only
    wan douzaine.

De English peep dat only got wan familee
    small size
Mus' be feel glad dat tam dere is no honder
    acre prize
For fader of twelve chil'ren—dey know dat
    mus' be so,
De Canayens would boss Kebeck—mebbe
    Ontario.

But dat is not de story dat I was gone tole
    you
About de fun we use to have w'en we leev a
    chez nous
We 're never lonesome on dat house, for many
    cavalier
Come at our place mos' every night—especially
    Sun-day.

But tam I 'member bes' is w'en I 'm twenty
    wan year—me—
An' so for mak' some pleasurement—we geev
    wan large soirée
De whole paroisse she be invite—de Curé he 's
    come too—
Wit plaintee peep from 'noder place—dat 's
    more I can tole you.

De night she 's cole an' freeze also, chemin
    she 's fill wit snow
An' on de chimley lak phantome, de win' is
    mak' it blow—
But boy an' girl come all de sam an' pass on
    grande parloir
For warm itself on beeg box stove, was mak'
    on Trois Rivières—

An' w'en Bonhomme Latour commence for
    tune up hees fidelle
It mak' us all feel very glad—l' enfant! he play
    so well,
Musique suppose to be firs' class, I offen hear,
    for sure
But mos' bes' man, beat all de res', is ole
    Bateese Latour—

An' w'en Bateese play Irish jeeg, he 's learn
    on Mattawa
Dat tam he 's head boss cook Shaintee—den
    leetle Joe Leblanc
Tak' hole de beeg Marie Juneau an' dance
    upon de floor
Till Marie say "Excuse to me, I cannot dance
    no more."—

An' den de Curé 's mak' de speech—ole Curé
    Ladouceur!
He say de girl was spark de boy too much on
    some cornerre—
An' so he 's tole Bateese play up ole fashion
    reel a quatre
An' every body she mus' dance, dey can't get
    off on dat.

Away she go—hooraw! hooraw! plus fort
   Bateese, mon vieux
Camille Bisson, please watch your girl—dat 's
   bes' t'ing you can do.
Pass on de right an' tak' your place Mamzelle
   Des Trois Maisons
You 're s'pose for dance on Paul Laberge, not
   Telesphore Gagnon.

Mon oncle Al-fred, he spik lak' dat—'cos he is
   boss de floor,
An' so we do our possibill an' den commence
   encore.
Dem crowd of boy an' girl I 'm sure keep up
   until nex' day
If ole Bateese don't stop heseff, he come so
   fatigué.

An' affer dat, we eat some t'ing, tak' leetle
   drink also
An' de Curé, he 's tole story of many year
   ago—
W'en Iroquois sauvage she 's keel de Canayens
   an' steal deir hair,
An' say dat 's only for Bon Dieu, we don't be
   here—he don't be dere.

But dat was mak' de girl feel scare—so all de
    cavalier
Was ax hees girl go home right off, an' place
    her on de sleigh,
An' w'en dey start, de Curé say, "Bonsoir et
    bon voyage
Menagez-vous—tak' care for you—prenez
    garde pour les sauvages."

An' den I go meseff also, an' tak' ma belle
    Elmire—
She 's nicer girl on whole Comté, an' jus' got
    eighteen year—
Black hair—black eye, an' chick rosée dat 's lak
    wan fameuse on de fall
But do n't spik much—not of dat kin', I can't
    say she love me at all.

Ma girl—she 's fader beeg farmeur—leev 'noder
    side St. Flore
Got five-six honder acre—mebbe a leetle
    more—
Nice sugar bush—une belle maison—de bes' I
    never see—
So w'en I go for spark Elmire, I don't be mak'
    de foolish me—

Elmire!—she's pass t'ree year on school—Ste.
    Anne de la Perade
An' w'en she's tak' de firs' class prize, dat's
    mak' de ole man glad;
He say "Ba gosh—ma girl can wash—can keep
    de kitchen clean
Den change her dress—mak' politesse before
    God save de Queen."

Dey's many way for spark de girl, an' you
    know dat of course,
Some way dey might be better way, an' some
    dey might be worse
But I lak' sit some cole night wit' my girl on
    ole burleau
Wit' lot of hay keep our foot warm—an'
    plaintee buffalo—

Dat's geev good chances get acquaint—an' if
    burleau upset
An' t'row you out upon de snow—dat's better
    chances yet—
An' if you help de girl go home, if horse he
    ronne away
De girl she's not much use at all—don't geev
    you nice baiser!

Dat 's very well for fun ma frien', but w'en
    you spark for keep
She 's not sam t'ing an' mak' you feel so scare
    lak' leetle sheep
Some tam you get de fever—some tam you 're
    lak snowball
An' all de tam you ack lak' fou—can't spik no
    t'ing at all.

Wall! dat 's de way I feel meseff, wit Elmire
    on burleau,
Jus' lak' small dog try ketch hees tail—roun'
    roun' ma head she go
But bimeby I come more brave—an' tak' El-
    mire she 's han'
"Laisse-moi tranquille" Elmire she say "You
    mus' be crazy man."

"Yass—yass I say" mebbe you t'ink I 'm wan
    beeg loup garou,
Dat 's forty t'ousand 'noder girl, I lef' dem all
    for you,
I s'pose you know Polique Gauthier your frien'
    on St. Cesaire
I ax her marry me nex' wick—she tak' me—I
    don't care."

Ba gosh; Elmire she don't lak' dat—it mak'
    her feel so mad—
She commence cry, say "'Poleon you treat me
    very bad—
I don't lak' see you t'row you'seff upon Polique
    Gauthier,
So if you say you love me sure—we mak' de
    marieé."—

Oh it was fine tam affer dat—Castor I t'ink he
    know,
We 're not too busy for get home—he go so
    nice an' slow,
He 's only upset t'ree—four tam—an' jus'
    about daylight
We pass upon de ole man's place—an' every
    t'ing 's all right.

Wall! we leev happy on de farm for nearly
    fifty year,
Till wan day on de summer tam—she die—ma
    belle Elmire
I feel so lonesome lef' behin'—I tink 't was
    bes' mebbe—
Dat w'en le Bon Dieu tak' ma famme—he
    should not forget me.

But dat is hees biz-nesse ma frien'—I know
    dat's all right dere
I'll wait till he call "'Poleon" den I will be
    prepare—
An' w'en he fin' me ready, for mak' de longue
    voyage
He guide me t'roo de wood hesef upon ma las'
    portage.

"De Papineau Gun"—An Incident of the Canadian Rebellion of 1837

BON jour, M'sieu'—you want to know
    'Bout dat ole gun—w'at good she's for?
W'y! Jean Bateese Bruneau—mon pere,
    Fight wit' dat gun on Pap'neau War!

Long tam since den you say—C'est vrai,
    An' me too young for 'member well,
But how de patriot fight an' die,
    I offen hear de ole folk tell.

De English don't ack square dat tam,
    Don't geev de habitants no show,
So 'long come Wolfred Nelson
    Wit' Louis Joseph Papineau.

An' swear de peep mus' have deir right.
  Wolfred he 's write Victoriaw,
But she 's no good, so den de war
  Commence among de habitants.

Mon pere he leev to Grande Brulé.
  So smarter man you never see,
Was alway on de grande hooraw!
  Plaintee w'at you call "Esprit!"

An' w'en dey form wan compagnie
  All dress wit' tuque an' ceinture sash
Ma fader tak' hees gun wit' heem
  An' marche away to Saint Eustache,

W'ere many patriots was camp
  Wit' brave Chenier, deir Capitaine,
W'en 'long come English Generale,
  An' more two t'ousan' sojer man.

De patriot dey go on church
  An' feex her up deir possibill;
Dey fight deir bes', but soon fin' out
  "Canon de bois" no good for kill.

An' den de church she come on fire,
  An' burn almos' down to de groun',
So w'at you t'ink our man can do
  Wit' all dem English armee roun'?

19

'Poleon, hees sojer never fight
    More brave as dem poor habitants,
Chenier, he try for broke de rank
    Chenier come dead immediatement.

He fall near w'ere de cross is stan'
    Upon de ole church cimitiere,
Wit' Jean Poulin an' Laframboise
    An' plaintee more young feller dere.

De gun dey rattle lak' tonnere
    Jus' bang, bang, bang! dat 's way she go,
An' wan by wan de brave man 's fall
    An' red blood 's cover all de snow

Ma fader shoot so long he can
    An' den he 's load hees gun some more,
Jomp on de ice behin' de church
    An' pass heem on de 'noder shore.

Wall! he reach home fore very long
    An' keep perdu for many day,
Till ev'ry t'ing she come tranquille,
    An' sojer man all gone away.

An' affer dat we get our right,
    De Canayens don't fight no more,
Ma fader's never shoot dat gun,
    But place her up above de door.

An' Papineau, an' Nelson too
   Dey 're gone long tam, but we are free,
Le Bon Dieu have 'em 'way up dere.
   Salut, Wolfred!   Salut, Louis!

How Bateese Came Home

W'EN I was young boy on de farm, dat 's
   twenty year ago
I have wan frien' he 's leev near me, call Jean
   Bateese Trudeau
An offen w'en we are alone, we lak for spik
   about
De tam w'en we was come beeg man, wit'
   moustache on our mout'.

Bateese is get it on hees head, he 's too moche
   educate
For mak' de habitant farmerre—he better go
   on State—
An' so wan summer evening we 're drivin'
   home de cow
He 's tole me all de whole beez-nesse—jus' lak
   you hear me now.

21

"W'at 's use mak' foolish on de farm? dere 's
no good chances lef'
An' all de tam you be poor man—you know
dat 's true you'se'f;
We never get no fun at all—don't never go on
spree
Onless we pass on 'noder place, an' mak' it
some monee .

"I go on Les Etats Unis, I go dere right
away
An' den mebbe on ten-twelve year, I be riche
man some day,
An' w'en I mak' de large fortune, I come back
I s'pose
Wit' Yankee famme from off de State, an'
monee on my clothes.

"I tole you somet'ing else also—mon cher
Napoleon
I get de grande majorité, for go on parlia-
ment
Den buil' fine house on borde l'eau—near w'ere
de church is stand
More finer dan de Presbytere, w'en I am come
riche man!"

I say "For w'at you spik lak dat? you must
    be gone crazee
Dere 's plaintee feller on de State, more smarter
    dan you be,
Beside she 's not so healtee place, an' if you
    mak' l'argent,
You spen' it jus' lak Yankee man, an' not lak
    habitant.

"For me Bateese! I tole you dis: I 'm very
    satisfy—
De bes' man don't leev too long tam, some
    day Ba Gosh! he die—
An' s'pose you got good trotter horse, an' nice
    famme Canadienne
Wit' plaintee on de house for eat—W'at more
    you want ma frien'?"

But Bateese have it all mak' up, I can't stop
    him at all
He 's buy de seconde classe tiquette, for go on
    Central Fall—
An' wit' two-t'ree some more de boy,—w'at
    t'ink de sam' he do
Pass on de train de very nex' wick, was lef'
    Rivière du Loup.

.   .   .   .

Wall! mebbe fifteen year or more, since Bateese
    go away
I fin' mesef Rivière du Loup, wan cole, cole
    winter day
De quick express she come hooraw! but stop
    de soon she can
An' beeg swell feller jomp off car, dat 's boss
    by nigger man.

He 's dressim on de première classe, an' got
    new suit of clothes
Wit' long moustache dat 's stickim out, de
    'noder side hees nose
Fine gol' watch chain—nice portmanteau—an'
    long, long overcoat
Wit' beaver hat—dat 's Yankee style—an' red
    tie on hees t'roat—

I say "Hello Bateese! Hello! Comment ça va
    mon vieux?"
He say "Excuse to me, ma frien' I t'ink I don't
    know you."
I say, "She 's very curis t'ing, you are Bateese
    Trudeau,
Was raise on jus' sam' place wit' me, dat 's
    fifteen year ago?"

He say, "Oh yass dat 's sure enough—I know
    you now firs' rate,
But I forget mos' all ma French since I go on
    de State.
Dere 's 'noder t'ing kip on your head, ma frien'
    dey. mus' be tole
Ma name 's Bateese Trudeau no more, but
    John B. Waterhole!"

"Hole on de water 's" fonny name for man
    w'at 's call Trudeau
Ma frien's dey all was spik lak dat, an' I am
    tole heem so—
He say "Trudeau an' Waterhole she 's jus'
    about de sam'
An' if you go for leev on State, you must have
    Yankee nam'."

Den we invite heem come wit' us, "Hotel du
    Canadaw"
W'ere he was treat mos' e'ry tam, but can't
    tak' w'isky blanc,
He say dat 's leetle strong for man jus' come
    off Central Fall
An' "tabac Canayen" bedamme! he won't
    smoke dat at all!—

But fancy drink lak "Collings John" de way
    he put it down
Was long tam since I don't see dat—I t'ink
    he 's goin' drown!—
An' fine cigar cos' five cent each, an' mak' on
    Trois-Rivières
L'enfant! he smoke beeg pile of dem—for
    monee he don't care!—

I s'pose meseff it 's t'ree o'clock w'en we are
    t'roo dat night
Bateese, hees fader come for heem, an' tak'
    heem home all right
De ole man say Bateese spik French, w'en he
    is place on bed—
An' say bad word—but w'en he wake—forget
    it on hees head—

Wall! all de winter w'en we have soirée dat 's
    grande affaire
Bateese Trudeau, dit Waterhole, he be de boss
    man dere—
You bet he have beeg tam, but w'en de spring
    is come encore
He 's buy de première classe tiquette for go on
    State some more.

You 'member w'en de hard tam come on Les
    Etats Unis
An' plaintee Canayens go back for stay deir
    own contrée?
Wall! jus' about dat tam again I go Rivière
    du Loup
For sole me two t'ree load of hay—mak' leetle
    visit too—

De freight train she is **jus' arrive**—only ten
    hour delay—
She 's never carry passengaire—dat 's w'at dey
    always say—
I see poor man on char caboose—he 's got
    heem small valise
Begosh! I nearly tak' de fit,—It is—it is
    Bateese!

He know me **very** well dis tam, an' say "Bon
    jour, mon vieux
I hope you know Bateese Trudeau was educate
    wit' you
I 'm jus' come off de State to see ma familee
    encore
I bus' mesef on Central Fall—I don't go dere
    no more."

"I got no monee— not at all—I 'm broke it up
   for sure—
Dat 's locky t'ing, Napoleon, de brakeman
   Joe Latour
He 's cousin of wan frien' of me call Camille
   Valiquette,
Conductor too 's good Canayen—don't ax me
   no tiquette."

I tak' Bateese wit' me once more "Hotel du
   Canadaw"
An' he was glad for get de chance drink some
   good w'isky blanc!
Dat 's warm heem up, an den he eat mos'
   ev'ryt'ing he see,
I watch de w'ole beez-nesse mese'f—Monjee!
   he was hongree!

Madame Charette wat 's kip de place get very
   much excite
For see de many pork an' bean Bateese put out
   of sight
Du pain doré—potate pie—an' 'noder t'ing be
   dere
But w'en Bateese is get heem t'roo—dey go I
   don't know w'ere.

28

It don't tak' long for tole de news "Bateese
    come off de State"
An' purty soon we have beeg crowd, lak vil-
    lage she 's en fête
Bonhomme Maxime Trudeau hese'f, he 's
    comin' wit' de pries'
An' pass' heem on de "Room for eat" w'ere
    he is see Bateese.

Den ev'rybody feel it glad, for watch de em-
    brasser
An' bimeby de ole man spik "Bateese you here
    for stay?"
Bateese he 's cry lak beeg bebè, "Bâ j'eux
    rester ici.
An if I never see de State, I 'm sure I don't
    care—me."

"Correc'," Maxime is say right off, "I place
    you on de farm
For help your poor ole fader, won't do you too
    moche harm
Please come wit' me on Magasin, I feex you
    up—bâ oui
An' den you 're ready for go home an' see de
    familee."

29

Wall! w'en de ole man an' Bateese come off de
    Magasin
Bateese is los' hees Yankee clothes—he 's dress
    lak Canayen
Wit' bottes sauvages—ceinture fléché—an'
    coat wit' capuchon
An' spik Français au naturel, de sam' as habi-
    tant.

     .   .   .   .

I see Bateese de oder day, he 's work hees
    fader's place
I t'ink mese'f he 's satisfy—I see dat on hees face
He say "I got no use for State, mon cher Na-
    poleon
Kebeck she 's good enough for me—Hooraw
    pour Canadaw."

De Nice Leetle Canadienne

YOU can pass on de worl' w'erever you lak,
    Tak' de steamboat for go Angleterre,
Tak' car on de State, an' den you come back,
    An' go all de place, I don't care—
Ma frien' dat 's a fack, I know you will say,
    W'en you come on dis contree again,
Dere 's no girl can touch, w'at we see ev'ry day,
       De nice leetle Canadienne.

DE NICE LEETLE CANADIENNE

Don't matter how poor dat girl she may be,
    Her dress is so neat an' so clean,
Mos' ev'rywan t'ink it was mak' on Paree
    An' she wear it, wall! jus' lak de Queen.
Den come for fin' out she is mak' it herse'f,
    For she ain't got moche monee for spen',
But all de sam' tam, she was never get lef',
        Dat nice leetle Canadienne.

W'en "un vrai Canayen" is mak' it mariée,
    You t'ink he go leev on beeg flat
An' bodder hese'f all de tam, night an' day,
    Wit' housemaid, an' cook, an' all dat?
Not moche, ma dear frien', he tak' de maison,
    Cos' only nine dollar or ten,
W'ere he leev lak blood rooster, an' save de
       l'argent,
        Wit' hees nice leetle Canadienne.

I marry ma famme w'en I'm jus' twenty year,
    An' now we got fine familee,
Dat skip roun' de place lak leetle small deer,
    No smarter crowd you never see—
An' I t'ink as I watch dem all chasin' about,
    Four boy an' six girl, she mak' ten,
Dat 's help mebbe kip it, de stock from run out.
        Of de nice leetle Canadienne.

O she 's quick an' she 's smart, an' got plaintee
       heart,
  If you know correc' way go about,
An' if you don't know, she soon tole you so
  Den tak' de firs' chance an' get out;
But if she love you, I spik it for true,
  She will mak' it more beautiful den,
An' sun on de sky can't shine lak de eye
      Of dat nice leetle Canadienne.

'Poleon Doré.—A Tale of the Saint Maurice

YOU have never hear de story of de young
    Napoleon Doré?
  Los' hees life upon de reever w'en de lumber
    drive go down?
W'ere de rapide roar lak tonder, dat 's de place
    he 's goin' onder,
  W'en he 's try save Paul Desjardins, 'Poleon
    hese'f is drown.

All de winter on de Shaintee, tam she 's good
    and work she 's plaintee,
  But we 're not feel very sorry, w'en de sun
    is warm hees face,

W'en de mooshrat an' de beaver, tak' some
      leetle swim on reever,
  An' de sout' win' scare de snowbird, so she
     fly some col'er place.

Den de spring is set in steady, an' we get de
      log all ready,
  Workin' hard all day an' night too, on de
     water mos' de tam,
An' de skeeter w'en dey fin' us, come so quickly
      nearly blin' us,
  Biz—biz—biz—biz—all aroun' us till we feel
     lak sacrédam,

All de sam' we 're hooraw feller, from de top
      of house to cellar,
  Ev'ry boy he 's feel so happy, w'en he 's
     goin' right away,
See hees fader an' hees moder, see hees sister
      an' hees broder,
  An' de girl he spark las' summer, if she 's
     not get mariée.

Wall we start heem out wan morning, an' de
      pilot geev us warning,
  "W'en you come on Rapide Cuisse, ma
     frien', keep raf' she 's head on shore,

'POLEON DORÉ

If you struck beeg rock on middle, w'ere le
    diable is play hees fiddle,
  Dat's de tam you pass on some place, you
    don't never pass before."

But we'll not t'ink moche of danger, for de
    rapide she's no stranger
  Many tam we're runnin' t'roo it, on de fall
    an' on de spring,
On mos' ev'ry kin' of wedder dat le Bon Dieu
    scrape togedder,
  An' we'll never drown noboddy, an' we'll
    never bus' somet'ing.

Dere was Telesphore Montbriand, Paul Desjar-
    dins, Louis Guyon,
  Bill McKeever, Aleck Gauthier, an' hees
    cousin Jean Bateese,
'Poleon Doré, Aimé Beaulieu, wit' some more
    man I can't tole you,
  Dat was mak' it bes' gang never run upon de
    St. Maurice.

Dis is jus' de tam I wish me, I could spik de
    good English—me—
  For tole you of de pleasurement we get upon
    de spring,

34

W'en de win' she 's all a sleepin', an' de raf'
    she go a sweepin'
  Down de reever on some morning, w'ile le
    rossignol is sing.

Ev'ryt'ing so nice an' quiet on de shore as we
    pass by it,
  All de tree got fine new spring suit, ev'ry
    wan she 's dress on green
W'y it mak' us all more younger, an' we don't
    feel any hunger,
  Till de cook say "'Raw for breakfas'," den
    we smell de pork an' bean.

Some folk say she 's bad for leever, but for man
    work hard on reever,
  Dat 's de bes' t'ing I can tole you, dat was
    never yet be seen,
Course dere 's oder t'ing ah tak' me, fancy dish
    also I lak me,
  But w'en I want somet'ing solid, please pass
    me de pork an' bean.

All dis tam de raf' she 's goin' lak steamboat
    was got us towin'
  All we do is keep de channel, an' dat 's easy
    workin' dere,

So we sing some song an' chorus, for de good
    tam dat 's before us,
  W'en de w'ole beez-nesse she 's finish, an'
    we come on Trois Rivieres.

But bad luck is sometam fetch us, for beeg
    strong win' come an' ketch us,
  Jus' so soon we struck de rapide—jus' so
    soon we see de smoke,
An' before we spik some prayer for ourse'f
    dat 's fightin' dere,
  Roun' we come upon de beeg rock, an' it 's
    den de raf' she broke.

Dat was tam poor Paul Desjardins, from de
    parish of St. Germain,
  He was long way on de fronte side, so he 's
    fallin' overboar'
Could n't swim at all de man say, but dat 's
    more ma frien', I can say,
  Any how he 's look lak drownin', so we 'll
    t'row him two t'ree oar.

Dat 's 'bout all de help our man do, dat 's
    'bout ev'ryt'ing we can do,
  As de crib we 're hangin' onto balance on
    de rock itse'f,

Till de young Napoleon Doré, heem I start for
      tole de story,
  Holler out, "Mon Dieu, I don't lak see poor
      Paul go drown hese'f."

So he's mak' beeg jomp on water, jus' de sam
      you see some otter
  An' he's pass on place w'ere Paul is tryin'
      hard for keep afloat,
Den we see Napoleon ketch heem, try hees
      possibill for fetch heem
  But de current she's more stronger, an' de
      eddy get dem bote.

O Mon Dieu! for see dem two man, mak' me
      feel it cry lak woman,
  Roun' an' roun' upon de eddy, quickly dem
      poor feller go,
Can't tole wan man from de oder, an' we'll
      know dem bote lak broder,
  But de fight she soon is finish—Paul an'
      'Poleon go below.

Yass, an' all de tam we stay dere, only t'ing
      we do is pray dere,
  For de soul poor drownin' feller, dat's enough
      mak' us feel mad,

Torteen voyageurs, all brave man, glad get any
    chances save man,
  But we don't see no good chances, can't do
    not'ing, dat's too bad.

Wall! at las' de crib she's come way off de
    rock, an' den on some way,
  By an' by de w'ole gang's passin' on safe
    place below de Cuisse,
Ev'ryboddy's heart she's breakin', w'en dey
    see poor Paul he's taken
  Wit' de young Napoleon Doré, bes' boy on
    de St. Maurice!

An' day affer, Bill McKeever fin' de bote man
    on de reever,
  Wit' deir arm aroun' each oder, mebbe pass
    above dat way—
So we bury dem as we fin' dem, w'ere de pine
    tree wave behin' dem
  An de Grande Montagne he's lookin' down
    on Marcheterre Bay.

You can't hear no church bell ring dere, but le
    rossignol is sing dere,
  An' w'ere ole red cross she's stannin', mebbe
    some good ange gardien,

Watch de place w'ere bote man sleepin', keep
    de reever grass from creepin'
On de grave of 'Poleon Doré, an' of poor
    Paul Desjardins.

De Notaire Publique

M'SIEU Paul Joulin, de Notaire Publique
    Is come I s'pose seexty year hees life
An' de mos' riche man on Sainte Angelique
    W'en he feel very sorry he got no wife—
So he 's paint heem hees buggy, lak new, by
    Gor!
    Put flower on hees coat, mak' hese'f more
    gay
Arrange on hees head fine chapeau castor
    An' drive on de house of de Boulanger.

For de Boulanger 's got heem une jolie fille
    Mos' bes' lookin' girl on paroisse dey say
An' all de young feller is lak Julie
    An' plaintee is ax her for mak' mariée,
But Julie she 's love only jus' wan man,
    Hees nam' it is Jérémie Dandurand
An' he 's work for her sak' all de hard he can'
    'Way off on de wood, up de Mattawa.

M'Sieu Paul he spik him "Bonjour Mamzelle,
  You lak promenade on de church wit' me?
Jus' wan leetle word an' we go ma belle
  An' see heem de Curé toute suite, chérie;
I dress you de very bes' style á la mode,
  If you promise for be Madame Paul Joulin,
For I got me fine house on Bord à Plouffe road
  Wit' mor'gage also on de Grande Moulin."

But Julie she say "Non, non, M'Sieu Paul,
  Dat 's not correc' t'ing for poor Jérémie
For I love dat young feller lak not'ing at all,
  An' I 'm very surprise you was not know me.
Jérémie w'en he 's geev me dat nice gol' ring,
  Las' tam he 's gone off on de Mattawa
Say he 's got 'noder wan w'en he 's come nex'
        spring
  Was mak' me for sure Madame Dandurand.

"I t'ank you de sam' M'Sieu Paul Joulin
  I s'pose I mus' be de wife wan poor man
Wit' no chance at all for de Grande Moulin,
  But leev all de tam on some small cabane."
De Notaire Publique den is tak' hees hat,
  For he t'ink sure enough dat hees dog she 's
        dead;
Dere 's no use mak' love on de girl lak dat,
  Wit' not'ing but young feller on de head.

Julie she's feel lonesome mos' all dat week,
  Don't know w'at may happen she wait till
      spring
Den t'ink de fine house of Notaire Publique
  An' plaintee more too— but love 's funny t'ing!
So nex' tam she see de Notaire again,
  She laugh on her eye an' say "M'Sieu Paul
Please pass on de house, or you ketch de rain,
  Dat 's very long tam you don't come at all."

She 's geev him so soon he 's come on de door
  Du vin de pays, an' some nice galettes,
She 's mak' dem herse'f only day before
  An' he say "Bigosh! dat is fine girl yet."
So he 's try hees chances some more—hooraw!
  Julie is not mak' so moche troub' dis tam;
She 's forget de poor Jérémie Dandurand
  An' tole de Notaire she will be hees famme.

W'en Jérémie come off de wood nex' spring,
  An' fin' dat hees girl she was get mariée
Everybody 's expec' he will do somet'ing,
  But he don't do not'ing at all, dey say;
For he 's got 'noder girl on Sainte Dorothée,
  Dat he 's love long tam, an' she don't say
      "No,"
So he 's forget too all about Julie
  An' mak' de mariée wit' hese'f also.

41

A Canadian Voyageur's Account of the Nile Expedition—"Maxime Labelle"

VICTORIAW: she have beeg war, E-gyp 's
    de nam' de place—
An' neeger peep dat 's leev 'im dere, got very
    black de face,
An' so she 's write Joseph Mercier, he 's stop
    on Trois Rivieres—
"Please come right off, an' bring wit' you t'ree
    honder voyageurs.

"I got de plaintee sojer, me, beeg feller six foot
    tall—
Dat 's Englishman, an' Scotch also, don't wear
    no pant at all;
Of course, de Irishman 's de bes', raise all de
    row he can,
But noboddy can pull batteau lak good Cana-
    dian man.

"I geev you steady job for sure, an' w'en you
    get 'im t'roo
I bring you back on Canadaw, don't cos' de
    man un sou,
Dat 's firs'-class steamboat all de way Kebeck
    an' Leeverpool,
An' if you don't be satisfy, you mus' be beeg,
    beeg fool."

We meet upon Hotel Dufresne, an' talk heem
    till daylight,
An' Joe he 's treat so many tam, we very near
    get tight,
Den affer w'ile, we mak' our min' dat 's not
    bad chance, an' so
Joseph Mercier he 's telegraph, "Correc', Ma-
    dame, we go."

So Joe arrange de whole beez-nesse wit' Queen
    Victoriaw;
Two dollar day—work all de tam—dat 's purty
    good l'argent!
An' w'en we start on Trois Rivieres, for pass
    on boar' de ship,
Our frien' dey all say, "Bon voyage," an' den
    Hooraw! E-gyp'!

Dat beeg steamboat was plonge so moche, I 'm
    'fraid she never stop—
De Capitaine 's no use at all, can't kip her on
    de top—
An' so we all come very sick, jus' lak one leetle
    pup,
An' ev'ry tam de ship 's go down, de inside
    she 's go up.

I 'm sorry spoke lak dis, ma frien', if you don't
    t'ink it 's so,
Please ax Joseph Mercier hese'f, or Aleck De
    Courteau,
Dat stay on bed mos' all de tam, so sick dey
    nearly die,
But lak' some great, beeg Yankee man, was
    never tole de lie.

De gang she 's travel, travel, t'roo many strange
    contree,
An' ev'ry place is got new nam', I don't re-
    member, me,
We see some fonny t'ing, for sure, more fonny
    I can tell,
But w'en we reach de Neel Riviere, dat 's feel
    more naturel

So many fine, beeg sojer man, I never see be-
    fore,
All dress heem on grand uniform, is wait upon
    de shore,
Some black, some green, an' red also, cos'
    honder dollar sure,
An' holler out, "She 's all right now, here come
    de voyageurs!"

We see boss Generale also, he's ride on beeg
    chameau.
Dat's w'at you call Ca-melle, I t'ink, I laugh
    de way she go!
Jomp up, jomp down, jomp ev'ry place, but
    still de Generale
Seem satisfy for stay on top, dat fonny an-i-
    mal.

He's holler out on Joe Mercier, "Comment
    câ va Joseph
You lak for come right off wit' me, tak' leetle
    ride yourseff?"
Joseph, he mak' de grand salut, an' tak' it off
    hees hat,
"Merci, Mon Generale," he say, "I got no use
    for dat."

Den affer we was drink somet'ing, an' sing
    "Le Brigadier,"
De sojer fellers get prepare, for mak' de em-
    barquer,
An' everybody's shout heem out, w'en we
    tak' hole de boat
"Hooraw pour Queen Victoriaw!" an' also
    "pour nous autres."

Bigosh; I do hard work mese'f upon de Ot-
tawa,
De Gatineau an' St. Maurice, also de Mat-
tawa,
But I don't never work at all, I 'sure you dat 's
a fack
Until we strike de Neel Riviere, an' sapré
Catarack!

"Dis way, dat way, can't keep her straight,"
"look out, Bateese, look out!"
"Now let her go"—"arrete un peu," dat 's
way de pilot shout,
"Don't wash de neeger girl on shore," an'
"prenez garde behin"
"W'at 's 'matter wit' dat rudder man? I t'ink
he 's goin' blin'!"

Some tam of course, de boat 's all right, an'
carry us along
An' den again, we mak portage, w'en current
she 's too strong
On place lak' dat, we run good chance, for sun-
struck on de neck,
An' plaintee tam we wish ourseff was back on
ole Kebeck.

46

De seconde Catarack we pass, more beeger dan
    de Soo,
She's nearly t orty mile for sure, it would as-
    tonish you,
Dat's place t'ree Irishman get drown, wan day
    we have beeg storm,
I s'pose de Queen is feel lak cry, los' dat nice
    uniform!

De night she's very, very cole, an' hot upon
    de day,
An' all de tam, you feel jus' lak you're goin'
    melt away,
But never min' an' don't get scare, you mak'
    it up all right,
An' twenty poun' you los' dat day, she's
    comin' back sam' night.

We got small bugle boy also, he's mebbe stan'
    four foot,
An' firs' t'ing ev'ry morning, sure, he mak' it
    toot! toot! toot!
She's nice enough upon de day, for hear de
    bugle call,
But w'en she play before daylight, I don't lak
    dat at all.

We mus' get up immediatement, dat leetle
    feller blow,
An' so we start heem off again, for pull de
    beeg batteau,
De sojer man he 's nice, nice boy, an' help us
    all he can,
An' geev heem chance, he 's mos' as good lak
    some Canadian man.

Wall all de tam, she go lak dat, was busy every
    day,
Don't get moche chance for foolishness, don't
    get no chance for play,
Dere 's plaintee danger all aroun', an' w'en
    we 're comin' back
We got look out for run heem safe, dem sapré
    Catarack.

But w'ere 's de war? I can't mak' out, don't
    see no fight at all!
She 's not'ing but une Grande Piqnique, dat 's
    las' in all de fall!
Mebbe de neeger King he 's scare, an' skip
    anoder place,
An' pour la Reine Victoriaw! I never see de
    face.

But dat's not ma beez-nesse, ma frien', I'm
    ready pull batteau
So long she pay two dollar day, wit' pork an'
    bean also;
An' if she geev me steady job, for mak' some
    more l'argent,
I say, "Hooraw! for all de tam, on Queen
    Victoriaw!"

Memories

O SPIRIT of the mountain that speaks to
    us to-night,
Your voice is sad, yet still recalls past visions
    of delight,
When 'mid the grand old Laurentides, old
    when the earth was new,
With flying feet we followed the moose and
    caribou.

And backward rush sweet memories, like frag-
    ments of a dream,
We hear the dip of paddle blades, the ripple of
    the stream,
The mad, mad rush of frightened wings from
    brake and covert start,
The breathing of the woodland, the throb of
    nature's heart.

Once more beneath our eager feet the forest
    carpet springs,
We march through gloomy valleys, where the
    vesper sparrow sings.
The little minstrel heeds us not, nor stays his
    plaintive song,
As with our brave coureurs de bois we swiftly
    pass along.

Again o'er dark Wayagamack, in bark canoe
    we glide,
And watch the shades of evening glance along
    the mountain side.
Anon we hear resounding the wizard loon's
    wild cry,
And mark the distant peak whereon the lin-
    g'ring echoes die.

But Spirit of the Northland! let the winter
    breezes blow,
And cover every giant crag with rifts of driving
    snow.
Freeze every leaping torrent, bind all the crys-
    tal lakes,
Tell us of fiercer pleasures when the Storm
    King awakes.

And now the vision changes, the winds are
    loud and shrill,
The falling flakes are shrouding the mountain
    and the hill,
But safe within our snug cabane with comrades
    gathered near,
We set the rafters ringing with "Roulant"
    and "Brigadier."

Then after Pierre and Telesphore have danced
    "Le Caribou,"
Some hardy trapper tells a tale of the dreaded
    Loup Garou,
Or phantom bark in moonlit heavens, with
    prow turned to the East,
Bringing the Western voyageurs to join the
    Christmas feast.

And while each backwoods troubadour is
    greeted with huzza
Slowly the homely incense of "tabac Cana-
    yen"
Rises and sheds its perfume like flowers of
    Araby,
O'er all the true-born loyal Enfants de la
    Patrie.

And thus with song and story, with laugh and
   jest and shout,
We heed not dropping mercury nor storms
   that rage without,
But pile the huge logs higher till the chimney
   roars with glee,
And banish spectral visions with La Chanson
   Normandie.

> "Brigadier! répondit Pandore
> Brigadier! vous avez raison,
> Brigadier! répondit Pandore,
> Brigadier! vous avez raison!"

O spirit of the mountain! that speaks to us
   to-night,
Return again and bring us new dreams of past
   delight,
And while our heart-throbs linger, and till our
   pulses cease,
We'll worship thee among the hills where
   flows the Saint-Maurice.

Phil-o-rum Juneau—A Story of the "Chasse Gallerie"

In the days of the "Old Régime" in Canada, the free
life of the woods and prairies proved too tempting for the

young men, who frequently deserted civilization for the
savage delights of the wilderness, These voyageurs and
coureurs de bois seldom returned in the flesh, but on every
New Year's Eve, back thro' snowstorm and hurricane—in
mid-air—came their spirits in ghostly canoes, to join, for
a brief spell, the old folks at home and kiss the girls, on
the annual feast of the "Jour de l'an," or New Year's
Day The legend which still survives in French-speaking
Canada is known as "La Chasse Gallerie."

HE sit on de corner mos' every night, ole
    Phil-o-rum Juneau,
Spik wit' hese'f an' shake de head, an' smoke
    on de pipe also—
Very hard job it 's for wake him up, no matter
    de loud we call
W 'en he 's feex hese'f on de beeg arm-chair,
    back on de kitchen wall.

He don't believe not'ing at all, at all 'bout
    lates' new fashion t'ing
Le char 'lectrique an' de telephome, was talk
    w'en de bell she ring
Dat 's leetle too moche for de ole bonhomme,
    mak' him shake it de head an' say
"Wat 's use mak' de foolish lak dat, sapré!
    I 'm not born only yesterday."

But if you want story dat's true, true, true, I
    tole you good wan moi-meme
An' de t'ing you was spik, dat I don't believe,
    for sure she was beat all dem.
So he's cough leetle cough, clear 'im up de
    t'roat, fill hees pipe wit' some more tabac,
An' w'en de chil'ren is come tranquille, de ole
    man begin comme câ.

L'enfant! l'enfant! it's very strange t'ing!
    mak' me laugh too w'en I hear
De young peep talk of de long, long tam of
    seventy, eighty year!
Dat's only be jus' eighty New Year Day, an'
    quickly was pass it by
It's beeg, beeg dream, an' you don't wake up,
    till affer you're comin' die.

Dat's true sure enough, you see curi's t'ing,
    if you only leev leetle w'ile,
So long you got monee go all de place, for
    mebbe t'ree t'ousan' mile,
But monee's not everyt'ing on dis worl', I tole
    you dat, mes amis,
An' man can be ole lak' two honder year, an'
    not see it, La Chasse Gal'rie.

I never forget de fine New Year night, nearly
    seexty year ago,
W'en I 'm lef' it our place for attend soiree, on
    ole Maxime Baribault,
Nine mile away, I can see tin roof, on church
    of de St. Joseph,
An' over de snow, de leaf dat die las' fall, was
    chasin' itse'f.

Dere was some of de neighbor house I call,
    dat 's be de ole fashion style,
An' very nice style too, mes amis, I hope she
    will las' long w'ile,
I shak' it de han', I drink santé, an' kiss it de
    girl she 's face,
So it 's come ten o'clock, w'en I pass on road,
    for visit Maxime hees place.

But I 'm not go more mebbe t'ree arpent, w'en
    de sky is get black all roun',
An' de win' she blow lak I never see, an' de
    beeg snowstorm come down.
I mak' it my min' she 's goin' be soon, de very
    bad night for true,
Dat 's locky I got plaintee whiskey lef', so I
    tak' it wan leetle "coup."

Purty quick affer dat, I'm comin' nice place,
    was stan'in' some fine beeg tree
W'ere de snow don't dreef', an' it seem jus'
    lak dat place it is mak' for me,
So I pass it on dere, for mak' safe mese'f, w'ile
    de storm is blow outside,
As if all de devil on hell below, was tak' heem
    some fancy ride.

Wan red fox he's comin' so close, so close, I
    could ketch him wit' de han',
But not on de tam lak dis ma frien', "Marche
    toi all de quick you can,"
Poor feller he's tire an' seem los' hees way,
    an' w'en he reach home dat night
Mebbe he fin' it all was close up, an' de door
    it was fassen tight.

But w'at is dat soun' mak' de hair stan' up,
    w'at is it mean, dat cry?
Comin' over de high tree top, out of de nor'-
    wes' sky
Lak cry of de wil' goose w'en she pass on de
    spring tam an' de fall,
But wil' goose fly on de winter night! I never
    see dat at all.

On, on t'roo de night, she is quickly come,
    more closer all de tam,
But not lak de cry of some wil' bird now, don't
    seem it at all de sam';
An' den wit' de rush of de win', I hear some-
    body sing chanson
An' de song dey sing is de ole, ole song, "Le
    Canayen Errant."

But it 's mak' me lonesome an' scare also, jus'
    sam' I be goin' for die
W'en I lissen dat song on night lak dis, so far
    away on de sky,
Don't know w'at to do at all mese'f, so I go
    w'ere I have good view,
An' up, up above t'roo de storm an' snow,
    she 's comin' wan beeg canoe.

Den somebody call it ma nam' out loud, firs'
    tam it was scare me so,
"We know right away, dat was you be dere,
    hello Phil-o-rum, hello!"
An' soon I see him dat feller spik, I 'member
    him too mese'f,
We go de sam' school twenty year before, hees
    nam's Telesphore Le Boeuf.

But I know on de way canoe she go, dat de
    crowd he mus' be dead man
Was come from de Grande Riviere du Nord,
    come from Saskatchewan,
Come too from all de place is lie on de Hòdson
    Bay Contree,
An' de t'ing I was see me dat New Year night,
    is le phantome Chasse Gal'rie.

An' many de boy I was see him dere, I know
    him so long before
He 's goin' away on de far contree—for never
    return no more—
An' now on phantome he is comin' home—t'roo
    de storm an' de hurricane
For kiss him de girl on jour de l'an, an' see de
    ole peep again.

De beeg voyageur w'at is steer canoe, wit'
    paddle hol' on hees han'
Got very long hair was hang down hees neck,
    de sam' as wil' Injin man
Invite me on boar' dat phantome canoe, for
    show it dead man de way—
Don't lak it de job, but no use refuse, so I 'll
    mak' it de embarquer.

Den wan of de gang, he mus' be foreman, say
    it 's tam for have leetle drink,
So he pass heem black bottle for tak' un "coup,"
    an' it 's look lak ma own I t'ink,
But it can't be de sam', I 'll be swear for dat,
    for w'en I was mak' de go,
I fin' dere is not'ing inside but win', an' de
    whiskey 's phantome also.

Dey be laugh affer dat, lak dey tak' some fit,
    so de boss spik him, "Tiens Phil-o-rum,
Never min' on dem feller—mus' have leetle
    sport, dat 's very long way we come,
Will you ketch it de paddle for steer us quick
    on place of Maxime Baribault?"
An' he 's ax me so nice, I do as he please', an'
    den away off she go.

Wan minute—two minute—we pass on dere,
    Maxime he is all hooraw!
An' we know by musique dat was play inside,
    mus' be de great Joe Violon,
Dat feller work fiddle on very bes' way, dat
    nobody never see
Mak' de boy an' de girl, ole peep also, dance
    lak dey was go crazee.

You s'pose dey was let me come on dat house?
    Not at all, for de boss he say,
"Phil-o-rum, it's long tam we don't see our
    frien' can't get heem chance ev'ry day,
Please stop on canoe so she won't blow off,
    w'ile we pass on de house an' see
Dem frien' we was lef' an' de girl we spark,
    before we go strange contree."

An' me I was sit on canoe outside, jus' lak I
    was sapré fou,
Watchin' dem feller dat's all dead man, dance
    heem lak Loup Garou.
De boss he kiss Marie Louise, ma girl, dat's
    way he spen' mos' de tam,
But of course she know not'ing of dat biz-nesse
    —don't lak it me jus' de sam'.

By tam I'm commence it for feel de col',
    dey're all comin' out encore,
An' we start off again t'roo de sky, hooraw!
    for mak' de visite some more,
All de place on de parish we go dat night,
    w'erever dey get some dance,
Till I feel it so tire, I could sleep right off, but
    dey don't geev it me no chance.

De las' place we're passin' dat's Bill Boucher,
    he's very good frien' of me,
An' I t'ink it's near tam I was lef' dat crowd,
    so I'll snub de canoe on tree,
Den affer dead man he was safe inside, an'
    ev'rywan start danser,
I go on de barn wat's behin' de house, for
    see I can't hide away.

She's nice place de barn, an' got plaintee
    warm, an' I'm feel very glad be dere,
So long dead feller don't fin' me out, an' ketch
    it me on de hair,
But s'pose I get col', work him hard all night,
    'cos I make it wan leetle cough,
W'en de rooster he's scare, holler t'ree, four
    tam, an' whole t'ing she bus' right off.

I'll never see not'ing so quick again—Canoe
    an' dead man go scat!
She's locky de rooster he mak' de noise, bus'
    ev'ryt'ing up lak dat,
Or mebbe dem feller get me encore, an' tak'
    me on Hodson Bay,
But it's all right now, for de morning's come,
    an' he see me ole Bill Boucher.

I 'm feel it so tire, an' sore all de place, wit' all
    de hard work I do'
'Cos I 'm not very use for mak' paddle, me, on
    beeg, beeg phantome canoe,
But Bill an' hees boy dey was leef me up, an'
    carry me on maison
W'ere plaintee nice t'ing dey was mak' me eat
    an' drink it some whiskey blanc.

An' now w'en I 'm finish, w'at you t'ink it
    youse'f, 'bout story dat you was hear?
No wonner ma hair she is all turn w'ite before
    I get eighty year!
But 'member dis t'ing, I be tole you firs, don't
    los' it mes chers amis,
De man he can leev him on long, long tam,
    an' not see it La Chasse Gal'rie!

   .   .   .   .

He sit on de corner mos' every night, ole Phil-
    o-rum Juneau,
Spik wit' hesef,' an' shak' de head, an' smoke
    on de pipe also,
But kip very quiet, don't wak' him up, let him
    stay on de kitchen wall,
For if you believe w'at de ole man say, you
    believe anyt'ing at all.

De Bell of Saint Michel

GO 'way, go 'way, don't ring no more, ole
    bell of Saint Michel,
For if you do, I can't stay here, you know dat
    very well,
No matter how I close ma ear, I can't shut out
    de soun',
It rise so high 'bove all de noise of dis beeg
    Yankee town.

An' w'en it ring, I t'ink I feel de cool, cool
    summer breeze
Dat's blow across Lac Peezagonk, an' play
    among de trees,
Dey're makin' hay, I know mese'f, can smell
    de pleasant smell
O! how I wish I could be dere to-day on Saint
    Michel!

It's fonny t'ing, for me I·'m sure, dat's travel
    ev'ryw'ere,
How moche I t'ink of long ago w'en I be leevin'
    dere;
I can't 'splain dat at all, at all, mebbe it's
    naturel,
But I can't help it w'en I hear de bell of Saint
    Michel.

Dere 's plaintee t'ing I don't forget, but I
    remember bes'
De spot I fin' wan day on June de small san'-
    piper's nes'
An' dat hole on de reever w'ere I ketch de
    beeg, beeg trout
Was very nearly pull me in before I pull heem
    out.

An' leetle Elodie Leclaire, I wonner if she
    still
Leev jus' sam' place she use to leev on 'noder
    side de hill.
But s'pose she marry Joe Barbeau, dat 's alway
    hangin' roun'
Since I am lef' ole Saint Michel for work on
    Yankee town.

Ah! dere she go, ding dong, ding, dong, its
    back, encore again
An' ole chanson come on ma head of "a la
    claire fontaine,"
I 'm not surprise it soun' so sweet, more sweeter
    I can tell
For wit' de song also I hear de bell of Saint
    Michel.

It 's very strange about dat bell, go ding dong
  all de w'ile
For when I 'm small garçon at school, can't
  hear it half a mile;
But seems more farder I get off from Church
  of Saint Michel,
De more I see de ole village an' louder soun'
  de bell.

O! all de monee dat I mak' w'en I be travel roun'
Can't kip me long away from home on dis beeg
  Yankee town,
I t'ink I 'll settle down again on Parish Saint
  Michel,
An' leev an' die more satisfy so long I hear dat
  bell.

Pelang

PELANG! Pelang! Mon cher garçon,
 I t'ink of you—t'ink of you night and
  day—
Don't mak' no difference, seems to me
 De long long tam you 're gone away.

PELANG

De snow is deep on de Grande Montagne—
    Lak tonder de rapide roar below—
De sam' kin' night, ma boy get los'
    On beeg, beeg storm forty year ago.

An' I never was hear de win' blow hard,
    An' de snow come sweesh on de window
        pane—
But ev'ryt'ing 'pear lak' it 's yesterday
    An' whole of ma troub' is come back again.

Ah me! I was foolish young girl den
    It 's only ma own plaisir I care,
An' w'en some dance or soirée come off
    Dat 's very sure t'ing you will see me dere.

Don't got too moche sense at all dat tam,
    Run ev'ry place on de whole contree—
But I change beeg lot w'en Pelang come 'long,
    For I love him so well, kin' o' steady me.

An' he was de bes' boy on Coteau,
    An' t'ink I am de bes' girl too for sure—
He 's tole me dat, geev de ring also
    Was say on de inside "Je t'aime toujours."

I geev heem some hair dat come off ma head,
    I mak' de nice stocking for warm hees feet,
So ev'ryt'ing 's feex, w'en de spring is come
    For mak' mariée on de church toute suite.

"W'en de spring is come!" Ah I don't see
    dat,
  Dough de year is pass as dey pass before,
An' de season come, an' de season go,
  But our spring never was come no more.

.   .   .   .

It's on de fête of de jour de l'an,
  An' de worl' outside is cole an' w'ite
As I sit an' watch for mon cher Pelang
  For he's promise come see me dis very night.

Bonhomme Peloquin dat is leev near us—
  He's alway keep look heem upon de moon—
See fonny t'ing dere only week before,
  An' say he's expec' some beeg storm soon.

So ma fader is mak' it de laugh on me
  "Pelang he's believe heem de ole Bon-
    homme
Dat t'ink he see ev'ryt'ing on de moon
  An' mebbe he's feel it too scare for come."

But I don't spik not'ing I am so sure
  Of de promise Pelang is mak' wit' me—
An' de mos' beeg storm dat is never blow
  Can't kip heem away from hees own Marie.

I open de door, an' pass outside
  For see mese'f how de night is look
An' de star is commence for go couché
  De mountain also is put on hees tuque.

No sooner, I come on de house again
  W'ere ev'ryt'ing feel it so nice an' warm,
Dan out of de sky come de Nor' Eas' win'—
  Out of de sky come de beeg snow storm.

Blow lak not'ing I never see,
  Blow lak le diable he was mak' grande tour;
De snow come down lak wan avalanche,
  An' cole! Mon Dieu, it is cole for sure!

I t'ink, I t'ink of mon pauvre garçon,
  Dat 's out mebbe on de Grande Montagne;
So I place chandelle w'ere it 's geev good light,
  An' pray Le Bon Dieu he will help Pelang.

De ole folk t'ink I am go crazee,
  An' moder she 's geev me de good night kiss;
She say "Go off on your bed, Marie,
  Dere 's nobody come on de storm lak dis."

But ma eye don't close dat long, long, night
  For it seem jus' lak phantome is near,
An' I t'ink of de terrible Loup Garou
  An' all de bad story I offen hear.

Dere was tam I am sure somet'ing call "Marie"
    So plainly I open de outside door,
But it 's meet me only de awful storm,
    An de cry pass away—don't come no more.

An' de morning sun, w'en he 's up at las',
    Fin' me w'ite as de face of de snow itse'f,
For I know very well, on de Grande Montagne,
    Ma poor Pelang he 's come dead hese'f.

It 's noon by de clock w'en de storm blow off,
    An' ma fader an' broder start out for see
Any track on de snow by de mountain side,
    Or down on de place w'ere chemin should be.

No sign at all on de Grande Montagne,
    No sign all over de w'ite, w'ite snow;
Only hear de win' on de beeg pine tree,
    An' roar of de rapide down below.

An' w'ere is he lie, mon cher Pelang!
    Pelang ma boy I was love so well?
Only Le Bon Dieu up above
    An' mebbe de leetle snow bird can tell.

An' I t'ink I hear de leetle bird say,
    "Wait till de snow is geev up its dead,
Wait till I go, an' de robin come,
    An' den you will fin' hees cole, cole bed."

An' it 's all come true, for w'en de sun
  Is warm de side of de Grande Montagne
An' drive away all de winter snow,
  We fin' heem at las', mon cher Pelang!

An' here on de fête of de jour de l'an,
  Alone by mese'f I sit again,
W'ile de beeg, beeg storm is blow outside,
  An' de snow come sweesh on de window
    pane.

Not all alone, for I t'ink I hear
  De voice of ma boy gone long ago;
Can hear it above de hurricane,
  An' roar of de rapide down below.

Yes—yes—Pelang, mon cher garçon!
  I t'ink of you, t'ink of you night an' day,
Don't mak' no difference seems to me
  How long de tam you was gone away.

Mon Choual "Castor"

I 'M poor man, me, but I buy las' May
  Wan horse on de Comp'nie Passengaire,
An' auction feller w'at sole heem say
  She 's out of de full-breed "Messengaire."

Good trotter stock, also galluppe,
  But work long tam on de city car,
Of course she 's purty well break heem up,
  So come leetle cheap—twenty-wan dollarre.

Firs' chance I sen' heem on St. Cesaire,
  W'ere I t'ink he 's have moche better sight,
Mebbe de grass an' de contree air
  Very soon was feex heem up all right.

I lef' heem dere till de fall come 'long,
  An' dat trotter he can't eat grass no more,
An' w'en I go dere, I fin' heem strong
  Lak not'ing I never see before.

I heetch heem up on de light sulkee,
  L'enfant! dat horse he is cover groun'!
Don't tak' long tam for de crowd to see
  Mon choual he was leek all trotter roun'.

Come down de race course lak' oiseau
  Tail over datch boar', nice you please,
Can't tell for sure de quick he go,
  S'pose somew'ere 'bout two, t'ree forties.

I treat ma frien' on de whiskey blanc,
  An' we drink "Castor" he 's bonne santé
From L'Achigan to St. Armand,
  He 's bes' horse sure on de whole comté.

71

'Bout week on front of dis, Lalime,
 Dat man drive horse call "Clevelan' Bay"
Was challenge, so I match wit' heem
 For wan mile heat on straight away.

Dat 's twenty dollarre on wan side,
 De lawyer 's draw de paper out,
But if dem trotter come in tied,
 Wall! all dat monee 's go on spout.

Nex' t'ing ma backer man, Labrie,
 Tak' off his catch-book vingt cinq cents,
An' toss Lalime bes' two on t'ree
 For see who 's go on inside fence.

Bateese Lalime, he 's purty smart,
 An' gain dat toss wit' jockey trick.
I don't care me, w'en "Castor" start,
 Very soon I t'ink he 's mak' heem sick.

Beeg crowd of course was dere for see
 Dem trotter on de grand match race
Some people come from St. Remi
 An' some from plaintee 'noder place.

W'en all is ready, flag was fall
 An' way dem trotter pass on fence
Lak not'ing you never see at all,
 It mak' me t'ink of "St. Lawrence."*

* "St. Lawrence," the Canadian "Dexter."

MON CHOUAL "CASTOR"

"Castor," hees tail was stan' so straight
    Could place chapeau on de en' of top
An' w'en he struck two forty gait
    Don't seem he 's never go for stop.

Wall! dat 's all right for firs' half mile
    W'en Clevelan' Bay commence for break,
Dat mak' me feel very moche lak smile,
    I 'm sure "Castor" he 's took de cake.

But Lalime pull heem hard on line
    An' stop "Clevelan'" before go far,
It 's all no good, he can't ketch mine
    I 'm go more quicker lak express car.

I 'm feel all right for my monee,
    For sure mon Choual he 's took firs' place,
W 'en 'bout arpent from home, sapré,
    Somet'ing she 's happen, I 'm los' de race.

Wan bad boy he 's come out on track,
    I cannot see dat bad boy's han';
He 's hol' somet'ing behin' hees back,
    It was small bell, I understan'.

Can spik for dat, ma horse go well,
    An' never show no sign of sweat,
Until dat boy he 's ring hees bell—
    Misere! I t'ink I hear heem yet!

Wall! jus' so soon mon Choual "Castor"
    Was hear dat bell go kling! klang! kling!
He 's t'ink of course of city car,
    An' s'pose mus' be conductor ring.

Firs' t'ing I know ma trotter 's drop
    Dat tail was stan' so straight before,
An' affer dat, mebbe he stop
    For me, I don't know not'ing more.

But w'en I 'm come alive again
    I fin' dat horse call "Clevelan' Bay"
Was got firs' place, an' so he 's gain
    Dat wan mile heat on straight away.

An' now w'erever I am go
    Bad boy he 's sure for holler an' yell
Dis donc! Dis donc! Paul Archambault!
    W'at's matter wit' your chestnutte bell?

Mak' plaintee troub' dem bad garçons,
    An' offen ring some bell also,
Was mad! Could plonge on de St. Laurent
    An' w'at to do, "Castor" don't know.

Las' tam I pass de railway track
    For drive avec mon frere Alfred,
In-jinne she 's ring, "Castor" he 's back,
    Monjee! it 's fonny I 'm not come dead!

Toujours comme ça! an' mak' me sick,
   But horse dat work long on les chars
Can't broke dem off on fancy trick
   So now I 'm busy for sole "Castor."

Ole Tam on Bord-a Plouffe

I LAK on summer ev'ning, w'en nice cool
   win' is blowin'
   An' up above ma head, I hear de pigeon on
      de roof,
To bring ma chair an' sit dere, an' watch de
      current flowin'
   Of ole Riviere des Prairies as she pass de
      Bord-a Plouffe.

But it seem dead place for sure now, on shore
      down by de lan'in'—
   No more de voyageurs is sing lak dey was
      sing alway—
De tree dey 're commence growin' w'ere
      shaintee once is stan'in',
   An' no one scare de swallow w'en she fly
      across de bay.

75

I don't lak see de reever she 's never doin'
    not 'in'
  But passin' empty ev'ry day on Bout de l'ile
    below—
Ma ole shaloup dat 's lyin' wit' all its timber
    rottin'
  An' tam so change on Bord-a Plouffe since
    forty year ago!

De ice dat freeze on winter, might jus' as well
    be stay dere,
  For w'en de spring she 's comin' de only
    t'ing I see
Is two, t'ree piqnique feller, hees girl was row
    away dere,
  Don't got no use for water now, on Riviere
    des Prairies.

'T was diff'rent on dem summer you could n't
    see de reever,
  Wit' saw-log an' squar' timber raf', mos' all
    de season t'roo—
Two honder man an' more too—all busy lak
    de beaver,
  An' me! I 'm wan de pilot for ronne 'em
    down de "Soo."

Don't 'member lak I use to, for now I 'm get-
    tin' ole, me—
  But still I can't forget Bill Wade, an' Guil-
    laume Lagassé,
Joe Monferrand, Bazile Montour—wit' plaintee
    I can't tole, me,
  An' king of all de Bord-a Plouffe, M'sieu'
    Venance Lemay.

Lak small boy on hees lesson, I learn de way
    to han'le
  Mos' beeges' raf' is never float upon de
    Ottawaw,
Ma fader show me dat too, for well he know
    de channel,
  From Dutchman Rapide up above to Bout
    de l'ile en bas.

He 's smart man too, ma fader, only t'ing he
    got de bow-leg,
  Ridin' log w'en leetle feller, mebbe dat 's
    de reason w'y.
All de sam', if he 's in hurry, den Bagosh!
    he 's got heem no leg
  But wing an' fedder lak oiseau, was fly upon
    de sky!

OLE TAM ON BORD-A PLOUFFE

O dat was tam we 're happy, an' man dey 're
    alway singin',
  For if it 's hard work on de raf', w'y dere 's
    your monee sure!
An' ev'ry summer evenin', ole Bord-a Plouffe
    she 's ringin'
  Wit' "En Roulant ma Boulé" an' "J'
    aimerai toujour."

Dere dey 're comin' on de wagon! fine young
    feller ev'ry wan too,
  Dress im up de ole tam fashion, dat I lak for
    see encore,
Yellin' hooraw! t'roo de village, all de horse
    upon de ronne too,
  Ah poor Bord-a Plouffe! she never have dem
    tam again no more!

Very offen w'en I 'm sleepin', I was feel as if
    I 'm goin'
  Down de ole Riviere des Prairies on de raf'
    de sam as den—
An' ma dream is only lef' me, w'en de rooster
    commence crowin'
  But it can't do me no harm, 'cos it mak' me
    young again.

An' upon de morning early, w'en de reever fog
    is clearin'
  An' sun is makin' up hees min' for drive
    away de dew,
W'en young bird want hees breakfas', I wak'
    an' t'ink I 'm hearin'
  Somebody shout "Hooraw, Bateese, de raf'
    she 's wait for you."

Dat 's voice of Guillaume Lagassé was call me
    on de morning
  Jus' outside on de winder w'ere you look
    across de bay,
But he 's drown upon de Longue "Soo," wit'
    never word of warning
  An' green grass cover over poor Guillaume
    Lagassé.

I s'pose dat 's meanin' somet'ing—mebbe I 'm
    not long for stay here,
  Seein' all dem strange t'ing happen—dead
    frien' comin' roun' me so—
But I 'm sure I die more happy, if I got jus'
    wan more day here,
  Lak we have upon de ole tam Bord-a Plouffe
    of long ago!

The Grand Seigneur

TO the hut of the peasant, or lordly hall,
    To the heart of the king, or humblest
        thrall,
Sooner or late, love comes to all,
And it came to the Grand Seigneur, my dear,
    It came to the Grand Seigneur.

The robins were singing a roundelay,
And the air was sweet with the breath of May,
As a horseman rode thro' the forest way,
And he was a Grand Seigneur, my dear,
    He was a Grand Seigneur.

Lord of the Manor, Count Bellefontaine,
Had spurr'd over many a stormy plain
With gallants of France at his bridle rein,
For he was a brave Cavalier, my dear—
    He was a brave Cavalier.

But the huntsman's daughter, La Belle Marie,
Held the Knight's proud heart in captivity,
And oh! she was fair as the fleur de lys,
Tho' only a peasant maid, my dear,
    Only a peasant maid.

THE GRAND SEIGNEUR

Thro' the woodland depths on his charger grey
To the huntsman's cottage he rides away,
And the maiden lists to a tale to-day
That haughtiest dame might hear, my dear,
      That haughtiest dame might hear.

But she cried "Alas! it may never be,
For my heart is pledged to the young Louis,
And I love him, O Sire, so tenderly,
Tho' he's only a poor Chasseur, my Lord,
      Only a poor Chasseur."

"Enough," spake the Knight with a courtly
    bow,
"Be true to thy lover and maiden vow,
For virtue like thine is but rare, I trow,
And farewell to my dream of love, and thee,
      Farewell to my dream of thee."

And they say the gallant Count Bellefontaine
Bestowed on the couple a rich domain,
But you never may hear such tale again,
For he was a Grand Seigneur, my dear,
      He was a Grand Seigneur!

M'sieu Smit', The Adventures of an Englishman in the Canadian Woods

WAN morning de walkim boss say "Damase,
  I t'ink you're good man on canoe
  d'ecorce,
So I'll ax you go wit' your frien' Philéas
  An' meet M'sieu Smit' on Chenail W'ite
  Horse.

"He'll have I am sure de grosse baggage—
  Mebbe some valise—mebbe six or t'ree—
But if she's too moche for de longue portage
  'Poleon he will tak' 'em wit' mail buggee."

W'en we reach Chenail, plaintee peep be dere,
  An' wan frien' of me, call Placide Chretien,
'Splain all dat w'en he say man from Angleterre
  Was spik heem de crowd on de "Parisien."

Fonny way dat Englishman he'll be dress,
  Leetle pant my dear frien' jus' come on
  knee,
Wit' coat dat's no coat at all—only ves'
  An' hat—de more stranger I never see!

Wall! dere he sit on de en' some log
  An' swear heem in English purty loud
Den talk Français, w'ile hees chièn boule dog
  Go smellim an' smellim aroun' de crowd.

I spik im "Bonjour, M'sieu Smit', Bonjour,
  I hope dat yourse'f and famille she 's well?"
M'sieu Smit' he is also say "Bonjour,"
  An' call off hees dog dat 's commence for
    smell.

I tell heem my name dat 's Damase Labrie
  I am come wit' Philéas for mak' de trip,
An' he say I 'm de firs' man he never see
  Spik English encore since he lef' de ship.

He is also ax it to me "Damase,
  De peep she don't seem understan' Français,
W'at 's matter wit' dat?" An' I say "Becos'
  You mak' too much talk on de Parisien."

De groun' she is pile wit' baggage—Sapré!
  An' I see purty quick we got plaintee troub—
Two tronk, t'ree valise, four-five fusil,
  An' w'at M'sieu Smit' he is call "bat' tubbe."

M'sieu Smit' he 's tole me w'at for 's dat t'ing,
  An' it seem Englishman he don't feel correc'
Until he 's go plonge on some bat' morning
  An' sponge it hees possibill high hees neck.

Of course dat's not'ing of my beez-nesse,
　　He can plonge on de water mos' ev'ry
　　　　day,
But I t'ink for mese'f it mak' foolishness
　　An' don't do no good w'en your bonne
　　　　santé.

W'en I tell 'Poleon he mus' mak' dat job,
　　Dere's leetle too moche for canoe d'écorce,
He's mad right away an' say "Sapré diable!
　　You t'ink I go work lak wan niggerhorse?

"I'm not manufacture dat way, bâ non,
　　Dat rich stranger man he have lot monee,
I go see my frien' Onésime Gourdon,
　　An' tole heem bring horse wit' some more
　　　　buggee."

Wall! affer some w'ile dey'll arrange all dat,
　　'Poleon an' hees frien' Onésime Gourdon,
But w'en 'Poleon is tak' hole of bat',
　　He receive it beeg scare immediatement!

Dat chien boule dog, I was tole you 'bout·
　　I am not understan' w'at good she's for,
Eat 'Poleon's leg w'it hees teet' an' mout,
　　'Poleon he is feel very mad—by Gor!

M'SIEU SMIT'

Of course I am poule heem hees tail toute suite
  But I don't know some reason mak' all dis
      troub',
W'en I hear me dat Englishman, M'sieu Smit'
  Say 'Poleon, w'at for you took my tubbe?

"Leff 'im dere—for I don't low nobodee
  Walk heem off on any such way lak dat;
You may tak' all de res', an' I don't care me—
  But de man he'll be keel who is tak' my
      bat'."

"I will carry heem wit' me," say M'sieu Smit'—
  "W'erever dat tubbe she mus' go, I go—
No matter de many place we visite,
  An' my sponge I will tak' mese'f also."

Philéas say "Damase, we mus' buil' some raf'
  Or mebbe some feller be sure get drown";
Dis geev me plaisir, but I'm scare mak' laf',
  So I'll do it mese'f, inside, way down.

At las' we are start on voyage, sure nuff,
  M'sieu Smit' carry tubbe on de top hees
     head,
Good job, I t'ink so, de lac is n't rough,
  Or probably dis tam, we're all come dead.

M'SIEU SMIT'

De dog go wit' Onésime Gourdon,
    An' Onésime afferwar' say to me,
"Dat chien boule dog is eat 'Poleon
    Was de more quiet dog I never see."

But fun she 's commence on very nex' day
    W'en we go camp out on de Castor Noir.
Dat Englishman he 'll come along an' say
    "I hope some wil' Injun she don't be dere.

"I have hear many tam, dat de wood be foule
    Of Injun w'at tak' off de hair your head.
But so surely my name she 's Johnnie Boule
    If I see use dem feller I shoot it dead."

Philéas den pray harder, more quick he can
    Mebbe he 's t'ink dat 's hees las' portage
De moder hees fader, she 's Injun man
    Derefore an' also, he is wan Sauvage.

I say "Don't mak' it some excitement;
    Saison she is 'close' on de spring an' fall,
An' dem peep dat work on de Gouvernement
    Don't lak you shoot Injun dis mont' at all."

Nex' day M'sieu Smit' is perform hees plonge
    We see heem go done it—Philéas an' me,
An' w'en he 's hang up bat' tubbe an' sponge
    We go on de wood for mak' Chasse perdrix.

M'SIEU SMIT'

An' mebbe you will not believe to me,
　　But w'en we come back on de camp encore
De sponge of dat Englishman don't be see,
　　An' we fin' beeg bear she's go dead on shore.

Very fonny t'ing how he's loss hees life,
　　But Philéas he'll know hese'f purty quick,
He cut M'sieu Bear wit' hees hunter knife,
　　An' sponge she's fall out on de bear stummick.

Day affer we get two fox houn' from Boss
　　Dat's good for ketch deer on de fall an' spring,
Den place Englishman w'ere he can't get los'
　　An' tole heem shoot quicker he see somet'ing.

Wat's dat leetle deer got no horn at all?
　　She'll be moder small wan en suite bimeby,
Don't remember mese'f w'at name she's call,
　　But dat's de kin' start w'en de dog is cry.

We see heem come down on de runaway
　　De dog she is not very far behin'
An' w'en dey pass place M'sieu Smit' is stay
　　We expec' he will shoot or make noise some kin'!

But he's not shoot at all, mon cher ami,
　　So we go an' we ax "Is he see some deer?"
He say "Dat's long tam I am stay on tree
　　But I don't see not'ing she's pass on here."

We spik heem once more, "He don't see fox
      houn'?"
W'at you t'ink he is say, dat Englishman?
"Yes, I see dem pass quickly, upon de groun',
    Wan beeg yellow dog, an' two small brown
    wan."

He's feel de more bad I don't see before
    W'en he know dat beeg dog, she's wan small
    deer,
An' for mak' ev'ryt'ing correc' encore
    We drink I am sure six bouteilles de bière.

Nex' day—dat's Dimanche—he is spik to me,
    "Damase, you mus' feel leetle fatigue,
You may sle'p wit' Philéas w'ile I go an' see
    I can't get some nice quiet tam to-day."

So for keep 'way skeeter, an' fly also
    Bouteille from de shelf M'sieu Smit' he tak',
Den he start wit' his chien boule dog an' go
    For nice quiet walk on shore of lac.

We don't sle'p half hour we'n dere's beeg, beeg
    yell,
    Lak somet'ing I'm sure don't hear long tam,
An' we see wan feller we cannot tell,
    Till he spik it, "Damase! Philéas!! dam
    dam!!!

Den we know it at once mon, cher ami,
　　But she 's swell up hees face—hees neck an'
　　　　han'!
It seem all de skeeter on w'ole contree
　　Is jump on de head of dat Englishman.

Some water on poor M'sieu Smit' we 'll t'row,
　　An' w'en he 's tranquille fin' out ev'ry-
　　　　t'ing;
Bouteille he 's rub on, got some nice sirop
　　I was mak' mese'f on de wood las' spring.

Dere was jus' 'noder t'ing he seem for care
　　An' den he is feel it more satisfy,
Dat t'ing, my dear frien', was for keel some
　　　　bear,
　　If he 'll do dat wan tam, he 's prepare for die.

Philéas say he know w'ere some blue berree
　　Mak' very good place for de bear have fonne,
So we start nex' day on morning earlee,
　　An' M'sieu Smit' go wit' hees elephan' gun.

Wan woman sauvage she is come be dere,
　　Mebbe want some blue berree mak' some
　　　　pie,
Dat' Englishman shoot, he is t'ink she 's bear,
　　An' de woman she 's holler, "Mon Dieu,
　　　　I 'm die!"

M'sieu Smit' he don't do no harm, becos
    He is shake hese'f w'en he shoot dat squaw,
But scare he pay hunder' dollar cos'
    For keel some sauvage on de "close" saison.

T'ree day affer dat, we start out on lac
    For ketch on de water wan Cariboo,
But win' she blow strong, an' we can't get
      back
    Till we t'row ourse'f out on dat canoe.

We t'ink M'sieu Smit' he is sure be drown,
    Leetle w'ile we can't see heem again no
      more,
An' den he's come up from de place go down
    An' jomp on hees bat' tubbe an' try go shore.

W'en he's pass on de bat', he say "Hooraw!"
    An' commence right away for mak' some
      sing;
I'm sure you can hear heem ten-twelve arpent
    'Bout "Brittanie, she alway' mus' boss some-
      t'ing."

Dat's all I will tole you jus' now, my frien';
    I s'pose you don't know de more fonny case,
But if Englishman go on wood again
    I'll have more storee w'en you pass my
      place.

When Albani Sang

WAS workin' away on de farm dere, wan
    morning not long ago,
Feexin' de fence for winter—'cos dat's w'ere
    we got de snow!
W'en Jeremie Plouffe, ma neighbor, come over
    an' spik wit' me,
"Antoine, you will come on de city, for hear
    Ma-dam All-ba-nee?"

"W'at you mean?" I was sayin' right off, me,
    "Some woman was mak' de speech,
Or girl on de Hooraw Circus, doin' high kick
    an' screech?"
"Non—non," he is spikin'—"Excuse me,
    dat's be Ma-dam All-ba-nee
Was leevin' down here on de contree, two mile
    'noder side Chambly.

"She's jus' comin' over from Englan', on
    steamboat arrive Kebeck,
Singin' on Lunnon, an' Paree, an' havin' beeg
    tam, I expec',
But no matter de moche she enjoy it, for travel
    all roun' de worl',
Somet'ing on de heart bring her back here, for
    she was de Chambly girl.

"She never do not'ing but singin' an' makin,
    de beeg grande tour
An' travel on summer an' winter, so mus' be
    de firs' class for sure!
Ev'ryboddy I 'm t'inkin' was know her, an' I
    also hear 'noder t'ing,
She 's frien' on La Reine Victoria an' show her
    de way to sing!"

"Wall," I say, "you 're sure she is Chambly,
    w'at you call Ma-dam All-ba-nee?
Don't know me dat nam' on de Canton—I
    hope you 're not fool wit' me?"
An' he say, "Lajeunesse, dey was call her, be-
    fore she is come mariée,
But she 's takin' de nam' of her husban'—I
    s'pose dat 's de only way."

"C'est bon, mon ami," I was say me, "if I
    get t'roo de fence nex' day
An' she don't want too moche on de monee,
    den mebbe I see her play."
So I finish dat job on to-morrow, Jeremie he
    was helpin' me too,
An' I say, "Len' me t'ree dollar quickly for
    mak' de voyage wit' you."

Correc'—so we 're startin' nex' morning, an'
    arrive Montreal all right,
Buy dollar tiquette on de bureau, an' pass on
    de hall dat night.
Beeg crowd, wall! I bet you was dere too, all
    dress on some fancy dress,
De lady, I don't say not'ing, but man 's all
    w'ite shirt an' no ves'.

Don't matter, w'en ban' dey be ready, de fore-
    man strek out wit' hees steek,
An' fiddle an' ev'ryt'ing else too, begin for
    play up de musique.
It 's fonny t'ing too dey was playin' don't lak
    it mese'f at all,
I rader be lissen some jeeg, me, or w'at you
    call "Affer de ball."

An' I 'm not feelin' very surprise den, w'en de
    crowd holler out, "Encore,"
For mak' all dem feller commencin' an try
    leetle piece some more,
'T was better wan' too, I be t'inkin', but slow
    lak you 're goin' to die,
All de sam', noboddy say not'ing, dat mean
    dey was satisfy.

Affer dat come de Grande piano, lak we got on
    Chambly Hotel,
She 's nice lookin' girl was play dat, so of
    course she 's go off purty well,
Den feller he 's ronne out an' sing some, it 's
    all about very fine moon,
Dat shine on Canal, ev'ry night too, I 'm sorry
    I don't know de tune.

Nex' t'ing I commence get excite, me, for I
    don't see no great Ma-dam yet,
Too bad I was los' all dat monee, an' too late
    for de raffle tiquette!
W'en jus' as I feel very sorry, for come all de
    way from Chambly,
Jeremie he was w'isper, "Tiens, Tiens, prenez
    garde, she 's comin' Ma-dam All-ba-nee!"

Ev'ryboddy seem glad w'en dey see her, come
    walkin' right down de platform,
An' way dey mak' noise on de han' den, w'y!
    it 's jus' lak de beeg tonder storm!
I 'll never see not'ing lak dat, me, no matter
    I travel de worl',
An' Ma-dam, you t'ink it was scare her? Non,
    she laugh lak de Chambly girl!

Dere was young feller comin' behin' her, walk
    nice, comme un Cavalier,
An' before All-ba-nee she is ready an' piano
    get startin' for play,
De feller commence wit' hees singin' more
    stronger dan all de res',
I t'ink he 's got very bad manner, know not'ing
    at all politesse.

Ma-dam, I s'pose she get mad den, an' before
    anyboddy can spik,
She settle right down for mak' sing too, an'
    purty soon ketch heem up quick,
Den she 's kip it on gainin' an' gainin', till de
    song it is tout finis,
An' w'en she is beatin' dat feller, Bagosh! I am
    proud Chambly!

I 'm not very sorry at all, me, w'en de feller
    was ronnin' away,
An' man he 's come out wit' de piccolo, an'
    start heem right off for play,
For it 's kin' de musique I be fancy, Jeremie
    he is lak it also,
An' wan de bes' t'ing on dat ev'ning is man
    wit' de piccolo!

Den mebbe ten minute is passin', Ma-dam she
    is comin' encore,
Dis tam all alone on de platform, dat feller
    don't show up no more,
An' w'en she start off on de singin' Jeremie
    say, "Antoine, dat's Français,"
Dis give us more pleasure, I tole you, 'cos
    w'y? We're de pure Canayen!

Dat song I will never forget me,' t was song of
    de leetle bird,
W'en he's fly from it's nes' on de tree top,
    'fore res' of de worl' get stirred,
Ma-dam she was tole us about it, den start off
    so quiet an' low,
An' sing lak de bird on de morning, de poor
    leetle small oiseau.

I 'member wan tam I be sleepin' jus' onder
    some beeg pine tree
An song of de robin wak' me, but robin he
    don't see me,
Dere's not'ing for scarin' dat bird dere, he's
    feel all alone on de worl',
Wall! Ma-dam she mus' lissen lak dat too, w'en
    she was de Chambly girl!

'Cos how could she sing dat nice chanson, de
    sam' as de bird I was hear,
Till I see it de maple an' pine tree an' Riche-
    lieu ronnin' near,
Again I 'm de leetle feller, lak young colt upon
    de spring
Dat 's jus' on de way I was feel, me, w'en Ma-
    dam All-ba-nee is sing!

An' affer de song it is finish, an' crowd is mak'
    noise wit' its han',
I s'pose dey be t'inkin' I 'm crazy, dat mebbe
    I don't onderstan',
Cos I 'm set on de chair very quiet, mese'f an'
    poor Jeremie,
An' I see dat hees eye it was cry too, jus' sam'
    way it go wit' me.

Dere 's rosebush outside on our garden, ev'ry
    spring it has got new nes',
But only wan bluebird is buil' dere, I know her
    from all de res',
An' no matter de far she be flyin' away on de
    winter tam,
Back to her own leetle rosebush she 's comin'
    dere jus' de sam'.

7

We 're not de beeg place on our Canton, mebbe
    cole on de winter, too,
But de heart 's "Canayen" on our body, an'
    dat 's warm enough for true!
An' w'en All-ba-nee was got lonesome for
    travel all roun' de worl'
I hope she 'll come home, lak de bluebird an'
    again be de Chambly girl!

De Camp on de " Cheval Gris"

YOU 'member de ole log-camp, Johnnie, up
    on de Cheval Gris,
W'ere we work so hard all winter, long ago
    you an' me?
Dere was fourteen man on de gang, den, all
    from our own paroisse,
An' only wan lef' dem feller is ourse'f an'
    Pierre Laframboise.

But Pierre can't see on de eye, Johnnie, I t'ink
    it 's no good at all!
An' it was n't for not'ing you 're gettin' rheu-
    mateez on de leg las' fall!
I t'ink it 's no use waitin', for neider can come
    wit' me,
So alone I mak' leetle visit dat camp on de
    Cheval Gris.

An' if only you see it, Johnnie, an' change dere
    was all aroun',
Ev'ryt'ing gone but de timber an' dat is all
    fallin' down;
No sign of portage by de reever w'ere man dey
    was place canoe,
W'y, Johnnie, I 'm cry lak de bebé, an' I 'm
    glad you don't come, mon vieux!

But strange t'ing's happen me dere, Johnnie,
    mebbe I go asleep,
As I lissen de song of de rapide, as pas' de
    Longue Soo she sweep,
Ma head she go biz-z-z lak de sawmeel, I don't
    know w'at 's wrong wit' me,
But firs' t'ing I don't know not'ing, an' den
    w'at you t'ink I see?

Yourse'f an' res' of de boy, Johnnie, by light
    of de coal oil lamp,
An you 're singin' an' tolin' story, sittin
    aroun' de camp,
We hear de win' on de chimley, an' we know
    it was beeg, beeg storm,
But ole box stove she is roarin', an' camp's
    feelin' nice an' warm.

I t'ink you 're on boar' of de raf', Johnnie,
    near head of Riviere du Loup,
W'en LeRoy an' young Patsy Kelly get drown
    comin' down de Soo,
Wall! I see me dem very same feller, jus' lak
    you see me to-day,
Playin' dat game dey call checker, de game dey
    was play alway!

An' Louis Charette asleep, Johnnie, wit' hees
    back up agen de wall,
Makin' soche noise wit' hees nose, dat you
    t'ink it was moose on de fall,
I s'pose he 's de mos' fattes' man dere 'cept
    mebbe Bateese La Rue,
But if I mak fonne on poor Louis, I know he
    was good boy too!

W'at you do over dere on your bunk, Johnnie,
    lightin' dem allumettes,
Are you shame 'cos de girl she write you, is
    dat de las' wan you get?
It 's fonny you can't do widout it ev'ry tam
    you was goin' bed,
W'y readin' dat letter so offen, you mus' have
    it all on de head!

Dat 's de very sam' letter, Johnnie, was comin'
    t 'ree mont' ago,
I t'ink I know somet'ing about it, 'cos I fin' it
    wan day on de snow.
An' I see on de foot dat letter, Philomene she
    is do lak dis: ***
I 'm not very moche on de school, me, but I
    t'ink dat was mean de kiss.

Wall! nobody 's kickin' de row, Johnnie, an'
    if allumettes' fini,
Put Philomene off on your pocket, an' sing
    leetle song wit' me;
For don't matter de hard you be workin' tou-
    jours you 're un bon garçon,
An' nobody sing lak our Johnnie, Kebeck to
    de Mattawa!

An' it 's den you be let her go, Johnnie, till
    roof she was mos' cave in,
An' if dere 's firs' prize on de singin', Bagosh!
    you 're de man can win!
Affer dat come fidelle of Joe Pilon, an' he 's
    feller can make it play,
So we 're clearin' de floor right off den, for
    have leetle small danser.

An' w'en dance she was tout finis, Johnnie, I
    go de sam' bunk wit' you
W'ere we sleep lak two broder, an' dream of
    de girl on Riviere du Loup,
Very nice ontil somebody call me, it soun' lak
    de boss Pelang,
"Leve toi, Jeremie ma young feller, or else
    you 'll be late on de gang."

An' den I am wak' up, Johnnie, an' w'ere do
    you t'ink I be?
Dere was de wood an' mountain, dere was de
    Cheval Gris,
But w'ere is de boy an' musique I hear only
    w'ile ago?
Gone lak de flower las' summer, gone lak de
    winter snow!

An' de young man was bring me up, Johnnie,
    dat 's son of ma boy Maxime,
Say, "Gran'fader, w'at is de matter, you
    havin' de bad, bad dream?
Come look on your face on de well dere, it 's
    w'ite lak I never see,
Mebbe 't was better you 're stayin', an' not
    go along wit' me."

An' w'en I look down de well, Johnnie, an' see
    de ole feller dere,
I say on mese'f "you be makin' fou Jeremie
    Chateauvert,
For t'ink you 're garçon agen. Ha! ha! jus'
    'cos you are close de eye,
An' only commence for leevin' w'en you 're
    ready almos' for die!"

Ah! dat 's how de young day pass, Johnnie,
    purty moche lak de t'ing I see,
Sometam dey be las' leetle longer, sam' as wit'
    you an' me,
But no matter de ole we 're leevin', de tam
    she must come some day,
W'en boss on de place above, Johnnie, he 's
    callin' us all away.

I 'm glad I was go on de camp, Johnnie, I
    t'ink it will do me good,
Mebbe it 's las' tam too, for sure, I 'll never
    pass on de wood,
For I don't expec' moche longer ole Jeremie
    will be lef',
But about w'at I see dat day, Johnnie, tole
    nobody but yourse'f.

De Stove Pipe Hole

DAT 's very cole an' stormy night on Vil-
lage St. Mathieu,
W'en ev'ry wan he 's go couché, an' dog was
quiet, too—
Young Dominique is start heem out see Em-
meline Gourdon,
Was leevin' on her fader's place, Maxime de
Forgeron.

Poor Dominique he 's lak dat girl, an'
love her mos' de tam,
An' she was mak' de promise—sure—some day
she be his famme,
But she have worse ole fader dat 's never on de
worl',
Was swear onless he 's riche lak diable, no
feller 's get hees girl.

He 's mak' it plaintee fuss about hees daughter
Emmeline,
Dat 's mebbe nice girl, too, but den, Mon Dieu,
she 's not de queen!
An' w'en de young man 's come aroun' for
spark it on de door,
An' hear de ole man swear "Bapteme!" he 's
never come no more.

Young Dominique he 's sam' de res',—was scare
    for ole Maxime,
He don't lak risk hese'f too moche for chances
    seein' heem,
Dat 's only stormy night he come, so dark you
    cannot see,
An dat 's de reason w'y also, he 's climb de
    gallerie.

De girl she 's waitin' dere for heem—don't
    care about de rain,
So glad for see young Dominique he 's comin'
    back again,
Dey bote forget de ole Maxime, an' mak de
    embrasser
An affer dey was finish dat, poor Dominique is
    say—

"Good-bye, dear Emmeline, good-bye; I 'm
    goin' very soon,
For you I got no better chance, dan feller on de
    moon—
It 's all de fault your fader, too, dat I be go
    away,
He 's got no use for me at all—I see dat ev'ry
    day.

"He's never meet me on de road but he is say
    'Sapré!'
An' if he ketch me on de house I'm scare he's
    killin' me,
So I mus' lef' ole St. Mathieu, for work on
    'noder place,
An' till I mak de beeg for-tune, you never see
    ma face."

Den Emmeline say "Dominique, ma love
    you'll alway be
An' if you kiss me two, t'ree tam I'll not tole
    noboddy—
But prenez garde ma fader, please, I know
    he's gettin' ole—
All sam' he offen walk de house upon de stock-
    in' sole.

"Good-bye, good-bye, cher Dominique! I
    know you will be true,
I don't want no riche feller me, ma heart she
    go wit' you,"
Dat's very quick he's kiss her den, before de
    fader come,
But don't get too moche pleasurement—so
    'fraid de ole Bonhomme.

Wall! jus' about dey 're half way t'roo wit all
    dat love beez-nesse
Emmeline say, "Dominique, w'at for you 're
    scare lak all de res'?
Don't see mese'f moche danger now de ole man
    come aroun',"
W'en minute affer dat, dere 's noise, lak' house
    she 's fallin' down.

Den Emmeline she holler "Fire! will no wan
    come for me?"
An Dominique is jomp so high, near bus' de
    gallerie,—
"Help! help! right off," somebody shout,
    "I 'm killin' on ma place,
It 's all de fault ma daughter, too, dat girl
    she 's ma disgrace."

He 's kip it up long tam lak dat, but not hard
    tellin' now,
W'at 's all de noise upon de house—who 's
    kick heem up de row?
It seem Bonhomme was sneak aroun' upon de
    stockin' sole,
An' firs' t'ing den de ole man walk right t'roo
    de stove pipe hole.

W'en Dominique is see heem dere, wit' wan
    leg hang below,
An' 'noder leg straight out above, he 's glad
    for ketch heem so—
De ole man can't do not'ing, den, but swear
    and ax for w'y
Noboddy tak' heem out dat hole before he 's
    comin' die.

Den Dominique he spik lak dis, "Mon cher
    M'sieur Gourdon
I 'm not riche city feller, me, I 'm only habi-
    tant,
But I was love more I can tole your daughter
    Emmeline,
An' if I marry on dat girl, Bagosh! she 's lak de
    Queen.

"I want you mak de promise now, before it 's
    come too late,
An' I mus' tole you dis also, dere 's not moche
    tam for wait.
Your foot she 's hangin' down so low, I 'm
    'fraid she ketch de cole,
Wall! if you give me Emmeline, I pull you out
    de hole."

Dat mak' de ole man swear more hard he never
    swear before,
An' wit' de foot he 's got above, he 's kick it
    on de floor,
"Non, non," he say "Sapré tonnerre! she
    never marry you,
An' if you don't look out you get de jail on
    St. Mathieu."

"Correc'," young Dominique is say, "mebbe
    de jail 's tight place,
But you got wan small corner, too, I see it on
    de face,
So if you don't lak geev de girl on wan poor
    habitant,
Dat 's be mese'f, I say, Bonsoir, mon cher
    M'sieur Gourdon."

"Come back, come back," Maxime is shout—
    "I promise you de girl,
I never see no wan lak you—no never on de
    worl'!
It 's not de nice trick you was play on man
    dat 's gettin' ole,
But do jus' w'at you lak, so long you pull me
    out de hole."

"Hooraw! Hooraw!" Den Dominique is pull
    heem out tout suite
An' Emmeline she 's helpin' too for place heem
    on de feet,
An' affer dat de ole man 's tak' de young peep
    down de stair,
W'ere he is go couchè right off, an' dey go on
    parloir.

Nex' Sunday morning dey was call by M'sieur
    le Curé.
Get marry soon, an' ole Maxime geev Emme-
    line away;
Den affer dat dey settle down lak habitant is
    do,
An' have de mos' fine familee on Village St.
    Mathieu.

"De Snowbird"

O LEETLE bird dat 's come to us w'en
    stormy win' she 's blowin',
  An' ev'ry fiel' an' mountain top is cover wit'
    de snow,
How far from home you 're flyin', noboddy 's
    never knowin'
  For spen' wit' us de winter tam, mon cher
    petit oiseau!

We alway know you 're comin', w'en we hear
      de firs' beeg storm,
  A sweepin' from de sky above, an' screamin'
      as she go—
Can tell you 're safe inside it, w'ere you 're
      keepin' nice an' warm,
  But no wan 's never see you dere, mon cher
      petit oiseau!

Was it 'way behin' de mountain, dat de nort'
      win' ketch you sleepin'
  Mebbe on your leetle nes' too, an' before de
      wing she grow,
Lif' you up an' bring you dat way, till some
      morning fin' you peepin'
  Out of new nes' on de snow dreef, mon pauv'
      petit oiseau!

All de wood is full on summer, wit' de many
      bird is sing dere,
  Dey mus' offen know each oder, mebbe mak'
      de frien' also,
But w'en you was come on winter, never seein'
      wan strange wing dere
  Was it mak' you feelin' lonesome, mon pauv'
      petit oiseau?

Plaintee bird is alway hidin' on some place no
    wan can fin' dem,
  But ma leetle bird of winter, dat was not de
    way you go—
For de chil'ren on de roadside, you don't seem
    to care for min' dem
  W'en dey pass on way to schoolhouse, mon
    cher petit oiseau!

No wan say you sing lak robin, but you got no
    tam for singin'
  So busy it was keepin' you get breakfas' on
    de snow,
But de small note you was geev us, w'en it join
    de sleigh bell ringin'
  Mak' de true Canadian music, mon cher petit
    oiseau!

O de long an' lonesome winter, if you 're never
    comin' near us'
  If we miss you on de roadside, an' on all de
    place below!
But le bon Dieu he will sen' you troo de storm
    again for cheer us,
  W'en we mos' was need you here too, mon
    cher petit oiseau!

The Habitant's Jubilee Ode

I READ on de paper mos' ev'ry day, all about
    Jubilee
An' grande procession movin' along, an' passin'
    across de sea,
Dat 's chil'ren of Queen Victoriaw comin' from
    far away
For tole Madame w'at dey t'ink of her, an'
    wishin' her bonne santé.

An' if any wan want to know pourquoi les
    Canayens should be dere
Wit' res' of de worl' for shout "Hooraw" an'
    t'row hees cap on de air,
Purty quick I will tole heem de reason, w'y we
    feel lak de oder do,
For if I 'm only poor habitant, I 'm not on de
    sapré fou.

Of course w'en we t'ink it de firs' go off, I
    know very strange it seem
For fader of us dey was offen die for flag of
    L'Ancien Regime.
From day w'en de voyageurs come out all de
    way from ole St. Malo,
Flyin' dat flag from de mas' above, an' long
    affer dat also.

De English fight wit' de Frenchman den over
    de whole contree,
Down by de reever, off on de wood, an' out on
    de beeg, beeg sea,
Killin' an' shootin', an' raisin' row, half tam
    dey don't know w'at for,
W'en it's jus' as easy get settle down, not
    makin' de crazy war.

Sometam' dey be quiet for leetle w'ile, you
    t'ink dey don't fight no more,
An' den w'en dey're feelin' all right agen,
    Bang! jus' lak' she was before.
Very offen we're beatin' dem on de fight,
    sometam' dey can beat us, too,
But no feller's scare on de 'noder man, an'
    bote got enough to do.

An' all de long year she be go lak' dat, we
    never was know de peace,
Not'ing but war from de wes' contree down to
    de St. Maurice;
Till de las' fight's comin' on Canadaw, an'
    brave Generale Montcalm
Die lak' a sojer of France is die, on Battle of
    Abraham.

Dat 's finish it all, an' de English King is axin'
    us stayin' dere
W'ere we have sam' right as de 'noder peep
    comin' from Angleterre.
Long tam' for our moder so far away de poor
    Canayens is cry,
But de new step-moder she 's good an' kin',
    an' it 's all right bimeby.

If de moder come dead w'en you 're small garçon
    leavin' you dere alone,
Wit' nobody watchin' for fear you fall, an hurt
    youse'f on de stone,
An' 'noder good woman she tak' your han' de
    sam' your own moder do,
Is it right you don't call her moder, is it right
    you don't love her too?

Bâ non, an' dat was de way we feel, w'en de
    ole Regime 's no more,
An' de new wan come, but don't change
    moche, w'y it 's jus' lak' it be before.
Spikin' Français lak' we alway do, an' de Eng-
    lish dey mak no fuss,
An' our law de sam', wall, I don't know me,
    't was better mebbe for us.

So de sam' as two broder we settle down,
    leevin' dere han' in han',
Knowin' each oder, we lak' each oder, de French
    an' de Englishman,
For it 's curi's t'ing on dis worl', I 'm sure you
    see it agen an' agen,
Dat offen de mos' worse ennemi, he 's comin'
    de bes', bes' frien'.

So we 're kipin' so quiet long affer dat, w'en
    las' of de fightin's done,
Dat plaintee is say, de new Canayens forget
    how to shoot de gun;
But Yankee man 's smart, all de worl' know
    dat, so he 's firs' fin' mistak' wan day
W'en he 's try cross de line, fusil on hee's han',
    near place dey call Chateaugay.

Of course it 's bad t'ing for poor Yankee man,
    De Salaberry be dere
Wit' habitant farmer from down below, an'
    two honder Voltigeurs,
Dem feller come off de State, I s'pose, was
    fightin' so hard dey can
But de blue coat sojer he don't get kill, is de
    locky Yankee man!

Since den w'en dey 're comin' on Canadaw, we
    alway be treat dem well,
For dey 're spennin' de monee lak' gentil-
    hommes, an' stay on de bes' hotel,
Den "Bienvenu," we will spik dem, an' "Come
    back agen nex' week,
So long you was kip on de quiet an' don't talk
    de politique!"

Yass, dat is de way Victoriaw fin' us dis
    jubilee,
Sometam' we mak' fuss about not'ing, but
    it 's all on de familee,
An' w'enever dere 's danger roun' her, no
    matter on sea or lan',
She 'll find that les Canayens can fight de
    sam' as bes' Englishman.

An' onder de flag of Angleterre, so long as
    dat flag was fly—
Wit' deir English broder, les Canayens is satisfy
    leev an' die.
Dat 's de message our fader geev us w'en dey
    're fallin' on Chateaugay,
An' de flag was kipin' dem safe den, dat 's de
    wan we will kip alway!

Ole Docteur Fiset

OLE Docteur Fiset of Saint Anicet,
   Sapré tonnerre! he was leev long tam!
I 'm sure he 's got ninety year or so,
Beat all on de Parish 'cept Pierre Courteau,
   An' day affer day he work all de sam'.

Dat house on de hill, you can see it still,
   She 's sam' place he buil' de firs' tam' he come
Behin' it dere 's one leetle small jardin
Got plaintee de bes' tabac Canayen
   Wit' fameuse apple an' beeg blue plum.

An' dey 're all right dere, for de small boy 's
      scare
   No matter de apple look nice an' red,
For de small boy know if he 's stealin' some
Den Docteur Fiset on dark night he come,
   An' cut leetle feller right off hees head!

But w'en dey was rap, an' tak' off de cap,
   M'sieu' le Docteur he will say "Entrez,"
Den all de boy pass on jardin behin'
W'ere dey eat mos' ev'ryt'ing good dey fin',
   Till dey can't go on school nearly two, t'ree
      day.

118

But Docteur Fiset, not moche fonne he get,
   Drivin' all over de whole contree,
If de road she's bad, if de road she's good,
W'en ev'ryt'ing's drown on de Spring-tam
     flood,
   An' workin' for not'ing half tam' mebbe!

Let her rain or snow, all he want to know
   Is jus' if anywan 's feelin' sick,
For Docteur Fiset 's de ole fashion kin'
Doin' good was de only t'ing on hees min'
   So he got no use for de politique.

An' he's careful too, 'cos firs' t'ing he do,
   For fear dere was danger some fever case,
Is tak' w'en he's come leetle w'isky chaud,
Den 'noder wan too jus' before he go,
   He's so scare carry fever aroun' de place!

On nice summer day w'en we're makin'
     hay
   Dere's not'ing more pleasant for us I'm
     sure
Dan see de ole man come joggin' along,
Alway singin' some leetle song,
   An' hear heem say "Tiens, mes amis, Bon
     jour!"

An' w'en de cole rain was commence again
   An' we 're sittin' at home on some warm
      cornerre,
If we hear de buggy an' see de light
Tearin' along t'roo de black, black night,
   We know right off dat 's de ole Docteur!

An' he 's smart horse sure, w'at he call "Fau-
      bourg,"
   Ev'ry place on de Parish he know dem all,
An' you ought to see de nice way he go
For fear he 's upsettin' upon de snow,
   W'en ole man 's asleep on de cariole!

I 'member w'en poor Hormisdas Couture
   Get sick on hees place twenty mile away
An' hees boy Ovide he was come "Raquette"
W'at you call "Snowshoe," for Docteur Fiset,
   An' Docteur he start wit' hees horse an'
      sleigh.

All de night before, de beeg storm she
      roar,
   An' mos' of de day it 's de sam' also,
De drif' was pilin' up ten feet high
You can't see not'ing dis side de sky,
   Not'ing but wan avalanche of snow.

I 'm hearin' de bell w'en I go on de well
    For water de cattle on barn close by,
But I only ketch sight of hees cheval blanc
An' hees coonskin coat wit' de capuchon
    An' de storm tak' heem off, jus' de sam' he fly.

Mus' be le Bon Dieu dat is help him t'roo,
    Ole Docteur Fiset an' hees horse "Fau-
        bourg,"
'T was somet'ing for splain-me, wall I don't
    care,
But somehow or 'noder he 's gettin' dere,
    An' save de life Hormisdas Couture.

But it 's sam' alway, lak' dat ev'ry day,
    He never was spare hese'f pour nous autres,
He don't mak' moche monee, Docteur Fiset,
An' offen de only t'ing he was get
    Is de prayer of poor man, an' wan bag of oat.

   .   .   .   .

Wall! Docteur Fiset of Saint Anicet
    He is not dead yet! an' I 'm purty sure
If you 're passin' dat place about ten year more
You will see heem go roun' lak he go before
    Wit' de ole cariole an' hees horse "Fau-
        bourg!"

Johnnie   Courteau

JOHNNIE COURTEAU of de mountain
  Johnnie Courteau of de hill
Dat was de boy can shoot de gun
Dat was de boy can jomp an' run
An' it 's not very offen you ketch heem still
                                    Johnnie Courteau!

Ax dem along de reever
Ax dem along de shore
Who was de mos' bes' fightin' man
From Managance to Shaw-in-i-gan?
De place w'ere de great beeg rapide roar,
                                    Johnnie Courteau!

Sam' t'ing on ev'ry shaintee
Up on de Mekinac
Who was de man can walk de log,
W'en w'ole of de reever she 's black wit' fog
An' carry de beeges' load on hees back?
                                    Johnnie Courteau!

On de rapide you want to see heem
If de raf' she 's swingin' roun'
An' he 's yellin' "Hooraw Bateese! good man!"
W'y de oar come double on hees han'
W'en he 's makin' dat raf' go flyin' down
                                    Johnnie Courteau!

JOHNNIE COURTEAU

An' Tête de Boule chief can tole you
De feller w'at save hees life
W'en beeg moose ketch heem up a tree
Who 's shootin' dat moose on de head, sapree!
An' den run off wit' hees Injun wife?
Johnnie Courteau!

An' he only have pike pole wit' heem
On Lac a la Tortue
W'en he meet de bear comin' down de hill
But de bear very soon is get hees fill!
An' he sole dat skin for ten dollar too,
Johnnie Courteau!

Oh he never was scare for not'ing
Lak de ole coureurs de bois,
But w'en he 's gettin' hees winter pay
De bes' t'ing sure is kip out de way
For he 's goin' right off on de Hip Hooraw!
Johnnie Courteau!

Den pullin' hees sash aroun' heem
He dance on hees botte sauvage
An' shout "All aboar' if you want to fight!"
Wall! you never can see de finer sight
W'en he go lak dat on de w'ole village!
Johnnie Courteau!

But Johnnie Courteau get marry
On Philomene Beaurepaire
She 's nice leetle girl was run de school
On w'at you call Parish of Sainte Ursule
An' he see her off on de pique-nique dere
                                    Johnnie Courteau!

Den somet'ing come over Johnnie
W'en he marry on Philomene
For he stay on de farm de w'ole year roun'
He chop de wood an' he plough de groun'
An' he 's quieter feller was never seen,
                                    Johnnie Courteau!

An' ev'ry wan feel astonish
From La Tuque to Shaw-in-i-gan
W'en dey hear de news was goin' aroun'
Along on de reever up an' down
How wan leetle woman boss dat beeg man
                                    Johnnie Courteau!

He never come out on de evening
No matter de hard we try
'Cos he stay on de kitchen an' sing hees song
          "A la claire fontaine,
          M'en allant promener,
          J'ai trouvé l'eau si belle

Que je m'y suis baigner!
Lui y'a longtemps que je t'aime
Jamais je ne t'oublierai."

Rockin' de cradle de w'ole night long
Till baby 's asleep on de sweet bimeby
                              Johnnie Courteau!

An' de house, wall! I wish you see it
De place she 's so nice an' clean
Mus' wipe your foot on de outside door,
You 're dead man sure if you spit on de floor,
An' he never say not'ing on Philomene,
                              Johnnie Courteau!

An' Philomene watch de monee
An' put it all safe away
On very good place; I dunno w'ere
But anyhow nobody see it dere
So she 's buyin' new farm de noder day
                              MADAME Courteau!

The Corduroy Road

DE corduroy road go bompety bomp,
   De corduroy road go jompety jomp,
An' he 's takin' beeg chances upset hees load
De horse dat 'll trot on de corduroy road.

125

Of course it 's purty rough, but it 's handy t'ing
    enough
An' dey mak' it wit' de log all jine togeder
W'en dey strek de swampy groun' w'ere de water
    hang aroun'
Or passin' by some tough ole beaver medder.

But it 's not macadamize, so if you 're only
    wise
You will tak' your tam an' never min' de worry
For de corduroy is bad, an' will mak' you plaintee
    mad
By de way de buggy jomp, in case you hurry.

An' I 'm sure you don't expec' leetle Victorine
    Leveque
She was knowin' moche at all about dem places,
'Cos she 's never dere before, till young Zeph-
    irin Madore
He was takin' her away for see de races.

O, I wish you see her den, dat 's before she marry,
    w'en
She 's de fines' on de lan' but no use talkin'
I can bet you w'at you lak, if you meet her you
    look back
Jus' to watch de fancy way dat girl is walkin'.

Yass de leetle Victorine was de nices' girl between
De town of Yamachiche an' Maskinongé,
But she's stuck up an' she's proud, an' you'll
    never count de crowd
Of de boy she geev' it w'at dey call de congé.

Ah! de moder spoil her sure, for even Joe
    D'Amour
W'en he's ready nearly ev'ry t'ing to geev
    her
If she mak' de mariée, only say, "please go
    away"
An' he's riches habitant along de reever.

Zephirin he try it too, an' he's workin' some-
    t'ing new
For he's makin' de ole woman many presen'
Prize package on de train, umbrella for de
    rain
But she's grompy all de tam, an' never pleasan'.

Wall, w'en he ax Ma-dame tak' de girl away dat
    tam
See dem races on Sorel wit' all de trotter
De moder say "All right if you bring her home
    to-night
Before de cow's milk, I let her go, ma daughter."

So Victorine she go wit' Zephirin her beau
On de yankee buggy mak' it on St. Bruno
An' w'en dey pass hotel on de middle of Sorel
Dey 're puttin' on de beeges' style dat you
    know.

Wall! dey got some good horse dere, but Zeph-
    irin don't care
He 's back it up hees own paroisse, ba golly,
An' he mak' it t'ree doll-arre w'en Maskinongé
    Star
On de two mile heat was beatin' Sorel Molly.

Victorine don't min' at all, till de "free for all"
    dey call
Dat 's de las' race dey was run before de snow
    fly
Den she say "I t'ink de cow mus' be gettin'
    home soon now
An' you know it 's only clock ole woman go by.

"An' if we 're comin' late w'en de cow pass on
    de gate
You 'll be sorry if you hear de way she talk
    dere,
So w'en I see de race on Sorel or any place
Affer dis, you may be sure I got to walk dere."

Den he laugh dat Zephirin, an' he say "Your
    poor mama
I know de pile she t'ink about her daughter
So we 'll tak' de short road back on de corduroy
    race track
Don't matter if we got to sweem de water."

No wonder he is smile till you hear heem half a
    mile
For dat morning he was tole hees leetle broder
Let de cattle out de gate, so he know it 's purty
    late
By de tam dem cow was findin' out each oder.

So along de corduroy de young girl an' de boy
Dey was kipin' up a joggin' nice an' steady
It is n't heavy load, an' Guillaume he know de
    road
For many tam he 's been dat way already.

But de girl she fin' it slow, so she ax de boy to
    go
Somet'ing better dan a mile on fifteen minute
An' he 's touch heem up Guillaume; so dat
    horse he lay for home
An' de nex' t'ing Victorine she know she 's
    in it.

"O, pull him in," she yell, "for even on Sorel
I am sure I never see de quicker racer,"
But it 's leetle bit too late, for de horse is get
      hees gait
An' de worse of all ba gosh! Guillaume 's a pacer.

See hees tail upon de air, no wonder she was scare
But she hang on lak de winter on T'ree Reever.
Cryin' out—"please hol' me tight, or I 'm comin
      dead to-night
An' ma poor ole moder dear, I got to leave her."

Wit' her arm aroun' hees wais'; she was doin'
      it in case
She bus' her head, or keel herse'f, it 's not so
      easy sayin'
Dey was comin' on de jomp t'roo dat dam ole
      beaver swamp
An' meet de crowd is lookin' for dem cow was go
      a-strayin'.

Den she 's cryin', Victorine, for she 's knowin'
      w'at it mean
De parish dey was talkin' firse chances dey be
      gettin',
But no sooner dat young man stop de horse, he
      tak' her han'
An' w'isper "never min', ma chere, won't do no
      good a-frettin'."

Non! she is n't cryin' long, for he tole her it was
    wrong
She 's sure he save her life too, or she was moche
    mistaken,
An' de ole Ma-dame Leveque also kiss heem on
    de neck
An' quickly affer dat Hooraw! de man an' wife
    dey 're makin'.

The Curé of Calumette

[The Curé of a French Canadian parish, when summoned
to the bedside of a dying member of his flock, always carries
in his buggy or sleigh a bell.   This bell serves two purposes:
first, it has the effect of clearing a way for the passage of
the good priest's vehicle, and, secondly, it calls to prayer
those of the faithful who are within hearing of its solemn
tones.]

DERE 's no voyageur on de reever never run
    hees canoe d'ecorce
T'roo de roar an' de rush of de rapide, w'ere it
    jump lak a beeg w'ite horse,
Dere 's no hunter man on de prairie, never wear
    w'at you call racquette
Can beat leetle Fader O'Hara, de Curé of
    Calumette.

Hees fader is full-blooded Irish, an' hees moder
    is pure Canayenne,
Not offen dat stock go togedder, but she 's fine
    combination ma frien'
For de Irish he 's full of de devil, an' de French
    dey got savoir faire,
Dat 's mak' it de very good balance an' tak'
    you mos' ev'ry w'ere.

But dere 's wan t'ing de Curé wont stan' it; mak'
    fun on de Irlandais
An' of course on de French we say not'ing, 'cos de
    parish she 's all Canayen,
Den you see on account of de moder, he can't
    spik hese'f very moche,
So de ole joke she 's all out of fashion, an' wan
    of dem t'ing we don't touch.

Wall! wan of dat kin' is de Curé, but w'en he be
    comin' our place
De peop' on de parish all w'isper, "How young
    he was look on hees face;
Too bad if de wedder she keel heem de firse tam
    he got leetle wet,
An' de Bishop might sen' beeger Curé, for it 's
    purty tough place, Calumette!"

Ha! ha! how I wish I was dere, me, w'en he go on
    de mission call
On de shaintee camp way up de reever, drivin'
    hees own cariole,
An' he meet blaggar' feller been drinkin', jus'
    enough mak' heem ack lak fou,
Joe Vadeboncoeur, dey was call heem, an' he 's
    purty beeg feller too!

Mebbe Joe he don't know it 's de Curé, so he 's
    hollerin', "Get out de way,
If you don't geev me whole of de roadside,
    sapree! you go off on de sleigh."
But de Curé he never say not'ing, jus' poule on
    de line leetle bit,
An' w'en Joe try for kip heem hees promise, hees
    nose it get badly hit.

Maudit! he was strong leetle Curé, an' he go for
    Jo-zeph en masse
An' w'en he is mak' it de finish, poor Joe is n't
    feel it firse class,
So nex' tam de Curé he 's goin' for visit de shain-
    tee encore
Of course he was mak' beeges' mission never see
    on dat place before.

An' he know more, I 'm sure dan de lawyer, an'
    dere 's many poor habitant
Is glad for see Fader O'Hara, an' ax w'at he t'ink
    of de law
W'en dey get leetle troub' wit' each oder, an'
    don't know de bes' t'ing to do,
Dat 's makin' dem save plaintee monee, an' kip
    de good neighbor too.

But w'en we fin' out how he paddle till canoe she
    was nearly fly
An' travel racquette on de winter, w'en snow-
    dreef is pilin' up high
For visit some poor man or woman dat 's waitin'
    de message of peace,
An' get dem prepare for de journey, we 're proud
    on de leetle pries' !

O! many dark night w'en de chil'ren is put away
    safe on de bed
An' mese'f an' ma femme mebbe sittin' an
    watchin' de small curly head
We hear somet'ing else dan de roar of de tonder,
    de win' an' de rain;
So we 're bote passin' out on de doorway, an'
    lissen an' lissen again.

An' it 's lonesome for see de beeg cloud sweepin'
    across de sky
An' lonesome for hear de win' cryin' lak some-
    body 's goin' to die,
But de soun' away down de valley, creepin'
    aroun' de hill
All de tam gettin' closer, closer, dat 's de soun'
    mak' de heart stan' still!

It 's de bell of de leetle Curé, de music of deat'
    we hear,
Along on de black road ringin', an' soon it was
    comin' near
Wan minute de face of de Curé we see by de lan-
    tern light,
An' he 's gone from us, jus' lak a shadder, into de
    stormy night.

An' de buggy rush down de hill side an' over de
    bridge below,
W'ere creek run so high on de spring-tam, w'en
    mountain t'row off de snow,
An' so long as we hear heem goin', we kneel on de
    floor an' pray
Dat God will look affer de Curé, an' de poor soul
    dat 's passin' away.

I dunno if he need our prayer, but we geev' it
 heem jus' de sam',
For w'en a man 's doin' hees duty lak de Curé do
 all de tam
Never min' all de t'ing may happen, no matter
 he 's riche or poor
Le bon Dieu was up on de heaven, will look
 out for dat man, I 'm sure.

I 'm only poor habitant farmer, an' mebbe know
 not'ing at all,
But dere 's wan t'ing I 'm alway wishin', an'
 dat 's w'en I get de call
For travel de far-away journey, ev'ry wan on de
 worl' mus' go
He 'll be wit' me de leetle Curé 'fore I 'm leffin'
 dis place below.

For I know I 'll be feel more easy, if he 's sittin'
 dere by de bed
An' he 'll geev' me de good-bye message, an'
 place hees han' on ma head,
Den I 'll hol' if he 'll only let me, dat han' till
 de las' las' breat'
An' bless leetle Fader O'Hara, de Curé of
 Calumette.

The Oyster Schooner

W'AT 's all dem bell a ringin' for, can hear
    dem ev'ry w'ere?
W'at 's bring de peop' togeder on de w'arf at
    Trois Rivieres,
Dat happy crowd is look so glad, w'y are dey
    comin' dere?
O! de reason dey 're so happy w'ile dey 're
    waitin' dere to-day
Is becos de oyster schooner she 's sailin' up de
    bay
An' de caraquette an' malpecque will quickly
    melt away
Affer she was t'row de anchor on T'ree Reever.

For w'y dey mak' de fuss lak dat, an' nearly
    broke deir neck,
Ain't dey got de noder oyster more better dan
    malpecque
Or caraquette, dat leetle wan from down below
    Kebęck?
Wall! ax de crowd dat question w'ile dey 're
    waitin' dere to-day,
So glad to see "La Belle Marie" sailin' up de bay,
An' dey 'll drown you on de water, so you 'll
    know about de way
She was t'rowin' out de anchor on T'ree Reever.

Dere 's ole Joe Lachapelle, he 's blin', can hardly
    see at all,
He 's bring de man got wooden leg call Jimmie
    Sauriol,
An' bote dem feller jomp aroun' lak mooshrat on
    de fall,
For dey know de schooner 's comin', she 's sailin'
    up de bay,
An' de reason she don't hurry w'ile dey 're
    waitin' dere to-day,
Is becos she 's full of oyster, will quickly pass
    away
W'en dat schooner t'row de anchor on T'ree
    Reever.

We 've trottin' race las' winter, an' circus on de
    spring,
Wit' elephan' an' monkey too, all playin' cn de
    ring,
But beeger crowd she 's comin' now, for w'y? it 's
    differen' t'ing,
For dey 're waitin' on dat schooner, she 's sailin'
    up de bay
Dey smell de malpecque oyster an' caraquette
    to-day
An' O! ba gosh, dey 'll eat dem! it 's alway be de
    way
W'en dat schooner t'row de anchor on T'ree
    Reever.

"She 's comin' in—she 's comin' in," jus' lissen
    to de cry!
"Get out de line an' hol' her fas', for fear she 's
    passin' by,
For if dere 's somet'ing happen now, de peop' will
    surely die."
Affer waitin' on dat schooner, she 's sailin' up de
    bay
Lak de sparrow on de wood-pile watchin' all de
    day,
But dey got her safe enough now, she 'll never sail
    away
Till dem oyster she was finish on T'ree Reever.

"All aboar'—comment câ va, Captinne Beli-
    veau?
We 're glad to see you back again from Cara-
    quette below,
But we 're sorry you don't hurry, w'en you got
    such nice car-go."
So dey ketch dat oyster schooner, she 's sailin'
    up de bay,
Dey ketch her an' dey hol' her till de oyster 's
    gone away
An' she 's two foot out de water "La Belle Marie" ·
    nex' day
Affer she was t'row de anchor on T'ree Reever.

My Leetle Cabane

I 'M sittin' to-night on ma leetle cabane, more
   happier dan de king,
An' ev'ry corner 's ringin' out wit' musique de
   ole stove sing
I hear de cry of de winter win', for de storm-
   gate 's open wide
But I don't care not'ing for win' or storm, so long
   I was safe inside.

Viens 'ci, mon chien, put your head on dere,
   let your nose res' on ma knee—
You 'member de tam we chase de moose back on
   de Lac Souris
An' de snow come down an' we los' ourse'f till
   mornin' is bring de light,
You t'ink we got place to sleep, mon chien, lak
   de place we got here to-night

Onder de roof of de leetle cabane, w'ere fire
   she 's blazin' high
An' bed I mak' of de spruce tree branch, is lie on
   de floor close by,
O! I lak de smell of dat nice fresh bed, an' I
   dream of de summer tam
An' de spot w'ere de beeg trout jomp so moche
   down by de lumber dam.

But lissen dat win', how she scream outside,
    mak me t'ink of de loup garou,
W'y to-night, mon chien, I be feelin' glad if even
    de carcajou
Don't ketch hese'f on de trap I set to-day on de
    Lac Souris
Let heem wait till to-morrow, an' den if he lak,
    I geev heem good chance, sapree!

I see beeg cloud w'en I 'm out to-day, off on de
    nor'-eas' sky,
An' she block de road, so de cloud behin', don't
    get a chance passin' by,
An' I t'ink of boom on de grande riviere, w'en
    log 's fillin' up de bay,
Wall! sam' as de boom on de spring-tam flood,
    dat cloud she was sweep away.

Dem log 's very nice an' quiet, so long as de
    boom 's all right,
But soon as de boom geev way, l'enfant! it 's
    den is begin de fight.
Dey run de rapide, an' jomp de rock, dey leap on
    de air an' dive,
Can hear dem roar from de reever shore, jus'
    lak dey was all alive.

An' dat was de way wit' de cloud to-day, de res'
    of dem push aside,
For dey 're comin' fas' from de cole nor'-eas' an'
    away t'roo de sky dey ride
Shakin' de snow as along dey go, lak grain from
    de farmer's han'
Till to-morrow you can't see not'ing at all, but
    smoke of de leetle cabane.

I 'm glad we don't got no chimley, only hole on
    de roof up dere,
An' spark fly off on w'ole of de worl', so dere 's
    no use gettin' scare,
Mus' get more log! an' it 's lucky too, de wood
    pile is stannin' near
So blow away storm, for harder you go, de
    warmer she 's comin' here—

I wonder how dey get on, mon chien, off on de
    great beeg town,
W'ere house is so high, near touch de sky, mus'
    be danger of fallin' down.
An' worser too on de night lak dis, ketchin' dat
    terrible win',
O! leetle small place lak de ole cabane was de
    right place for stayin' in.

I s'pose dey got plaintee bodder too, dem feller
    dat 's be riche man,
For dey 're never knowin' w'en t'ief may come
    an' steal all de t'ing he can
An' de monee was kip dem busy too, watchin'
    it night an' day,
Dunno but we 're better off here, mon chien, wit'
    beeg city far away.

For I look on de corner over dere, an' see it ma
    birch canoe,
I look on de wall w'ere ma rifle hang along wit'
    de good snowshoe,
An' ev'ry t'ing else on de worl' I got, safe on dis
    place near me.
An' here you are too, ma brave old dog, wit'
    your nose up agen ma knee.

An' here we be stay t'roo de summer day, w'en
    ev'ry t'ing 's warm an' bright
On winter too w'en de stormy win' blow lak she
    blow to-night
Let dem stay on de city, on great beeg house,
    dem feller dat 's be riche man
For we 're happy an' satisfy here, mon chien, on
    our own leetle small cabane.

Bateese the Lucky Man

HE 's alway ketchin' doré, an' he 's alway
    ketchin' trout
  On de place w'ere no wan else can ketch at all
He 's alway ketchin' barbotte, dat 's w'at you
    call bull-pout,
  An' he never miss de wil' duck on de fall.

O! de pa'tridge do some skippin' w'en she see
    heem on de swamp
  For she know Bateese don't go for not'ing
    dere,
An' de rabbit if he 's comin', wall! you ought to
    see heem jomp.
  W'y he want to climb de tree he feel so scare.

Affer two hour by de reever I hear hees leetle song
  Den I meet heem all hees pocket full of snipe,
An' me, I go de sam' place, an' I tramp de w'ole
    day long
  An' I 'm only shootin' two or t'ree, Ba Cripe!

I start about de sun-rise, an' I put out ma decoy,
  An' I see Bateese he sneak along de shore,
An' before it 's comin' breakfas', he 's holler on
    hees boy
  For carry home two dozen duck or more.

An' I 'm freezin' on de blin'—me—from four
      o'clock to nine
  An' ev'ry duck she 's passin' up so high.
Dere 's blue-bill an' butter-ball, an' red-head,
      de fines' kin
  An' I might as well go shootin' on de sky.

Don't see de noder feller lak Bateese was lucky
      man,
  He can ketch de smartes' feesh is never sweem,
An' de bird he seldom miss dem, let dem try de
      hard dey can
  W'y de eagle on de mountain can't fly away
    from heem.

But all de bird, an' feesh too, is geev' up feelin'
      scare,
  An' de rabbit he can stay at home in bed,
For he feesh an' shoot no longer, ole Jean
      Bateese Belair,
  'Cos he 's dead.

The Hill of St. Sebastien

I OUGHT to feel more satisfy an' happy dan
  I be,
  For better husban' dan ma own, it 's very hard
    to fin'

An' plaintee woman if dey got such boy an' girl
    as me
  Would never have no troub' at all, an' not'ing
    on deir min'
But w'ile dey 're alway wit' me, an' dough I love
    dem all
  I can't help t'inkin' w'en I watch de chil'ren
    out at play
Of tam I 'm just' lak dat mese'f, an' den de tear
    will fall
  For de hill of St. Sebastien is very far away!

It seem so pleasan' w'en I come off here ten year
    ago
  An' hardes' work I 'm gettin' den, was never
    heavy load,
De roughes' place is smoot' enough, de quickes'
    gait is slow
  For glad I am to foller w'ere Louis lead de
    road
But somet'ing 's comin' over me, I feel it more
    an' more
  It 's alway pullin' on de heart, an' stronger
    ev'ry day,
An' O! I long to see again de reever an' de
    shore
  W'ere de hill of St. Sebastien is lookin' on
    de bay!

I use to t'ink it 's fine t'ing once, to stan' upon
de door
 An' see de great beeg medder dere, stretchin'
far an' wide,
An' smell de pleasan' flower dat grow lak star
on de prairie floor,
 An' watch de spotted antelope was feedin'
ev'ry side,
How did we gain it, man an' wife, dis lan' was
no man's lan'?
 By rifle, an' harrow an' plow, shovel an' spade
an' hoe
De blessin' of good God up above, an' work of our
own strong han'
 Till it stan' on de middle, our leetle nes', w'ere
de wheat an' cornfiel' grow.

An' soon de chil'ren fill de house, wit' musique
all day long,
 De sam' ma moder use to sing on de cradle over
me,
I 'm almos' sorry it 's be ma fault dey learn dem
ole tam song
 W'at good is it tak' me off lak dat back on ma
own contree?
Till de reever once more I see again, an' lissen
its current flow
 An' dere 's Hercule de ferry man comin' across
de bay!

Wat 's use of foolin' me lak dat? for surely I
    mus' know
  De hill of St. Sebastien is very far away!

W'en Louis ketch me dat summer night watchin'
        de sky above,
    Seein' de mountain an' de lake, wit' small boat
        sailin' roun'
He kiss me an' say—"Toinette, I 'm glad dis
        prairie lan' you love
    For travel de far you can, ma belle, it 's fines'
        on top de groun'!"
Jus' w'en I 'm lookin' dat beeg cloud too, stand-
        in' dere lak a wall!
    Sam' as de hill I know so well, home on ma own
        contree,
Good job I was cryin' quiet den, an' Louis can't
        hear at all
    But I kiss de poor feller an' laugh, an' never
        say not'ing—me.

W'at can you do wit' man lak dat, an' w'y am
        I bodder so?
    De firse t'ing he might fin' it out, den hees
        heart will feel it sore
An' if he say "Come home Toinette," I 'm sure
        I mus' answer "No,"
    For if I 'm seein' dat place again, I never
        return no more!

So let de heart break—I don't care, I won't
    say not'ing—me—
  I 'll mak' dat promise on mese'f, an' kip it
    night an' day
But O! Mon Dieu! how glad, how glad, an'
    happy I could be
  If de hill of St. Sebastien was not so far away!

Marie Louise

DIS was de story of boy an' girl
    Dat 's love each oder above de worl'
But it 's not easy job for mak' l'amour
W'en de girl she 's riche an' de boy he 's poor
All de sam' he don't worry an' she don't cry,
But wait for good chances come bimeby.

Young Marie Louise Hurtubuise
Was leev wit' her moder la veuve Denise
On fines' house on de w'ole chemin
From Caribou reever to St. Germain
For ole woman 's boss on de grande moulin.

W'ere dere 's nice beeg dam, water all de tam
An' season t'roo runnin' jus' de sam'
Wit' good leetle creek comin' off de hill
Was helpin' de reever for work de mill
So de grande moulin she is never still.

MARIE LOUISE

No wonder Denise she was hard to please
W'en de boy come sparkin' Marie Louise
For affer de foreman Bazile is pay
De mill she 's bringin' t'ree dollar a day
An' for makin' de monee, dat 's easy way.

An' de girl Marie, O! she 's tres jolie,
Jompin' aroun lak de summer bee
She 's never short plaintee t'ing to do
An' mebbe she ketch leetle honey too,
'Cos she 's jus' as sweet as de morning dew.

An' w'en she was dress on her Sunday bes'
An' walk wit' her moder on seconde messe
Dere 's not'ing is bring de young man so fas'
An' dey stan' on door of church en masse
So res' of de peop' dey can hardly pass.

An' she know musique, 'cos on Chris'mas week
W'en organ man on de church is sick
(S'pose he got de grippe) dat girl she play
Lak college professor, de pries' is say
Till de place it was crowd nearly ev'ry day.

Ole Curé Belair of St. Pollinaire,
Dat 's parish ten mile noder side riviere,
If he 's not gettin' mad, it was funny t'ing
W'en hees young man fly lak bird on de wing
Wit' nobody lef' behin' to sing.

An' nex' t'ing dey know it 's comin' so
Dat mos' of de girl she got no beau,
An' of course dat 's makin' de jealousie
For w'en de young feller he see Marie
He see not'ing else on hees eye, sapree!

Mus' be somet'ing done sure as de gun,
It 's all very well for de boy have fun
But dere 's noder t'ing too, must n't be forget,
Dere 's two fine parish dat 's all upset
An' mebbe de troub' is n't over yet.

So ev'ry wan say de only way
Is gettin' young Marie Louise mariée,
Den dey have beeg meetin' on magasin,
W'ere he sit on de chair Aleck Sanschagrin,
An' dey 'point heem for go on de grande moulin.

But w'en Aleck come dere for arrange affaire,
Ole Madame Denise she was mak' heem scare
For jus' on de minute she see hees face
She know right away all about de case
An' she tole Bazile t'row heem off de place.

Now de young Bazile he was t'ink good deal
Of Marie Louise an' he 's ready for keel
Any feller come foolin' aroun' de door
So he kick dat man till he 's, feelin' sore,
An' Aleck he never go back no more.

MARIE LOUISE

If it 's true w'at dey say, Joe Boulanger
Was crazy to fight Irish man wan day
W'en he steal all de pork on hees dinner can,
Den it is n't so very hard onderstan'
Bazile Latour mus' be darn smart man.

For nobody know de poor feller Joe
W'en he 's come from de grande moulin below
'Cept hees moder, dat 's tole heem mak' promise
     sure
Kip off on de mill, an' Bazile Latour,
(But it 's long before doctor can mak' heem cure).

Den de ole Denise she was very please,
An' nex' day spik wit' Marie Louise,
"Ma girl, I got de right man for you
If you can only jus' love heem true,
Bazile dat young feller, I t'ink he 'll do."

"Wall! Moder he 's poor, Bazile Latour,
But if you t'ink you will lak heem sure
I 'll try an' feex it mese'f some day
For you 've been de good moder wit' me alway"
An' dat 's w'at Marie Louise she say.

So it 's comin' right affer all de fight,
An' de parish don't see de more finer sight
Dan w'en dey get marry on St. Germain
W'y de buggy she 's pilin' de w'ole chemin
All de way from de church to de grande moulin.

The Old House and the New

IS it only twelve mont' I play de fool,
　　You 're sure it 's correc', ma dear?
I 'm glad for hearin' you spik dat way
　　For I t'ink it was twenty year,
Since leffin' de leetle ole house below,
　　I mak' wit' ma own two han'
For go on dat fine beeg place, up dere—
　　Mon Dieu! I 'm de crazy man!

You 'member we 're not very riche, cherie,
　　Dat tam we 're beginnin' life!
Mese'f I 'm twenty, an' you eighteen
　　W'en I 'm bringin' you home ma wife,
Many de worry an' troub' we got
　　An' some of dem was n't small,
But not very long dey bodder us
　　For we work an' forget dem all.

An' you was de savin' woman too,
　　Dere 's nobody beat you dere!
An' I laugh w'en I t'ink of de tam you go
　　Over on Trois Rivieres
For payin' de bank—you know how moche
　　We 're owin' for dat new place
W'at was he sayin' de nice young man
　　Smilin' upon hees face.

W'en he got dat monee was all pure gole
    Come down on your familee
For honder year an' mebbe more?
    "Ma-dame you 're excusin' me,
·But w'ere was you gettin' dis nice gole coin
    Of Louis Quatorze, hees tam
Wit' hees face on back of dem ev'ry wan?
    For dey 're purty scase, now Ma-dame?"

An' you say "Dat 's not'ing at all M'sieu'
    Ma familee get dem t'ing,
I suppose it 's very long tam ago,
    W'en Louis Quatorze is King,
An' I 'm sorry poor feller he 's comin' dead
    An' not leevin' here to-day
'Cos man should be good on hees frien', M'sieu'
    W'en de monee he mak' dat way."

Yass, ev'ry wan know we 're workin' hard
    An' savin' too all dem year,
But nobody see us starve ourse'f
    Dere 's plaintee to eat, don't fear—
Bimeby our chil'ren dey 're growin' up
    So we 're doin' de bes' we can
Settle dem off on de firse good chance
    An' geevin' dem leetle lan'.

THE OLD HOUSE AND THE NEW

An' den de troub' is begin to show
   W'en our daughter poor Caroline
She marry dat lawyer on Trois Rivieres
   De beeges' fool never seen!
Alway come home ev'ry summer sure
   Bringin' her familee,
All right for de chil'ren, I don't min' dem;
   But de husban'! sapree maudit!

I wish I was close ma ear right off
   W'en he talk of our leetle house
Dough I know w'en familee's comin' home
   Dere is n't moche room for a mouse,
He say "Riche man lak youse'f can't leev'
   On shaintee lak dis below,
W'en t'ousan' dollar will buil' fin' place
   Up on de hill en haut."

An' he talk about gallerie all aroun'
   W'ere we sit on de summer night
Watchin' de star on de sky above
   W'ile de moon she was shinin' bright,
Could plant some apple-tree dere, also,
   An' flower, an' I dunno w'at,
An' w'en de sun he 's begin to rise
   Look at de view we got!

Den he bring 'noder feller from Trois Rivieres
    An' show w'at he call de plan
For makin' dem house on de w'ole contree—
    Mon Dieu! how I hate dat man!
'Cos he 's talkin' away nearly all de tam
    Lak trotter upon de race—
Wall! affer a w'ile we mak' our min'
    For havin' dat nice new place.

So dey go ahead, an' we let dem go,
    But stuff dey was t'row away;
I 'm watchin' for dat, an' I save mese'f
    Mebbe twenty-five cent a day,
For you 're surely cheat if you don't tak' care
    Very offen we fin' dat 's true,
An' affer de house she was finish up,
    We're geevin' it nam' Bellevue.

O! yass, I know we enjoy ourse'f
    W'en our frien' dey was comin' roun'
An' say "Dat 's very fine place you got;
    Dere 's not'ing upon de town,
Or anyw'ere else for honder mile
    Dis house Bellevue can touch,"
An' den let de horse eat de garden fence
    Non! we don't enjoy dat so moche.

THE OLD HOUSE AND THE NEW

An' of course we can't say not'ing at all
    For it 's not correc' t'ing you know—
But "Never min' dat, an' please come again,
    I 'm sorry you got to go."
Baptême! w'en I 'm seein' beeg feller bus'
    Our two dollar easy chair—
Can't help it at all, I got to go
    Down on de cellar an' swear!

An' w'ere did we leev' on dat belle maison?
    Wan room an' de kitchen, dat 's all
An' plaintee too for de man an' wife!
    An' you 'member de tam I fall
Off on de gallerie wan dark night,
    I los' mese'f tryin' fin'
De winder dere on de grande parloir,
    For closin' it up de blin'?

An' all de tam de poor leetle house
    Is down on de road below,
I t'ink she was jealous dat fine new place
    Up on de hill en haut,
For O! she look lonesome by herse'f
    De winder all broke an' gone—
No smoke on de chimley comin' out
    No frien' stannin' dere—not wan.

You 'member too, w'en de fever come
  An' ketch us wan winter day?
W'at he call de shaintee, our son-in-law,
  Dat 's w'ere dey pass away
Xavier, Zoë, an' Euchariste
  Our chil'ren wan, two, t'ree—
I offen t'ink of de room dey die,
  An' I can't help cryin'—me.

So we 'll go on de ole house once again,
  Long enough we been fool lak dis
Never min' w'at dey say bimeby, ma chere
  But geev me de leetle kiss,
Let dem stay on dat fine new place up dere
  Our daughter an' son-in-law
For to-morrow soon as de sun will rise
  We 're goin' back home—Hooraw!

The Canadian Country Doctor

I S'POSE mos' ev'ry body t'ink hees job 's
  about de hardes'
From de boss man on de Gouvernement to poor
  man on de town
From de curé to de lawyer, an' de farmer to de
  school boy
An' all the de noder feller was mak' de worl' go
  roun'.

But dere 's wan man got hees han' full t'roo
    ev'ry kin' of wedder
  An' he 's never sure of not'ing but work an'
    work away—
Dat 's de man dey call de doctor, w'en you ketch
    heem on de contree
  An' he 's only man I know-me, don't got no
    holiday.

If you 're comin' off de city spen' de summer-
    tam among us
  An' you walk out on de mornin w'en de leetle
    bird is sing
Mebbe den you see de doctor w'en he 's passin
    wit' hees buggy
  An' you t'ink "Wall! contree doctor mus' be
    very pleasan' t'ing.

"Drivin' dat way all de summer up an' down
    along de reever
  W'ere de nice cool win' is blowin' among de
    maple tree
Den w'en he 's mak' hees visit, comin' home
    before de night tam
  For pass de quiet evening wit' hees wife an'
    familee."

An' w'en off across de mountain, some wan 's
    sick an' want de doctor
  "Mus' be fine trip crossin' over for watch de
    sun go down
Makin' all dem purty color lak w'at you call de
    rainbow,"
  Dat 's way de peop' is talkin' was leevin' on
    de town.

But it is n't alway summer on de contree, an' de
    doctor
  He could tole you many story of de storm dat
    he 's been in
How hees coonskin coat come handy, w'en de
    win' blow off de reever
  For if she 's sam' ole reever, she 's not alway
    sam' old win'.

An' de mountain dat 's so quiet w'en de w'ite
    cloud go a-sailin'
  All about her on de summer w'ere de sheep
    is feedin' high
You should see her on December w'en de snow
    is pilin' roun' her
  An' all de win' of winter come tearin' t'roo de
    sky.

THE CANADIAN COUNTRY DOCTOR

O! le bon Dieu help de doctor w'en de message
  come to call heem
 From hees warm bed on de night-tam for visit
   some poor man
Lyin' sick across de hill side on noder side de
  reever
 An' he hear de mountain roarin' lak de beeg
   Shawinigan.

Ah! well he know de warning but he can't stay
  till de morning
 So he 's hitchin' up hees leetle horse an' put
   heem on burleau
Den w'en he 's feex de buffalo, an' wissle to hees
  pony
 Away t'roo storm an' hurricane de contree
   doctor go.

O! de small Canadian pony! dat 's de horse can
  walk de snowdreef.
 Dat 's de horse can fin' de road too he 's never
   been before ·
Kip your heart up leetle feller, for dere 's many
  mile before you
 An' it 's purty hard job tellin' w'en you see
   your stable door.

Yass! de doctor he can tole you, if he have de tam
    for talkin'
  All about de bird was singin' before de summer
    lef'
For he 's got dem on hees bureau an' he 's doin'
    it hese'f too
  An' de las' tam I was dere, me, I see dem all
    mese'f.

But about de way he travel t'roo de stormy
    night of winter
  W'en de rain come on de spring flood, an' de
    bridge is wash away
All de hard work, all de danger dat was offen
    hang aroun' heem
  Dat 's de tam our contree doctor don't have
    very moche to say.

For it 's purty ole, ole story, an' he alway have
    it wit' heem
  Ever since he come among us on parish Saint
    Mathieu
An' no doubt he 's feelin' mebbe jus' de sam' as
    noder feller
  So he rader do hees talkin' about somet'ing
    dat was new.

Mon Frere Camille

MON frere Camille he was firse class blood
   W'en he come off de State las' fall,
Wearin' hees boot a la mode box toe
An' diamon' pin on hees shirt also
Sam' as dem feller on Chi-caw-go;
  But now he 's no blood at all,
                Camille, mon frere.

W'at 's makin' dat change on mon frere Camille?
  Wall! lissen for minute or two,
An' I 'll try feex it up on de leetle song
Dat 's geevin' some chance kin' o' help it
    along
So wedder I 'm right or wedder I 'm wrong
  You 'll know all about heem w'en I get
    t'roo,
                Mon frere Camille.

He never sen' letter for t'orteen year
  So of course he mus' be all right
Till telegraph 's comin' from Kan-Ka-Kee
"I 'm leffin' dis place on de half pas' t'ree
W'at you want to bring is de bes' buggee
  An' double team sure for me t'orsday night
              Ton frere Camille."

MON FRERE CAMILLE

I wish you be dere w'en Camille arrive
 I bet you will say "W'at 's dat?"
For he 's got leetle cap very lak tuque bleu
Ole habitant 's wearin' in bed, dat 's true,
An' w'at do you t'ink he carry too?
  Geev it up? Wall! small valise wit' de fine
   plug hat.
         Mon frere Camille.

"Very strange." I know you will say right off,
 For dere 's not'ing wrong wit' hees clothes,
An' he put on style all de bes' he can
Wit' diamon' shinin' across hees han'
An' de way he 's talkin' lak Yankee man
 Mus' be purty hard on hees nose,
         Mon frere Camille.

But he 'splain all dat about funny cap,
 An' tole us de reason w'y,
It seem no feller can travel far,
An' specially too on de Pullman car,
'Less dey wear leetle cap only cos' dollarre,
 Dat 's true if he never die,
         Mon frere Camille.

Don't look very strong dem fancy boot
 But he 's 'splain all dat also
He say paten' ledder she 's nice an' gay

You don't need to polish dem ev'ry day,
Besides he 's too busy for dat alway,
 W'en he 's leevin' on Chi-caw-go,
       Mon frere Camille.

But de State she was n't de only place
 He visit all up an' down,
For he 's goin' Cu-baw an' de Mex-i-co,
W'ere he 's killin' two honder dem wil' taureau,
W'at you call de bull: on de circus show,
 O! if you believe heem he travel roun'.
       Mon frere Camille.

So of course w'en ma broder was gettin' home
 All the peop' on de parish come
Every night on de parlor for hear heem tell
How he foller de brave Generale Roosvel'
W'en rough rider feller dey fight lak hell
 An' he walk on de front wit' great beeg drum,
       Mon frere Camille.

An' how is he gainin' dat diamon' ring?
 Way off on de Mex-i-co
W'ere he 's pilin' de bull wan summer day
Till it 's not easy haulin' dem all away,
An' de lady dey 're t'rowin' heem large bouquet
 For dey lak de style he was keel taureau,
       Mon frere Camille.

MON FRERE CAMILLE

Wall! he talk dat way all de winter t'roo,
   An' hees frien' dey was tryin' fin'
Some bull on de county dat 's wil' enough
For mon frere Camille, but it 's purty tough
'Cos de farmer 's not raisin' such fightin'
     stuff
   An' he don't want not'ing but mos' worse
    kin'

               Mon frere Camille.

Dat 's not pleasan' t'ing mebbe los' hees trade,
   If we don't hurry up, for sure,
I s'pose you t'ink I was goin' it strong?
Never min', somet'ing happen 'fore very long
It 'll all come out on dis leetle song
   W'en he pass on de house of Ma-dame
    Latour

               Camille, mon frere.

We 're makin' pique-nique on Denise Latour
   For helpin' put in de hay
Too bad she 's de moder large familee
An' los' de bes' husban' she never see
W'en he drown on de reever, poor Jeremie,
   So he come wit' de res' of de gang dat
    day,

               Camille, mon frere.

An' affer de hay it was put away
    Don't tak' very long at all,
De boy an' de girl she was lookin' 'roun'
For havin' more fun 'fore dey lef' de groun'
An' dey see leetle bull, mebbe t'ree honder poun'
    An' nex' t'ing I hear dem call
                        Mon frere Camille.

So nice leetle feller I never see
    Dat bull of Ma-dame Latour
Wit' curly hair on de front hees head
An' quiet? jus' sam' he was almos' dead
An' fat? wall! de chil'ren dey see heem fed
    So he 's not goin' keel heem I 'm very sure,
                        Mon frere Camille.

But de girl kip teasin' an' ole Ma-dame
    She say, "You can go ahead
He cos' me four dollarre six mont' ago
So if anyt'ing happen ma small taureau,
Who 's pay me dat monee I lak to know?"
    An' he answer, "Dat 's me w'en I keel heem
        dead"
                        Mon frere Camille.

Den he feex beeg knife on de twelve foot pole,
    So de chil'ren commence to cry
An' he jomp on de fence, an' yell, "Hooraw"
167

An' shout on de leetle French bull, "Dis donc!
Ain't you scare w'en you see feller from Cubaw?"
   An' he show heem hees red necktie,
                  Mon frere Camille.

L'petit taureau w'en he see dat tie
   He holler for half a mile
Den he jomp on de leg an' he raise de row
Ba Golly!   I 'm sure I can see heem now.
An' dey run w'en dey hear heem, de noder cow
   Den he say, "Dat bull must be surely wil'"
                  Mon frere Camille.

But de bull don't care w'at he say at all,
   For he 's watchin' dat red necktie
An' w'en ma broder he push de pole
I 'm sure it 's makin' some purty large hole,
If de bull be dere, but ma blood run col'
   For de nex' t'ing I hear heem cry,
                  Camille, mon frere.

No wonder he cry, for dat sapree bull
   He 's yell leetle bit some more,
Den he ketch ma broder dat small taureau
Only cos' four dollarre six mont' ago
An' he 's t'rowin' heem up from de groun' below
   Wan tam, two tam, till he 's feelin' sore,
                  Camille, mon frere.

An' w'en ma broder 's come down agen
  I s'pose he mus' change hees min'
An' mebbe t'ink if it 's all de sam'
He 'll keel dat bull w'en he get more tam
For dere he was runnin' wit' ole Ma-dame
  De chil'ren, de bull, an' de cow behin'
                        Camille, mon frere.

So dat 's de reason he 's firse class blood
  W'en he come off de State las' fall
Wearin' hees boot a la mode box toe
An' diamon' pin on hees shirt also
Sam' as dem feller on Chi-caw-go
  But now he 's no blood at all,
                        Camille, mon frere.

The Habitant's Summer

O WHO can blame de winter, never min' de
    hard he 's blowin'
  'Cos w'en de tam is comin' for passin' on hees
    roun'
De firse t'ing he was doin' is start de sky a
    snowin'
  An' mak' de nice w'ite blanket, for cover up de
    groun'.

An' de groun' she go a'sleepin' t'roo all de stormy
    season,
  Restin' from her work las' summer, till she 's
    waken by de rain
Dat le bon Dieu sen' some morning, an' of
    course dat 's be de reason
  Ev'ry year de groun' she 's lookin' jus' as
    fresh an' young again.

Den you geev her leetle sunshine, w'en de snow
    go off an' leave her
  Let de sout' win' blow upon her, an' you see
    beeg changes now
Wit' de steam arisin' from her jus' de sam' she
    got de fever,
  An' not many day is passin' w'en she 's ready
    for de plow.

We don't bodder wit' no spring-tam w'ere de
    rain she 's alway fallin',
  Two, t'ree mont', or mebbe longer, on de
    place beyon' de sea,
W'ere some bird he 's nam' de cuckoo, spen' de
    mos' hees tam a-callin'
  But for fear he wet hees fedder, hide away
    upon de tree.

On de swamp beside de reever, mebbe jus' about
        de fly-tam
    W'ere it 's very hard to see heem, we hear de
        wo-wa-raw,
Dat 's w'at you call de bull-frog, singin' "more
        rum," all de night-tam.
    He 's only kin' of cuckoo we got on Canadaw.

No, we have n't got dat feller, but we got some
        bird can beat heem,
    An' we hear dem, an' we see dem, jus' so soon
        de winter go,
So never min' de cuckoo for we 're not afraid to
        meet heem,
    W'enever he was ready, wit' our own petits
        oiseaux.

An' dey almos' come togeder, lak de spring an'
        summer wedder,
    Blue-bird wan day, pie-blanche nex' day,
        geevin' out deir leetle note,
Affer dat we see de robin, an' de gouglou on de
        medder,
    Den le roi, de red bird 's comin', dressim on
        hees sojer coat.

W'en de grosbec on de pine tree, wak' you early
    wit' hees singin',
  W'en you lissen to de pa'tridge a-beatin' on
    hees drum,
W'en de w'ole place roun' about you wit' musi-
    que is a-ringin',
  Den you know de winter 's over, an' de sum-
    mer day is come.

See de apple blossom showin', see de clover how
    it 's growin'
  Watch de trout, an' way dey 're playin' on de
    reever down below,
Ah! de cunning leetle feller, easy see how well
    dey 're knowin'
  We 're too busy now for ketch dem an' dat 's
    w'y dey 're jompin' so.

For de mos' fine summer season don't las' too
    long, an' we know it,
  So we 're workin' ev'rybody, w'ile de sun is
    warm an' clear,
Dat 's de tam for plant de barley, an' de injun
    corn we sow it,
  W'en de leaf upon de maple 's jus' de size of
    squirrel's ear.

'Noder job is feexin' fences, if we don't be lak de
    las' year,
  W'en de Durham bull he 's pullin' nearly all
    de fence away,
An' dat sapree champion taureau let de cattle
    out de pasture
  So dey 're playin' on de dévil wit' de oat an'
    wit' de hay.

Yass, de farmer 's offen worry, an' it sometam
    mak' heem snappy,
  For no sooner wan job 's finish, dan he got two
    t'ousan' more,
But he 's glad for see de summer, w'en all de
    worl' she 's happy,
  An' ev'ryt'ing aroun' heem was leevin' out
    o' door.

Now de ole sheep 's takin' young wan up de hill-
    side, an' dey feed dem
  W'ere de nice short grass is growin' sweeter
    dan it grow below,
Ev'ry morning off dey 're goin' an' it 's pleasan'
    t'ing to see dem
  Lookin' jus' lak leetle snow-ball all along de
    green coteau.

Dere 's de hen too, wit' her chicken, O how
     moche dey mak' her bodder
  Watchin' dem mos' ev'ry minute, fearin' dey
     was go astray
But w'en mountain hawk he 's comin' den how
     quick dey fin' de moder
  An' get onderneat' her fedder till de danger 's
     pass away.

An' jus' see de turkey gobbler, an' lissen to heem
     talkin'
  No wonder he 's half crazee, an' spikin' out
     so loud,
W'en you meet heem on de roadside wit' hees
     wife an' chil'ren walkin',
  It 's kipin' heem so busy lookin' affer such a
     crowd.

Dat 's about de way we 're leevin', dat 's a few
     t'ing we 're seein',
  W'en de nice warm summer sun is shinin' down
     on Canadaw,
An' no matter w'at I 'm hearin', still I never feel
     lak bein'
  No oder stranger feller, me, but only habitant.

For dere 's no place lak our own place, don't
      care de far you 're goin'
    Dat 's w'at de whole worl's sayin', w'enever
      dey come here,
'Cos we got de fines' contree, an' de beeges'
      reever flowin'
    An' le bon Dieu sen' de sunshine nearly twelve
      mont' ev'ry year.

Little Lac Grenier
(Gren-Yay)

LEETLE Lac Grenier, she 's all alone,
    Right on de mountain top,
But cloud sweepin' by, will fin' tam to stop
No matter how quickly he want to go,
So he 'll kiss leetle Grenier down below.

Leetle Lac Grenier, she 's all alone,
Up on de mountain high
But she never feel lonesome, 'cos for w'y?
So soon as de winter was gone away
De bird come an' sing to her ev'ry day.

Leetle Lac Grenier, she 's all alone,
Back on de mountain dere,
But de pine tree an' spruce stan' ev'rywhere
Along by de shore, an' mak' her warm
For dey kip off de win' an' de winter storm.

LITTLE LAC GRENIER

Leetle Lac Grenier, she 's all alone,
No broder, no sister near,
But de swallow will fly, an' de beeg moose
    deer
An' caribou too, will go long way
To drink de sweet water of Lac Grenier.

Leetle Lac Grenier, I see you now,
Onder de roof of spring
Ma canoe 's afloat, an' de robin sing,
De lily 's beginnin' her summer dress,
An' trout 's wakin' up from hees long long
    res'.

Leetle Lac Grenier, I 'm happy now,
Out on de ole canoe,
For I 'm all alone, ma chere, wit' you,
An' if only a nice light rod I had
I 'd try dat fish near de lily pad!

Leetle Lac Grenier, O! let me go,
Don't spik no more,
For your voice is strong lak de rapid's roar,
An' you know youse'f I 'm too far away,
For visit you now—leetle Lac Grenier!

The Windigo

G<small>O</small> easy wit' de paddle, an' steady wit' de
   oar
  Geev rudder to de bes' man you got among de
    crew,
Let ev'ry wan be quiet, don't let dem sing no
   more
  W'en you see de islan' risin' out of Grande
    Lac Manitou.

Above us on de sky dere, de summer cloud may
   float
  Aroun' us on de water de ripple never show,
But somet'ing down below us can rock de
   stronges' boat,
  W'en we 're comin' near de islan' of de spirit
    Windigo!

De carcajou may breed dere, an' otter sweem de
   pool
  De moosh-rat mak' de mud house, an' beaver
    buil' hees dam
An' beeges' Injun hunter on all de Tête de Boule
  Will never set hees trap dere from spring to
    summer tam.

But he 'll bring de fines' presen' from upper St.
    Maurice
    De loup marin an' black-fox from off de Hod-
        son Bay
An' hide dem on de islan' an' smoke de pipe of
    peace
    So Windigo will help heem w'en he travel far
        away.

We shaintee on dat islan' on de winter seexty-
    nine
    If you look you see de clearin' aroun' de Coo
        Coo Cache,
An' pleasan' place enough too among de spruce
    an' pine
    If foreman on de shaintee is n't Cyprien
        Palache.

Beeg feller, alway watchin' on hees leetle weasel
    eye,
    De gang dey can't do not'ing but he see dem
        purty quick
Wit' hees "Hi dere, w'at you doin'?" ev'ry tam
    he 's passin' by
    An' de bad word he was usin', wall! it offen
        mak' me sick.

An' he carry silver w'issle wit' de chain aroun'
    hees neck
  For fear he mebbe los' it, an' ev'rybody
    say
He mus' buy it from de devil w'en he 's passin'
    on Kebeck
  But if it 's true dat story, I dunno how moche
    he pay.

Dere 's plaintee on de shaintee can sing lak ros-
    signol
  Pat Clancy play de fiddle, an' Jimmie Char-
    bonneau
Was bring hees concertina from below St.
    Fereol
  So we get some leetle pleasure till de long,
    long winter go.

But if we start up singin' affer supper on de
    camp
  "Par derriere chez ma tante," or "Mattawa
    wishtay,"
De boss he 'll come along den, an' put heem out
    de lamp,
  An' only stop hees swearin' w'en we all go
    marche coucher.

We 've leetle boy dat winter from Po-po-lo-be-
      lang
   Hees fader an' hees moder dey 're bote
      A-ben-a-kee
An' he 's comin', Injun Johnnie, wit' some man
      de lumber gang
   Was fin' heem nearly starvin' above on Lac
      Souris.

De ole man an' de woman is tryin' pass de Soo
   W'en water 's high on spring tam, an' of course
      dey 're gettin' drown',
For even smartes' Injun should n't fool wit'
      birch canoe,
   W'ere de reever lak toboggan on de hill is
      runnin' down.

So dey lef' de leetle feller all alone away up
      dere
   Till lumber gang is ketchin' him an' bring him
      on de Cache,
But better if he 's stayin' wit' de wolf an' wit'
      de bear
   Dan come an' tak' hees chances wit' Cyprien
      Palache.

I wonder how he stan' it, w'y he never run
    away
  For Cyprien lak neeger he is treat heem all
    de sam'
An' if he 's wantin' Johnnie on de night or on de
    day
  God help heem if dat w'issle she was below de
    secon' tam!

De boy he don't say not'ing, no wan never see
    heem cry
  He 's got de Injun in heem, you can see it on
    de face,
An' only for us feller an' de cook, he 'll surely
    die
  Long before de winter 's over, long before we
    lef' de place,

But I see heem hidin' somet'ing wan morning
    by de shore
  So firse tam I was passin' I scrape away de
    snow
An' it 's rabbit skin he 's ketchin' on de swamp
    de day before,
  Leetle Injun Johnnie 's workin' on de spirit
    Windigo.

December 's come in stormy, an' de snow-dreef
  fill de road
 Can only see de chimley an' roof of our cabane,
An' stronges' team in stable fin' it plaintee
  heavy load
  Haulin' sleigh an' two t'ree pine log t'roo de
  wood an' beeg savane.

An' I travel off wan day me, wit' Cyprien
  Palache,
  Explorin' for new timber, w'en de win' begin
  to blow,
So we hurry on de snow-shoe for de camp on Coo
  Coo Cache
  If de nor' eas' storm is comin', was de bes'
  place we dunno—

An' we 're gettin' safe enough dere wit' de storm
  close on our heel,
  But w'en our belt we loosen for takin' off de
  coat
De foreman commence screamin' an' mon Dieu
  it mak' us feel
  Lak he got t'ree t'ousan' devil all fightin' on
  hees t'roat.

Cyprien is los' hees w'issle, Cyprien is los' hees
    chain
  Injun Johnnie he mus' fin' it, even if de win'
    is high
He can never show hese'f on de Coo Coo Cache
    again
  Till he bring dat silver w'issle an' de chain it 's
    hangin' by.

So he sen' heem on hees journey never knowin'
    he come back
  T'roo de rough an' stormy wedder, t'roo de
    pile of dreefin' snow
"Wat 's de use of bein' Injun if you can't smell
    out de track?"
  Dat 's de way de boss is talkin', an' poor
    Johnnie have to go.

If you want to hear de musique of de nort' win'
    as it blow
  An' lissen to de hurricane an' learn de way it
    sing
An' feel how small de man is w'en he 's leevin'
    here below,
  You should try it on de shaintee w'en she 's
    doin' all dem t'ing!

W'at 's dat soun' lak somet'ing cryin' all aroun'
    us ev'ryw'ere?
  We never hear no tonder upon de winter
    storm!
Dey 're shoutin' to each oder dem voices on de
    air,
  An' it 's red hot too de stove pipe, but no
    wan 's feelin' warm!

"Get out an' go de woodpile before I freeze to
    deat'"
  Cyprien de boss is yellin' an' he 's lookin' cole
    an' w'ite
Lak dead man on de coffin, but no wan go, you
    bet,
  For if it 's near de woodpile, 't is n't close
    enough to-night!

Non! we ain't afraid of not'ing, but we don't
    lak takin' chance,
  An' w'en we hear de spirit of de wil' A-ben-a-
    kee
Singin' war song on de chimley, makin' all dem
    Injun dance
  Raisin' row dere, you don't ketch us on no
    woodpile—no siree!

O! de lonesome night we 're passin' w'ile we 're
    stayin' on dat place!
  An' ev'rybody sheever w'en Jimmie Char-
    bonneau
Say he 's watchin' on de winder an' he see de
    Injun face
  An' it 's lookin' so he tole us, jus' de sam' as
    Windigo.

Den again mese'f I 'm hearin' somet'ing callin',
    an' it soun'
  Lak de voice of leetle Johnnie so I 'm passin'
    on de door
But de pine stump on de clearin' wit' de w'ite
    sheet all aroun'
  Mak' me t'ink of churchyar' tombstone, an'
    I can't go dere no more

Wat 's de reason we 're so quiet w'ile our heart
    she 's goin' fas'
  W'y is no wan ax de question? dat we 're all
    afraid to spik?
Was it wing of flyin' wil' bird strek de winder as
    it pass,
  Or de sweesh of leetle snow-ball w'en de win'
    is playin' trick?

W'en we buil' de Coo Coo shaintee, she 's as
    steady as a rock,
  Did you feel de shaintee shakin' de sam, she 's
    goin' to fall?
Dere 's somet'ing on de doorway! an' now we
    hear de knock
  An' up above de hurricane we hear de w'issle
    call.

Callin', callin' lak a bugle, an' he 's jompin' up
    de boss
  From hees warm bed on de corner an' open
    wide de door—
Dere 's no use foller affer for Cyprien is los'
  An' de Coo Coo Cache an' shaintee he 'll
    never see no more.

At las' de morning 's comin', an' storm is blow
    away
  An' outside on de shaintee young Jimmie
    Charbonneau
He 's seein track of snowshoe, 'bout de size of
    double sleigh
  Dere 's no mistak' it 's makin' by de spirit
    Windigo.

An' de leetle Injun Johnnie, he's all right I
    onderstan'
  For you 'll fin' heem up de reever above de
    Coo Coo Cache
Ketchin' mink and ketchin' beaver, an 'he 's
    growin' great beeg man
  But dat 's de las' we 're hearin' of Cyprien
    Palache.

National Policy

OUR fader lef' ole France behin', dat 's
    many year ago,
An' how we get along since den, wall! ev'ry
    body know,
Few t'ousan' firse class familee was only come
    dat tam,
An' now we got pure Canayens; t'ree million
    peop' bedamme!

Dat 's purty smart beez-nesse, I t'ink we done
    on Canadaw,
An' we don't mak' no grande hooraw, but do it
    tranquillement
So if we 're braggin' now an' den, we mus' be
    excuzay,
For no wan 's never see before de record bus'
    dat way.

An' w'y should we be feel ashame, 'cos we have
  boy an' girl?
No matter who was come along, we 'll match
  agen de worl';
Wit' plaintee boy lak w'at we got no danger be
  afraid,
An' all de girl she look too nice for never come
  ole maid.

If we have only small cor-nerre de sam' we have
  before
W'en ole Champlain an' Jacques Cartier firse
  jomp upon de shore
Dere 's no use hurry den at all, but now you
  understan'
We got to whoop it up, ba gosh! for occupy de
  lan'!

W'at 's use de million acre, w'at 's use de belle
  riviere,
An' t'ing lak dat if we don't have somebody
  leevin' dere?
W'at 's mak' de worl' look out for us, an' kip
  de nation free
Unless we 're raisin' all de tam some fine large
  familee?

Don't seem so long we buil' dat road, Chemin
    de Pacifique,
Tak' honder dollar pass on dere, an' nearly two
    t'ree week,
Den look dat place it freeze so hard, on w'at
    you call Klon-dak,
Wall! if we have to fill dem up, we got some large
    contrac'!

Of course we 're not doin' bad jus' now; so ev'ry-
    body say,
But we dunno de half we got on Canadaw to-
    day,
An' still she 's comin' beeger, an' never mak'
    no fuss,
So if we don't look out, firse t'ing, she 'll get
    ahead of us.

De more I t'ink, de more I 'm scare, de way
    she grow so fas',
An' worse of all it 's hard to say how long de
    boom 'll las'
But if she don't go slower an' ease up leetle
    bit,
Bimeby de Canayens will be some dead bird on
    de pit.

Den ev'ry body hip hooraw! an' sen' de familee
Along de reever, t'roo de wood, an' on de grande
    prairie,
Dat 's only way I 'm t'inkin' arrange de w'ole
    affaire
An' mebbe affer w'ile dere won't be too moche
    lan' for spare.

Autumn Days

IN dreams of the night I hear the call
    Of wild duck scudding across the lake,
In dreams I see the old convent wall,
    Where Ottawa's waters surge and break.

But Hercule awakes me ere the sun
    Has painted the eastern skies with gold.
Hercule! true knight of the rod and gun
    As ever lived in the days of old.

"Arise! tho' the moon hangs high above,
    The sun will soon usher in the day,
And the southerly wind that sportsmen love
    Is blowing across St. Louis Bay."

The wind is moaning among the trees,
    Along the shore where the shadows lie,
And faintly borne on the fresh'ning breeze
    From yonder point comes the loon's wild cry

Like diamonds flashing athwart the tide
  The dancing moonbeams quiver and glow,
As out on the deep we swiftly glide
  To our distant Mecca, Ile Perrot.

Ile Perrot far to the southward lies,
  Pointe Claire on the lee we leave behind,
And eager we gaze with longing eyes,
  For faintest sign of the deadly "blind."

Past the point where Ottawa's current flows—
  A league from St. Lawrence golden sands—
Out in the bay where the wild grass grows
  We mark the spot where our ambush stands.

We enter it just as the crimson flush
  Of morn illumines the hills with light,
And patiently wait the first mad rush
  Of pinions soaring in airy flight.

A rustle of wings from over there,
  Where all night long on watery bed
The flocks have slept—and the morning air
  Rings with the messenger of lead.

Many a pilgrim from far away
  Many a stranger from distant seas,
Is dying to-day on St. Louis Bay,
  To requiem sung by the southern breeze.

And thus till the sound of the vesper bell
   Comes stealing o'er Ottawa's dusky stream,
And the ancient light-house we know so well
   Lights up the tide with its friendly gleam.

Then up with the anchor and ply the oar,
   For homeward again our course must bear,
Farewell to the "blind" by Ile Perrot 's shore,
   And welcome the harbor of old Pointe Claire!

Madeleine Vercheres

I 'VE told you many a tale, my child, of the old heroic days
Of Indian wars and massacre, of villages ablaze
With savage torch, from Ville Marie to the Mission of Trois Rivieres
But never have I told you yet, of Madeleine Vercheres.

Summer had come with its blossoms, and gaily the robin sang
And deep in the forest arches the axe of the woodman rang
Again in the waving meadows, the sun-browned farmers met
And out on the green St. Lawrence, the fisherman spread his net.

And so through the pleasant season, till the
    days of October came
When children wrought with their parents, and
    even the old and lame
With tottering frames and footsteps, their feeble
    labors lent
At the gathering of the harvest le bon Dieu
    himself had sent.

For news there was none of battle, from the
    forts on the Richelieu
To the gates of the ancient city, where the
    flag of King Louis flew
All peaceful the skies hung over the seigneurie
    of Vercheres,
Like the calm that so often cometh, ere the
    hurricane rends the air.

And never a thought of danger had the Seigneur
    sailing away,
To join the soldiers of Carignan, where down at
    Quebec they lay,
But smiled on his little daughter, the maiden
    Madeleine,
And a necklet of jewels promised her, when
    home he should come again.

And ever the days passed swiftly, and careless
    the workmen grew
For the months they seemed a hundred, since
    the last war-bugle blew.
Ah! little they dreamt on their pillows, the
    farmers of Vercheres,
That the wolves of the southern forest had
    scented the harvest fair.

Like ravens they quickly gather, like tigers
    they watch their prey
Poor people! with hearts so happy, they sang
    as they toiled away.
Till the murderous eyeballs glistened, and the
    tomahawk leaped out
And the banks of the green St. Lawrence echoed
    the savage shout.

"Oh mother of Christ have pity," shrieked the
    women in despair
"This is no time for praying," cried the young
    Madeleine Vercheres,
"Aux armes! aux armes! les Iroquois! quick to
    your arms and guns
Fight for your God and country and the lives
    of the innocent ones."

And she sped like a deer of the mountain, when
 beagles press close behind
And the feet that would follow after, must be
 swift as the prairie wind.
Alas! for the men and women, and little ones
 that day
For the road it was long and weary, and the fort
 it was far away.

But the fawn had outstripped the hunters, and
 the palisades drew near,
And soon from the inner gateway the war-bugle
 rang out clear;
Gallant and clear it sounded, with never a note
 of despair,
'T was a soldier of France's challenge, from the
 young Madeleine Vercheres.

"And this is my little garrison, my brothers
 Louis and Paul?
With soldiers two—and a cripple? may the
 Virgin pray for us all.
But we 've powder and guns in plenty, and we 'll
 fight to the latest breath
And if need be for God and country, die a brave
 soldier's death.

"Load all the carabines quickly, and whenever
　　you sight the foe
Fire from the upper turret, and the loopholes
　　down below.
Keep up the fire, brave soldiers, though the
　　fight may be fierce and long
And they 'll think our little garrison is more
　　than a hundred strong."

So spake the maiden Madeleine, and she roused
　　the Norman blood
That seemed for a moment sleeping, and sent
　　it like a flood
Through every heart around her, and they
　　fought the red Iroquois
As fought in the old time battles, the soldiers
　　of Carignan.

And they say the black clouds gathered, and a
　　tempest swept the sky
And the roar of the thunder mingled with the
　　forest tiger's cry
But still the garrison fought on, while the
　　lightning's jagged spear
Tore a hole in the night's dark curtain, and
　　showed them a foeman near.

And the sun rose up in the morning, and the
    color of blood was he
Gazing down from the heavens on the little
    company.
"Behold! my friends!" cried the maiden, "'t is
    a warning lest we forget
Though the night saw us do our duty, our work
    is not finished yet."

And six days followed each other, and feeble
    her limbs became
Yet the maid never sought her pillow, and the
    flash of the carabines' flame
Illumined the powder-smoked faces, aye, even
    when hope seemed gone
And she only smiled on her comrades, and told
    them to fight, fight on.

And she blew a blast on the bugle, and lo! from
    the forest black
Merrily, merrily ringing, an answer came peal-
    ing back
Oh! pleasant and sweet it sounded, borne on
    the morning air,
For it heralded fifty soldiers, with gallant De
    la Monniere.

And when he beheld the maiden, the soldier
of Carignan,
And looked on the little garrison that fought
the red Iroquois
And held their own in the battle, for six long
weary days,
He stood for a moment speechless, and mar-
velled at woman's ways.

Then he beckoned the men behind him and
steadily they advance
And with carabines uplifted, the veterans of
France
Saluted the brave young Captain so timidly
standing there
And they fired a volley in honor of Madeleine
Vercheres.

And this, my dear, is the story of the maiden
Madeleine
God grant that we in Canada may never see
again
Such cruel wars and massacres, in waking or in
dream
As our fathers and mothers saw, my child, in
the days of the old regime.

The "Rose Delima"

YOU can sew heem up in a canvas sack,
　　An' t'row heem over boar'
You can wait till de ship she 's comin' back
　　Den bury heem on de shore
For dead man w'en he 's dead for sure,
　　Ain't good for not'ing at all
An' he 'll stay on de place you put heem
　　Till he hear dat bugle call
Dey say will soun' on de las', las' day
W'en ev'ry t'ing 's goin' for pass away,
But down on de Gulf of St. Laurent
　　W'ere de sea an' de reever meet
An' off on St. Pierre de Miquelon,
　　De chil'ren on de street
Can tole you story of Pierre Guillaume,
　　De sailor of St. Yvonne
Dat 's bringin' de "Rose Delima" home
　　Affer he 's dead an' gone.

———

He was stretch heem on de bed an' he could n't
　　　　raise hees head
　　So dey place heem near de winder w'ere he
　　　　can look below,
An' watch de schooner lie wit' her topmas' on
　　　　de sky,
　　An' oh! how mad it mak' heem, ole Captinne
　　　　Baribeau.

199

For she's de fines' boat dat never was afloat
  From de harbor of St. Simon to de shore of
      New-fun-lan'
She can almos' dance a reel, an' de sea shell on
    her keel
  Wall! you count dem very easy on de finger
    of your han'.

But de season's flyin' fas', an' de fall is nearly
      pas'
  An' de leetle "Rose Delima" she's doin'
    not'ing dere
Only pullin' on her chain, an' wishin' once
    again
  She was w'ere de black fish tumble, an jomp
    upon de air.

But who can tak' her out, for she's got de tender
      mout'
  Lak a trotter on de race-course dat's mebbe
    run away
If he's not jus' handle so—an' ole Captinne
    Baribeau
  Was de only man can sail her, dat's w'at dey
    offen say.

An' now he 's lyin' dere, w'ere de breeze is
    blow hees hair
  An' he 's hearin' ev'ry morning de "Rose
    Delima" call,
Sayin', "Come along wit' me, an' we 'll off across
    de sea,
  For I 'm lonesome waitin' for you, Captinne
    Paul.

"On Anticosti shore we hear de breaker
    roar
  An' reef of Dead Man's Islan' too we
    know,
But we never miss de way, no matter night or
    day,
  De 'Rose Delima' schooner an' Captinne
    Baribeau."

De Captinne cry out den, so de house is shake
    again,
  "Come here! come here, an' quickly, ma
    daughter Virginie,
An' let me hol' your han', for so long as I can
    stan'
  I 'll tak' de 'Rose Delima,' an' sail her off to
    sea."

"No, no, ma fader dear, you 're better stayin'
here
Till de cherry show her blossom on de spring,
For de loon he 's flyin' sout' an' de fall is nearly
out,
W'en de wil' bird of de nort' is on de wing.

"But fader dear, I know de man can go below
Wit' leetle 'Rose Delima' on St. Pierre de
Miquelon
Hees nam' is Pierre Guillaume, an' he 'll bring
de schooner home
Till she 's t'rowin' out her anchor on de port
of St. Simon."

"Ha! Ha! ma Virginie, it is n't hard to see
You lak dat smart young sailor man youse'f,
I s'pose he love you too, but I tole you w'at
I do
W'en I have some leetle talk wit' heem mese'f.

"So call heem up de stair:" an' w'en he 's stan-
nin' dere,
De Captinne say, "Young feller, you see
how sick I be?
De poor ole Baribeau has n't very much below
Beside de 'Rose Delima,' an' hees daughter
Virginie.

"An' I know your fader well, he's fine man
    too, Noël,
  An' hees nam' was comin' offen on ma
    prayer—
An' if your sailor blood she's only half as good
  You can sail de 'Rose Delima' from here to
    any w'ere.

"You love ma Virginie? wall! if you promise me
  You bring de leetle schooner safely home
From St. Pierre de Miquelon to de port of St.
  Simon
  You can marry on ma daughter, Pierre Guil-
    laume."

An' Pierre he answer den, "Ma fader was your
    frien'
  An' it's true your daughter Virginie I love,
Dat schooner she 'll come home, or ma nam' 's
  not Pierre Guillaume
  I swear by all de angel up above."

So de wil' bird goin' sout', see her shake de
    canvas out,
  An' soon de "Rose Delima" she's flyin' down
  de bay
An' poor young Virginie so long as she can see
  Kip watchin' on dat schooner till at las' she's
    gone away.

Ho! ho! for Gaspé cliff w'en de win' is blowin'
   stiff,
   Ho! ho! for Anticosti w'ere bone of dead man
      lie!
De sailor cimetiere! God help de beeg ship
      dere
   If dey come too near de islan' w'en de wave
      she's runnin' high.

It's locky t'ing he know de way he ought to go
   It's locky too de star above, he know dem
      ev'ry wan
For God he mak' de star, was shinin' up so far,
   So he trus' no oder compass, young Pierre
      of St. Yvonne.

An' de schooner sail away pas' Wolf Islan' an'
      Cape Ray—
   W'ere de beeg wave fight each oder roun'
      de head of ole Pointe Blanc
Only gettin' pleasan' win', till she tak' de
      canvas in
   An' drop de anchor over on St. Pierre de
      Miquelon.

We 're glad to see some more, de girl upon de
 shore,
 An' Jean Barbette was kipin' Hotel de Sans-
  souci
He 's also glad we come, 'cos we mak' de rafter
 hum;
 An' w'en we 're stayin' dere, ma foi! we spen'
  de monee free.

But Captinne Pierre Guillaume, might jus' as
 well be home,
 For he don't forget his sweetheart an' ole
  man Baribeau,
An' so he stay on boar', an' fifty girl or more
 Less dey haul heem on de bowline, dey
  could n't mak' heem go.

Wall! we 're workin' hard an' fas', an' de cargo 's
 on at las'
 Two honder cask of w'isky, de fines' on de
  worl'!
So good-bye to Miquelon, an' hooraw for St.
 Simon—
 An' au revoir to Jean Barbette, an' don't for-
  get de girl.

You can hear de schooner sing, w'en she open
    out her wing
  So glad to feel de slappin' of de sea wave on
    her breas'
She did n't los' no tam, but travel jus' de
    sam',
  As de small bird w'en he 's flyin' on de evening
    to hees nes'.

But her sail 's not blowin' out wit' de warm
    breeze of de sout'
  An' it 's not too easy tellin' w'ere de snow-
    flake meet de foam
Stretchin' out on ev'ry side, all across de Gulf so
    wide
  W'en de nor'-eas' win' is chasin' de "Rose
    Delima" home.

An' we 're flyin' once again pas' de Isle of
    Madeleine
  An' away for Anticosti we let de schooner
    go
Lak a race-horse on de track, we could never
    hol' her back—
  She mebbe hear heem callin' her, ole Captinne
    Baribeau!

But we 're ketchin' it wan night w'en de star
    go out of sight
  For de storm dat 's waitin' for us, come before
    we know it 's dere—
An' it blow us near de coas' w'ere dey leev' de
    sailor's ghos'
  On de shore of Dead Man's Islan' till dey
    almos' fill de air.

So de Captinne tak' de wheel, an' it mak' de
    schooner feel
  Jus' de sam' as ole man Baribeau is workin'
    dere hese'f
Well she know it 's life or deat', so she 's fightin'
    hard for breat'
  For wit' all dem wave a chokin' her, it 's leetle
    she got lef'.

Den de beeges' sea of all, stannin' up dere lak
    a wall
  Come along an' sweep de leetle "Rose Delima"
    fore an' af'
An' above de storm a cry, "Help, mon Dieu!
    before I die."
  An' dere 's no wan on de wheel house, an'
    we hear dem spirit laugh.

Dey 're lookin' for dead man, an' dey 're shoutin'
    all dey can
  Don't matter all de pile dey got dey want
    anoder wan—
An' now dey 're laughin' loud, for out of all de
    crowd
  Dey got no finer sailor boy dan Pierre of St.
    Yvonne!

But look dere on de wheel! w'at 's dat was seem
    to steal
  From now'ere, out of not'ing, till it reach de
    pilot's place
An' steer de rudder too, lak de Captinne used
    to do
  So lak de Captinne's body, so lak de Cap-
    tinne's face.

But well enough we know de poor boy 's gone
    below,
  W'ere hees bone will join de oder on de place
    w'ere dead man be—
An' we only see phantome of young Captinne
    Pierre Guillaume
  Dat sail de "Rose Delima" all night along de
    sea.

So we help heem all we can, kip de schooner
    off de lan'
  W'ere bad spirit work de current dat was
    pullin' us inside—
But we fool dem all at las', an' we know de
    danger 's pas'
  W'en de sun come out an' fin' us floatin' on
    de morning tide.

So de Captinne's work is done, an' nex' day de
    schooner run
  Wit' de sail all hangin' roun' her, to de port
    of St. Simon.
Dat 's de way young Pierre Guillaume bring
    de "Rose Delima" home
  T'roo de wil' an' stormy wedder from St.
    Pierre de Miquelon.

An' de leetle Virginie never look upon de sea
  Since de tam de "Rose Delima" 's comin'
    home,
For she 's lef' de worl' an' all! but behin' de
    convent wall
  She don't forget her fader an' poor young
    Pierre Guillaume.

Little Mouse

GET along leetle mouse, kick de snow up
      behin' you
  For it 's fine winter road we 're travel to-night
Wit' de moon an' de star shinin' up on de sky
      dere
    W'y it 's almos' de sam' as de broad day light.

De bell roun' your body it 's quick tune dey 're
      playin'
  But your foot 's kipin' tam jus' as steady can
      be,
Ah! you dance youse'f crazy if only I let you,
  Ma own leetle pony—petite souris.

You 'member w'en firse we be tryin' for broke
      you
  An' Joe Sauvageau bet hees two dollar bill
He can drive you alone by de bridge on de
      reever
  An' down near de place w'ere dey got de
      beeg mill.

An' it 's new cariole too, is come from St. Felix
  Jo-seph 's only buyin' it week before,
An' w'en he is passin' de road wit' hees trotter
  Ev'ry body was stan' on de outside door.

An' dere he sit, sam' he don't care about not'ing
    Hees foot on de dashboar', hees han' on de
        line
Ev'ry dog on de place is come out for barkin'
    An' all de young boy he was ronnin' behin'.

Wall! sir, Joe 's put on style leetle soon for hees
        pleasure
    For w'en de mill w'issle, you jomp lak de cat
An' nex' t'ing poor Joe is commencin' get busy.
    Non! I never see fine run-away lak dat.

'Way go de pony den—'way go de cariole,
    Poor Joe say, "good-bye" on de foot of de
        hill
An' all he can see of de sleigh de nex' morning
    Is jus' about pay for hees two dollar bill.

Ah! your right nam' jus' den should be leetle
        devil
    An' not leetle mouse, de sam' you have now.
Wall! dat 's long ago, an' you 're gettin' more
        quiet
    Since tam you was never done kickin' de row.

But I 'm not very sorry de firse day I see you
    Settle down on de trot lak your fader he get
W'en he beat Sorel Boy on de ice at T'ree Reever
    Bes' two on t'ree heat, an' win all de bet.

Your moder she 's come off de Lachapelle stock
    too
  Ole Canayen blood from Berthier en haut
De bes' kin' of horse never look on de halter
  So it is n't moche wonder you know how to go.

Dat 's church bell we 're off dere on de hillside
  Get along leetle mouse, for we must n't be
    late,
Fin' your way t'roo de res' of dem crowdin' de
    roadside
  You 'll never get better chance showin' your
    gait.
   .   .   .   .   .   .

Wall! church is all over, an' Josephine 's comin'
  For drive wit' us home on her gran'moder's
    house
So tak' your own tam an' don't be on de hurry
  Your slowes' gait 's quick enough now, leetle
    mouse.

Strathcona's Horse

(Dedicated to Lord Strathcona)

O I was thine, and thou wert mine, and ours
  the boundless plain,
Where the winds of the North, my gallant steed,
  ruffled thy tawny mane,

But the summons hath come with roll of drum,
    and bugles ringing shrill,
Startling the prairie antelope, the grizzly of the
    hill.
'T is the voice of Empire calling, and the chil-
    dren gather fast
From every land where the cross bar floats out
    from the quivering mast;
So into the saddle I leap, my own, with bridle
    swinging free,
And thy hoof-beats shall answer the trumpets
    blowing across the sea.
Then proudly toss thy head aloft, nor think of
    the foe to-morrow,
For he who dares to stay our course drinks deep
    of the Cup of Sorrow.

Thy form hath pressed the meadow's breast,
    where the sullen grey wolf hides,
The great red river of the North hath cooled
    thy burning sides;
Together we 've slept while the tempest swept
    the Rockies' glittering chain;
And many a day the bronze centaur hath gal-
    loped behind in vain.
But the sweet wild grass of mountain pass, and
    the shimmering summer streams
Must vanish forevermore, perchance, into the
    land of dreams;

For the strong young North hath sent us forth
    to battlefields far away,
And the trail that ends where Empire trends,
    is the trail we ride to-day.
But proudly toss thy head aloft, nor think of
    the foe to-morrow,
For he who bars Strathcona's Horse, drinks
    deep of the Cup of Sorrow.

Johnnie's First Moose

D E cloud is hide de moon, but dere 's plain-
    tee light above,
Steady, Johnnie, steady—kip your head down
    low,
Move de paddle leetle quicker, an' de ole canoe
    we 'll shove
        T'roo de water nice an' quiet
        For de place we 're goin' try it
        Is beyon' de silver birch dere
        You can see it lak a church dere
W'en we 're passin' on de corner w'ere de lily
    flower grow.

Was n't dat correc' w'at I 'm tolin' you jus' now?
Steady, Johnnie, steady—kip your head down
    low,
Never min', I 'll watch behin'—me—an' you
    can watch de bow

An' you 'll see a leetle clearer
W'en canoe is comin' nearer—
Dere she is—now easy, easy,
For de win' is gettin' breezy,
An' we don't want not'ing smell us, till de
horn begin to blow—

I remember long ago w'en ma fader tak' me out,
Steady, Johnnie, steady—kip your head down
low,
Jus' de way I 'm takin' you, sir, hello! was
dat a shout?
Seems to me I t'ink I 'm hearin'
Somet'ing stirrin' on de clearin'
W'ere it stan' de lumber shaintee,
If it 's true, den you 'll have plaintee
Work to do in half a minute, if de moose don't
start to go.

An' now we 're on de shore, let us hide de ole
canoe,
Steady, Johnnie, steady—kip your head down
low,
An' lie among de rushes, dat 's bes' t'ing we
can do,
For de ole boy may be closer
Dan anybody know, sir,

An' look out you don't be shakin'
Or de bad shot you 'll be makin'
But I 'm feelin' sam' way too, me, w'en I
was young, also—

You ready for de call? here goes for number wan,
Steady, Johnnie, steady—kip your head down
low,
Did you hear how nice I do it, an' how it
travel on
Till it reach across de reever
Dat 'll geev' some moose de fever!
Wait now, Johnnie, don't you worry,
No use bein' on de hurry,
But lissen for de answer, it 'll come before you
know.

For w'y you jomp lak dat? w'at 's matter wit'
your ear?
Steady, Johnnie, steady—kip your head down
low—
Tak' your finger off de trigger, dat was only
bird you hear,
Can't you tell de pine tree crickin'
Or de boule frog w'en he 's spikin'?
Don't you know de grey owl singin'
From de beeg moose w'en he 's ringin'
Out hees challenge on de message your ole
gran'fader blow?

216

You 're lucky boy to-night, wit' hunter man
    lak me!
Steady, Johnnie, steady—kip your head down
    low—
Can tole you all about it! H-s-ssh! dat 's
    somet'ing now I see,
        Dere he 's comin' t'roo de bushes,
        So get down among de rushes,
        Hear heem walk! I t'ink, by tonder,
        He mus' go near fourteen honder!
Dat 's de feller I been watchin' all de evening,
    I dunno.

I 'll geev' anoder call, jus' a leetle wan or two,
Steady, Johnnie, steady—kip your head down
    low—
W'en he see dere 's no wan waitin' I wonder
    w'at he 'll do?
        But look out for here he 's comin'
        Sa-pris-ti! ma heart is drummin'!
        You can never get heem nearer
        An' de moon is shinin' clearer,
W'at a fine shot you 'll be havin'! now
    Johnnie let her go!

Bang! bang! you got heem sure! an' he 'll
    never run away
Nor feed among de lily on de shore of Wes-
    sonneau,

So dat's your firse moose, Johnnie! wall! re-
    member all I say—
        Does n't matter w'at you 're chasin',
        Does n't matter w'at you 're facin',
        Only watch de t'ing you 're doin'
        If you don't, ba gosh! you 're ruin!
An' steady, Johnnie, steady—kip your head
    down low.

The Old Pine Tree

(*Dedicated to the St. George Snowshoe Club*)

"LISTEN, my child," said the old pine
      tree to the little one nestling near,
"For the storm clouds troop together to-night,
    and the wind of the north I hear
And perchance there may come some echo of
    the music of long ago,
The music that rang when the White Host
    sang, marching across the snow."

"Up and away Saint George! up thro' the
    mountain gorge,
Over the plain where the tempest blows, and
    the great white flakes are flying
Down the long narrow glen! faster my merry
    men,
Follow the trail, tho' the shy moon hides, and
    deeply the drifts are lying."

THE OLD PINE TREE

"Ah! mother," the little pine tree replied,
      "you are dreaming again to-night
Of ghostly visions and phantom forms that
      forever mock your sight
'T is true the moan of the winter wind comes
      to my list'ning ear
But the White Host marching, I cannot see,
      and their music I cannot hear."

"When the northern skies were all aflame
      where the trembling banners swung,
When up in the vaulted heavens the moon of
      the Snow-Shoe hung,
When the hurricane swept the hillside, and the
      crested drifts ran high
Those were the nights," said the old pine tree,
      "the great White Host marched by."

And the storm grew fiercer, fiercer, and the
      snow went hissing past,
But the little pine tree still listened, till she
      heard above the blast
The music her mother loved to hear in the
      nights of the long ago
And saw in the forest the white-clad Host
      marching across the snow.

And loud they sang as they tramped along of
  the glorious bygone days
When valley and hill re-echoed the snow-
  shoer's hymn of praise
Till the shy moon gazed down smiling, and the
  north wind paused to hear
And the old pine tree felt young again as the
  little one nestling near.

"Up and away Saint George! up thro' the
  mountain gorge.
Over the plain where the tempest blows, and
  the great white flakes are flying.
Down the long narrow glen! faster my merry
  men.
Follow the trail, tho' the shy moon hides, and
  deeply the drifts are lying."

Little Bateese

YOU bad leetle boy, not moche you care
    How busy you 're kipin' your poor gran'-
  pere
Tryin' to stop you ev'ry day
Chasin' de hen aroun' de hay—
W'y don't you geev' dem a chance to lay?
                              Leetle Bateese!

LITTLE BATEESE

Off on de fiel' you foller de plough
Den w'en you 're tire you scare de cow
Sickin' de dog till dey jomp de wall
So de milk ain't good for not'ing at all—
An' you 're only five an' a half dis fall,
                        Leetle Bateese!

Too sleepy for sayin' de prayer to-night?
Never min' I s'pose it 'll be all right
Say dem to-morrow—ah! dere he go!
Fas' asleep in a minute or so—
An' he 'll stay lak dat till de rooster crow,
                        Leetle Bateese!

Den wake us up right away toute suite
Lookin' for somet'ing more to eat,
Makin' me t'ink of dem long leg crane
Soon as dey swaller, dey start again,
I wonder your stomach don't get no pain,
                        Leetle Bateese!

But see heem now lyin' dere in bed,
Look at de arm onderneat' hees head;
If he grow lak dat till he 's twenty year
I bet he 'll be stronger dan Louis Cyr
An' beat all de voyageurs leevin' here,
                        Leetle Bateese!

Jus' feel de muscle along hees back,
Won't geev' heem moche bodder for carry pack
On de long portage, any size canoe,
Dere 's not many t'ing dat boy won't do
For he 's got double-joint on hees body too,
                              Leetle Bateese!

But leetle Bateese! please don't forget
We rader you 're stayin' de small boy yet,
So chase de chicken an' mak' dem scare
An' do w'at you lak wit' your ole gran'pere
For w'en you 're beeg feller he won't be dere—
                              Leetle Bateese!

Donal' Campbell

DONAL' CAMPBELL—Donal' Bane—
    sailed away across the ocean
With the tartans of Clan Gordon, to the Indies'
    distant shore,
But on Dargai's lonely hillside, Donal' Camp-
    bell met the foeman,
And the glen of Athol Moray will never see
    him more!

O! the wailing of the women, O! the storm of
    bitter sorrow
Sweeping like the wintry torrent thro' Athol
    Moray's glen

When the black word reached the clansmen,
    that young Donal' Bane had fallen
In the red glare of the battle, with the gallant
    Gordon men!

Far from home and native sheiling, with the
    sun of India o'er him
Blazing down its cruel hatred on the white-
    faced men below
Stood young Donal' with his comrades, like the
    hound of ghostly Fingal
Eager, waiting for the summons to leap up
    against the foe—

Hark! at last! the pipes are pealing out the
    welcome Caber Feidh
And wild the red blood rushes thro' every
    Highland vein
They breathe the breath of battle, the children
    of the Gael,
And fiercely up the hillside, they charge and
    charge again—

And the grey eye of the Highlands, now is
    dark as blackest midnight,
The history of their fathers is written on each face,
Of border creach and foray, of never yielding
    conflict
Of all the memories shrouding a stern uncon-
    quered race!

And up the hillside, up the mountain, while
    the war-pipes shrilly clamour
Bayonet thrusting, broadsword cleaving, the
    Northern soldiers fought
Till the sun of India saw them victors o'er the
    dusky foemen,
For who can stay the Celtic hand when Celtic
    blood is hot?

But the corse of many a clansman from the far-
    off Scottish Highlands
'Mid the rocks of savage Dargai is lying cold
    and still
With the death-dew on its forehead, and young
    Donal' Campbell's tartan
Bears a deeper stain of purple than the heather
    of the hill!

Mourn him!   Mourn him thro' the mountains,
    wail him women of Clan Campbell!
Let the Coronach be sounded till it reach the
    Indian shore
For your beautiful has fallen in the foremost
    of the battle
And the glen of Athol Moray will never see
    him more.

The Dublin Fusilier

HERE 's to you, Uncle Kruger! slainté!
    an' slainté galore.
You 're a dacint ould man, begorra; never
    mind if you are a Boer.
So with heart an' a half ma bouchal, we 'll
    drink to your health to-night
For yourself an' your farmer sojers gave us a
    damn good fight.

I was dramin' of Kitty Farrell, away in the
    Gap o' Dunloe,
When the song of the bugle woke me, ringin'
    across Glencoe;
An' once in a while a bullet came pattherin'
    from above,
That tould us the big brown fellows were send-
    in' us down their love.

'T was a kind of an invitation, an' written in
    such a han'
That a Chinaman could n't refuse it—not to
    spake of an Irishman.
So the pickets sent back an answer. "We 're
    comin' with right good will,"
Along what they call the kopje, tho' to me it
    looked more like a hill.

"Fall in on the left," sez the captain, "my
    men of the Fusiliers;
You 'll see a great fight this morning—like
    you have n't beheld for years."
"Faith, captain dear," sez the sergeant, "you
    can bet your Majuba sword
If the Dutch is as willin' as we are, you never
    spoke truer word."

So we scrambled among the bushes, the bowl-
    ders an' rocks an' all,
Like the gauger's men still-huntin' on the
    mountains of Donegal;
We doubled an' turned an' twisted the same
    as a hunted hare,
While the big guns peppered each other over
    us in the air.

Like steam from the divil's kettle the kopje
    was bilin' hot,
For the breeze of the Dutchman's bullets was
    the only breeze we got;
An' many a fine boy stumbled, many a brave
    lad died,
When the Dutchman's message caught him
    there on the mountainside.

Little Nelly O'Brien, God help her! over
    there at ould Ballybay,
Will wait for a Transvaal letter till her face an'
    her hair is grey,
For I seen young Crohoore on a stretcher, an'
    I knew the poor boy was gone
When I spoke to the ambulance doctor, an' he
    nodded an' then passed on.

"Steady there!" cried the captain, "we must
    halt for a moment here."
An' he spoke like a man in trainin', full winded
    an' strong an' clear.
So we threw ourselves down on the kopje,
    weary an' tired as death,
Waitin' the captain's orders, waitin' to get a
    breath.

It 's strange all the humors an' fancies that
    comes to a man like me;
But the smoke of the battle risin' took me
    across the sea—
It 's the mist of Benbo I 'm seein'; an' the rock
    that we 'll capture soon
Is the rock where I shot the eagle, when I was
    a small gossoon.

THE DUBLIN FUSILIER

I close my eyes for a minute, an' hear my poor
    mother say,
"Patrick, avick, my darlin', you 're surely not
    goin' away
To join the red-coated sojers?"—but the
    blood in me was strong—
If your sire was a Connaught Ranger, sure
    where would his son belong?

Hark! whisht! do you hear the music comin'
    up from the camp below?
An odd note or two when the Maxims take
    breath for a second or so,
Liftin' itself on somehow, stealin' its way up
    here,
Knowin' there 's waitin' to hear it, many an
    Irish ear.

Augh! Garryowen! you 're the jewel! an' we
    charged on the Dutchman's guns,
An' covered the bloody kopje, like a Galway
    greyhound runs,
At the top of the hill they met us, with faces
    all set and grim;
But they could n't take the bayonet—that 's
    the trouble with most of thim.

So of course, they 'll be praisin' the Royals
    an' men of the Fusiliers,
An' the newspapers help to dry up the widows
    an' orphans' tears,
An' they 'll write a new name on the colors—
    that is, if there 's room for more
An' we 'll follow them thro' the battle, the same
    as we 've done before.

But here 's to you, Uncle Kruger! slainté! an'
    slainté galore.
After all, your 're a dacint Christian, never
    mind if you are a Boer.
So with heart an' a half, ma bouchal, we 'll
    drink to your health to-night,
For yourself an' your brown-faced Dutchmen
    gave us a damn good fight.

Dreams

BORD à Plouffe, Bord à Plouffe,
    W'at do I see w'en I dream of you?
A shore w'ere de water is racin' by,
A small boy lookin', an' wonderin' w'y
He can't get fedder for goin' fly
Lak de hawk makin' ring on de summer sky,
        Dat 's w'at I see.

229

DREAMS

Bord à Plouffe, Bord à Plouffe,
W'at do I hear w'en I dream of you?
Too many t'ing for sleepin' well!
De song of de ole tam cariole bell,
De voice of dat girl from Sainte Angèle
(I geev' her a ring was mark "fidèle")
   Dat 's w'at I hear.

Bord à Plouffe, Bord à Plouffe,
W'at do I smoke w'en I dream of you?
Havana cigar from across de sea,
An' get dem for not'ing too? No siree!
Dere 's only wan kin' of tabac for me.
An' it grow on de Rivière des Prairies—
   Dat 's w'at I smoke.

Bord à Plouffe, Bord à Plouffe,
How do I feel w'en I t'ink of you?
Sick, sick for de ole place way back dere—
An' to sleep on ma own leetle room upstair
W'ere de ghos' on de chimley mak' me scare
I 'd geev' more monee dan I can spare—
   Dat 's how I feel.

Bord à Plouffe, Bord à Plouffe,
W'at will I do w'en I 'm back wit' you?
I 'll buy de farm of Bonhomme Martel,
Long tam he 's been waitin' a chance to sell,

Den pass de nex' morning on Sainte Angèle,
An' if she 's not marry—dat girl—very well,
      Dat 's w'at I 'll do.

The Old Sexton

I KNOW very well 't was purty hard case
   If dere 's not on de worl' some beeger place
Dan village of Cote St. Paul,
But we got mebbe sixty-five house or more
Wit' de blacksmit' shop an' two fine store
Not to speak of de church an' de city hall.

An' of course on village lak dat you fin'
Some very nice girl if you have a min'
To look aroun', an' we got dem too—
But de fines' of all never wear a ring,
Since firse I 'm t'inkin' of all dem t'ing,
Was daughter of ole Narcisse Beaulieu.

Narcisse he 's bedeau on de beeg church dere,
He also look affer de presbytere,
An' leev on de house close by,
On Sunday he 's watchin' de leetle boys,
Stoppin' dem kickin' up too much noise,
An' he bury de peop' w'en dey 're comin' die.

231

So dat 's w'at he do, Narcisse Beaulieu,
An' it 's not very easy I 'm tolin' you,
But a purty large heavy load,
For on summer de cow she was run aroun'
An' eat all de flower on de Curé's groun'.
An' before he can ketch her, p-s-s-t! she 's down
    de road.

Dat 's not'ing at all, for w'en winter come
Narcisse got plaintee more work ba gum!
Shovellin' snow till hees back was sore,
Makin' some track for de horse an' sleigh,
Kipin' look out dey don't run away,
An' freezin' outside on de double door.

But w'enever de vault on de church is fill
Wit' de peop' was waitin' down dere ontil
Dey can go on de cimetière,
For fear dem student will come aroun'
An' tak' de poor dead folk off to town
Narcisse offen watch for dem all night dere.

An' de girl Josephine she 's her fader's pet,
He never see nobody lak her yet,
So w'en he 's goin' on St. Jerome
For travel about on some leetle tour
An' lef' her alone on de house, I 'm sure
De house she 's all right w'en he 's comin'
    home.

THE OLD SEXTON

Wall! nearly t'ree year is come an' go,
De quietes' year de village know,
For dem student don't show hees face,
An' de peop' is beginnin' to ax w'at for
Dey 're alway goin' on Ile Bizard
An' never pass on our place.

But it 's bully tam for de ole Narcisse,
An' w'en he 's lettin' heem go de pries'
For stay away two t'ree day
He t'ink of course it was purty good chance,
So he buy heem new coat an' pair of pants,
An' go see hees frien' noder side de bay.

An' dat very sam' night, ba gosh! it seem
De girl 's not dreamin' some pleasan' dream
For she visit de worse place never seen
Down on T'ree Reever, an' near Kebeck
W'ere robber-man's chokin' her on de neck—
De poor leetle Josephine!

So she 's risin' up den and she tak' de gun
An' off on de winder she quickly run
For fear she might need a shot
An' dem student he 's comin' across de square
Right on de front of de cimetière
An' carryin' somet'ing—you know w'at!

So she 's takin' good aim on de beeges' man
An' pull de trigger de hard she can,
An' he 's yellin' an' down he go,
Hees frien' dey say not'ing, but clear out quick,
Dat 's way Josephine she was playin' trick
On feller was treatin' poor dead folk so!

Den she kick up a row an' begin to feel
Very sorry right off for de boy she keel
An' de nex' t'ing she 's startin' cry
An' call on her fader an' moder too,
Poor leetle Josephine Beaulieu,
An' wishin' she 'd lak to die.

But she did n't die den, an' he 's leevin' yet—
Dat feller was comin' so near hees deat'—
For she 's nursin' heem back to life,
Dey 're feexin' it someway, I dunno how,
But dey 're marry an' leev' in de city now
An' she 's makin' heem firse class wife.

An' Narcisse hese'f he was alway say,
"It 's fonny t'ing how it come dat way
But I 'm not very sorry at all,
Course I know ma son he 's not doin' right,
But man he was haulin' aroun' dat night
Is worse ole miser on Cote St. Paul."

Child Thoughts—Written to Commemorate the Anniversary of my Brother Tom's Birthday

O MEMORY, take my hand to-day
    And lead me thro' the darkened bridge
Washed by the wild Atlantic spray
    And spanning many a wind-swept ridge
Of sorrow, grief, of love and joy,
    Of youthful hopes and manly fears!
    O! let me cross the bridge of years
And see myself again a boy!

The shadows pass—I see the light,
    O morning light, how clear and strong!
My native skies are smiling bright,
    No more I grope my way along,
It comes, the murmur of the tide
    Upon my ear—I hear the cry
    Of wandering sea birds as they fly
In trooping squadrons far and near.

The breeze that blows o'er Mullaghmore
    I feel against my boyish cheek
The white-walled huts that strew the shore
    From Castlegal to old Belleek,

The fisher folk of Donegal,
    Kindly of heart and strong of arm,
    Who plough the ocean's treacherous farm,
How plainly I behold them all!

The thrush's song, the blackbird's note,
    The wren within the hawthorn hedge,
The robin's swelling vibrant throat,
    The leveret crouching in the sedge!
In those dear days, ah! what was school?
    When Nature made our pulses thrill!
    The lessons we remember still
Were learnt at Nature's own footstool!

"The hounds are out! the beagles chase
    Along the slopes of Tawley's plain!"
I rise and follow in the race
    Till fox, or hare, or both are slain,
With heart ablaze, I loose the reins
    Of all my childish fierce desire,
    My faith! 't is Ireland plants the fire
And iron in her children's veins!

The mountain linnet whistles sweet
    Among the gorse of summer-time,
As up the hill with eager feet
    The sun of morning sees me climb

Until at last I sink to rest
  Where heatherbells swing to the tune
  That Benbo breezes softly croon—
A tired child on the mother's breast!

And now in wisdom's riper years,
  Ah, wisdom! what a price we pay
Of sorrow, grief, of smiles and tears,
  Before we reach that wiser day!
We meet to greet in joy and mirth
  The white-haired parent of us all
  Our childhood's memories to recall
And bless the land that gave us birth.

Bateese and his Little Decoys

O I 'm very very tire Marie,
    I wonder if I 'm able hol' a gun
An' me dat 's alway risin' wit de sun
An' travel on de water, an' paddle ma canoe
An' trap de mink an' beaver de fall an' winter
        t'roo,
But now I t'ink dat fun is gone forever.

Wall! I 'm mebbe stayin' long enough,
  For eighty-four I see it on de spring;
Dough ma fader he was feelin' purty tough
  An' at ninety year can do mos' ev'ry t'ing,

237

But I never know de feller, don't care how ole
      he come,
Dat is n't sure to t'ink he 's got anoder year,
      ba gum!
Before he lif' de anchor for de las' tam!

It 's not so easy lyin' on de bed,
   An' lissen to de wil' bird on de bay,
Dey know dat poor Bateese is nearly dead,
   Or dey would n't have such good fun ev'ry
     day!
Put ma gun upon de piller near de winder, jus'
     for luck,
Den bring w'ere I can see dem, ma own nice
     leetle duck
So I have some talk wit' dem mese'f dis
     morning.

Ah! dere you 're comin' now! mes beaux
     canards!
   Dat 's very pleasan' day, an' how you feel?
Of course you dunno w'at I want you for,
   Wall! lately I 've been t'inkin' a good deal
Of all de fuss I 'm havin' show you w'at you
     ought to do
W'en de cole win' of October de blin' is blow-
     ing t'roo
An' de bluebill 's flyin' up an' down de reever.

BATEESE AND HIS LITTLE DECOYS

O! de bodder I 'm havin' wit' you all!
  It 's makin' me feel ole before ma tam!
Stan' over dere upon de right again de wall,
  Ma-dame Lapointe—I 'm geevin' you Ma-
      dame
'Cos you walk aroun' de sam' way as ma cousin
      Aurelie
An' lak youse'f she 's havin' de large large
      familee,
Now let us see you don't forget your lesson!

Qu-a-a-ck! you 're leetle hoarse to-day, don't
      you t'ink?
  Quack! quack! quack! dat 's right Mam-
      zelle Louise!
You go lak dat, an' quicker dan a wink,
  It 'll ring across de lake along de breeze,
Till de wil' bird dey will lissen up de reever
      far an' near,
An' tole de noder wan too, de musique dey was
      hear
An' dey 'll fly aroun' our head before we know it.

Come here, François, an' min' you watch
      youse'f!
  You can't forget de las' day we was out,
Your breat' dere 's very leetle of it lef'
  An' I tole you it was better shut your mout'

239

W'en you start dat fancy yellin,' for it soun'
  de sam' to me
Lak de devil he was goin' on de beeges' kin'
  of spree,
François! dat 's not de way for mak' de
  shootin'!

Wan—two—t'ree,—now let us hear you please,
  It is n't very hard job if you try,
Purten' you 're feelin' lonesome lak Louise
  An' want to see de sweetheart bimeby,
Quack! quack! quack!
O! stop dat screechin', don't never spik no more
For if anyt'ing, sapree, tonnerre! you 're worser
  dan before,
I wonder w'at you do wit' all your schoolin'!

Come out from onderneat' de bed, Lisette,
  I believe you was de fattes' of de lot;
It 's handy too of course, for you never feel de
  wet,
  An' w'en you lak to try it, O! w'at a voice
   you got!
So let us play it 's blowin' hard, an' duck is up
  de win'
An' you want to reach dem—sure—now we 're
  ready for begin,
Hooraw! an' never min' de noise dat you 're
  makin'.

Quack! quack! quack! quack! O! let me
    tak' de gun
  For I would n't be astonish w'en Lisette is
    get de start,
Roun' de house dey 'll come a-flyin', an' den
    we 'll have de fun!
  Yass, yass, kip up de flappin', O! ain't
    she got de heart!
Not many duck can beat her, an' I wish I had
    some more,
Can mak' de song lak dat upon de water!

Dat 's very funny how it ketch de crowd!
  An' now dey 're goin' all de younger wan!
But if you don't stop singin' out so loud,
  I 'm sorry I mus' tole you all begone,
'Cos I want to go to sleep, for I 'm very, very
    tire,
An' de shiver 's comin' on me! so Marie poke
    up de fire
An' mebbe I 'll feel better on de morning.
     .   .   .   .

De leetle duck may call on de spring tam an'
    de fall
W'en dey see de wil' bird flyin' on de air
Dey may cry aroun' hees door, but he 'll never
    come no more
For showin' dem de lesson! ole Jean Bateese
    Belair.

Phil-o-Rum's Canoe

"O MA ole canoe! w'at's matter wit' you,
  an' w'y was you be so slow?
Don't I work hard enough on de paddle, an'
  still you don't seem to go—
No win' at all on de fronte side, an' current
  she don't be strong,
Den w'y are you lak lazy feller, too sleepy for
  move along?

"I 'member de tam w'en you jomp de sam' as
  deer wit' de wolf behin'
An' brochet on de top de water, you scare
  heem mos' off hees min';
But fish don't care for you now at all, only jus'
  mebbe wink de eye,
For he know it's easy git out de way w'en you
  was a passin' by."

I'm spikin' dis way jus' de oder day w'en I'm
  out wit' de ole canoe,
Crossin' de point w'ere I see las' fall wan very
  beeg caribou,
W'en somebody say, "Phil-o-rum, mon vieux,
  wat's matter wit' you youse'f?"
An' who do you s'pose was talkin'? w'y de
  poor ole canoe shese'f.

242

O yass, I 'm scare w'en I 'm sittin' dere, an'
    she 's callin' ma nam' dat way:
"Phil-o-rum Juneau, w'y you spik so moche,
    you 're off on de head to-day
Can't be you forget ole feller, you an' me
    we 're not too young,
An' if I 'm lookin' so ole lak you, I t'ink I
    will close ma tongue.

"You should feel ashame; for you 're alway
    blame, w'en it is n't ma fault at all
For I 'm tryin' to do bes' I can for you on
    summer-tam, spring, an' fall.
How offen you drown on de reever if I 'm not
    lookin' out for you
W'en you 're takin' too moche on de w'isky
    some night comin' down de Soo.

"De firse tam we go on de Wessoneau no fel-
    ler can beat us den,
For you 're purty strong man wit' de paddle,
    but dat 's long ago ma frien',
An' win' she can blow off de mountain, an'
    tonder an' rain may come,
But camp see us bote on de evening—
    you know dat was true Phil-o-rum.

"An' who's your horse too, but your ole
    canoe, an' w'en you feel cole an' wet
Who was your house w'en I'm upside down
    an' onder de roof you get,
Wit' rain ronnin' down ma back, Baptême! till
    I'm gettin' de rheumateez,
An' I never say not'ing at all, moi-même, but
    let you do jus' you please.

"You t'ink it was right, kip me out all night
    on reever side down below,
An' even 'Bon Soir' you was never say, but
    off on de camp you go
Leffin' your poor ole canoe behin' lyin' dere
    on de groun'
Watchin' de moon on de water, an' de bat
    flyin' all aroun'.

"O! dat's lonesome t'ing hear de grey owl
    sing up on de beeg pine tree
An' many long night she kip me awake till sun
    on de eas' I see,
An' den you come down on de morning for
    start on some more voyage.
An' only t'ing decen' you do all day is carry
    me on portage.

"Dat's way Phil-o-rum, rheumateez she
    come, wit' pain ronnin' troo ma side
Wan leetle hole here, noder beeg wan dere, dat
    not'ing can never hide;
Don't do any good fix me up agen, no matter
    how moche you try,
For w'en we come ole an' our work she's
    done, bote man an' canoe mus' die."

Wall! she talk dat way mebbe mos' de day,
    till we're passin' some beaver dam
An' wan de young beaver he's mak' hees tail
    come down on de water flam!
I never see de canoe so scare, she jomp nearly
    two, t'ree feet
I t'ink she was goin' for ronne away, an' she
    shut up de mout' toute suite.

It mak' me feel queer, de strange t'ing I hear,
    an' I'm glad she don't spik no more,
But soon as we fin' ourse'f arrive over dere on
    de noder shore
I tak' dat canoe lak de lady, an' carry her off
    wit' me,
For I'm sorry de way I treat her, an' she
    know more dan me, sapree!

Yass! dat 's smart canoe, an' I know it 's true,
    w'at she 's spikin' wit' me dat day,
I 'm not de young feller I use to be w'en work
    she was only play;
An' I know I was comin' closer on place w'ere
    I mus' tak' care
W'ere de mos' worse current 's de las' wan too,
    de current of Dead Riviere.

You can only steer, an' if rock be near, wit'
    wave dashin' all aroun',
Better mak' leetle prayer, for on Dead Riviere
    some very smart man get drown;
But if you be locky an' watch youse'f, mebbe
    reever won't seem so wide,
An' firse t'ing you know you 'll ronne ashore,
    safe on de noder side.

The Log Jam

DERE 's a beeg jam up de reever, w'ere
    rapide is runnin' fas',
  An' de log we cut las' winter is takin' it all
    de room;
So boss of de gang is swearin', for not'ing at
    all can pass
  An' float away down de current till some-
    body break de boom.

"Here's for de man will tak' de job, holiday
      for a week
   Extra monee w'en pay day come, an' ten
      dollar suit of clothes.
'T is n't so hard work run de log, if only you
      do it quick—
   W'ere's de man of de gang den is ready
      to say, 'Here goes?'"

Dere was de job for a feller, handy an' young
      an' smart,
   Willin' to tak' hees chances, willin' to risk
      hees life.
'Cos many a t'ing is safer, dan tryin' de boom
      to start,
   For if de log wance ketch you, dey're cut-
      tin' you lak a knife.

Aleck Lachance he lissen, an' answer heem
      right away
   "Marie Louise dat's leevin' off on de shore
      close by
She's sayin' de word was mak' me mos' hap-
      pies' man to-day
   An' if you ax de reason I'm ready to go,
      dat's w'y."

247

Pierre Delorme he's spikin' den, an' O! but
    he's lookin' glad.
  "Dis morning de sam' girl tole me, she mus'
    say to me, 'Good-bye Pierre.'
So no wan can stop me goin', for I feel I was
    comin' mad
  An' wedder I see to-morrow, dat's not'ing,
    for I don't care."

Aleck Lachance was steady, he's bully boy all
    aroun',
  Alway sendin' de monee to hees moder
    away below,
Now an' den savin' a leetle for buyin' de house
    an' groun',
  An' never done t'inkin', t'inkin' of Marie
    Louise Lebeau.

Pierre was a half-breed feller, we call heem de
    grand Nor' Wes'—
  Dat is de place he's leevin' w'en he work
    for de Compagnie,
Dey say he's marry de squaw dere, never min'
    about all de res'—
  An' affer he get hees monee, he's de boy
    for de jamboree!

Ev'ry wan start off cheerin' w'en dey pass on
      de log out dere
  Jompin' about lak monkey, Aleck an' Pierre
      Delorme.
Workin' de sam' as twenty, an' runnin' off
      ev'ryw'ere,
  An' busy on all de places, lak beaver before
      de storm.

Den we hear some wan shoutin', an' dere was
      dat crazy girl,
  Marie Louise, on de hillside, cryin' an' raisin'
      row.
Could n't do not'ing worser! mos' foolish t'ing
      on de worl'
  For Pierre Delorme an' Aleck was n't
      workin' upon de scow.

Bote of dem turn aroun' dere w'en girl is com-
      mencin' cry,
  Lak woman I wance remember, got los' on
      de bush t'ree day,
"Look how de log is movin'! I 'm seein' it
      wit' ma eye,
  Come back out of all dem danger!" an' den
      she was faint away.

Ten year I been reever driver, an' mebbe
  know somet'ing too,
  An' dere was n't a man don't watch for de
    minute dem log she go;
But never a word from de boss dere, stannin'
  wit' all hees crew,
  So how she can see dem movin' don't ax
    me, for I dunno.

Hitch dem all up togeder, t'ousan' horse crazy
  mad—
  Only a couple of feller for han'le dem ev'ry
    wan,
Scare dem wit' t'onder, an' lightning, an' den 't
  is n't half so bad
  As log runnin' down de rapide, affer de
    boom she 's gone.

See dem nex' day on de basin, you t'ink dey
  was t'roo de fight
  Cut wit' de sword an' bullet, lyin' along de
    shore
You 'd pity de log, I 'm sure, an' say 't was
  terrible sight
  But man goin' t'roo de sam' t'ing, you 'd
    pity dat man some more.

An' Pierre w'en he see dem goin' an' log jom-
    pin' up an' down
  De sign of de cross he 's makin' an' drive on
    de water dere,
He know it 's all up hees chances, an' he rader
    be goin' drown
  Dan ketch by de rollin' timber, an' dat 's
    how he go, poor Pierre.

Aleck's red shirt is blazin' off w'ere we hear de
    log
  Crackin' away an' bangin', sam' as a honder
    gun,
Lak' sun on de morning tryin' to peep t'roo
    de reever fog—
  But Aleck's red shirt is redder dan ever I see
    de sun.

An' w'en dey 're tryin' wake her: Marie
    Louise Lebeau,
  On her neck dey fin' a locket, she 's kipin' so
    nice an' warm,
An' dey 're tolin' de funny story, de funnies'
    I dunno—
  For de face, Baptême! dey see dere, was de
    half-breed Pierre Delorme!

The Canadian Magpie

MOS' ev'rywan lak de robin
    An' it 's pleasan' for hear heem sing,
Affer de winter 's over
    An' it 's comin' anoder spring.
De snow 's hardly off de mountain
    An' it 's cole too among de pine
But you know w'en he sing, de sout' win'.
    Is crowdin' heem close behin'.

An' mebbe you hear de grosbec
    Sittin' above de nes'—
An' you see by de way he 's goin'
    De ole man 's doin' hees bes'
Makin' de wife an' baby
    Happy as dey can be—
An' proud he was come de fader
    Such fine leetle familee.

De gouglou of course he 's nicer
    Dan many de bird dat fly,
Dunno wa't we do widout heem,
    But offen I wonder w'y
He can't stay quiet a minute
    Lak res' of de small oiseaux
An' finish de song he 's startin'
    Till whish! an' away he go!

Got not'ing to say agen dem,
  De gouglou an' all de res'—
'Cept only dey lak de comfort,
  An' come w'en it suit dem bes'—
For soon as de summer 's passin'
  An' leaf is begin to fall—
You 'll walk t'roo de wood an' medder
  An' never hear wan bird call.

But come wit' me on de winter
  On place w'ere de beeg tree grow
De smoke of de log house chimley
  Will tole you de way to go—
An' if you 're not too unlucky
  De w'isky jack dere you 'll see
Flyin' aroun' de shaintee
  An' dat was de bird for me.

You 'll mebbe not lak hees singin'
  Dough it 's better dan not'ing too,
For affer he do hees bes', den
  W'at more can poor Johnnie do?
It 's easy job sing on summer
  De sam' as de rossignol—
But out of door on de winter
  Jus' try it youse'f—dat 's all.

THE CANADIAN MAGPIE

See heem dere, now he 's comin'
    Hoppin' an' hoppin' aroun'
W'en we start on de morning early
    For work till de sun go down—
T'row heem hees piece of breakfas'
    An' hear heem say "merci bien,"
For he 's fond of de pork, ba golly!
    Sam' as de Canayen.

De noise of de axe don't scare heem
He stay wit' us all de day,
    An' w'en he was feelin' lak' it
    Ride home wit' de horse an' sleigh
Den affer we reach de shaintee
    He 's waitin' to see us back
Jompin' upon de log dere
    Good leetle w'isky jack!

So here 's to de bird of winter
    Wearin' de coonskin coat,
W'enever it 's bird election
    You bet he can get ma vote—
Dat 's way I be feel about it,
    Voyageurs let her go today!
W'isky jack, get ready, we drink you
    Toujours à vot' bonne santé!
            Baptême!

The Red Canoe

DE win' is sleepin' in de pine, but O! de
    night is black!
An' all day long de loon bird cry on Lac Waya-
    gamack—
No light is shinin' by de shore for helpin' steer
    heem t'roo
W'en out upon de night, Ubalde he tak' de
    red canoe.

I hear de paddle dip, dip, dip! wance more I
    hear de loon—
I feel de breeze was show de way for storm
    dat 's comin' soon,
An' den de sky fly open wit' de lightning
    splittin' t'roo—
An' 'way beyon' de point I see de leetle red
    canoe.

It 's dark again, but lissen how across Waya-
    gamack
De tonder 's roarin' loud, an' now de mount-
    ains answer back—
I wonder wit' de noise lak dat, he hear me, le
    bon Dieu
W'en on ma knee I ax Heem save de leetle red
    canoe!

Is dat a voice, so far away, it die upon ma ear?
Or only win' was foolin' me, an' w'isperin'
    "Belzemire"?
Yaas, yaas, Ubalde, your Belzemire she 's
    prayin' hard for you—
An' den again de lightning come, but w'ere 's
    de red canoe?

.   .   .   .

Dey say I 'm mad, dem foolish folk, cos w'en
    de night is black
An' w'en de wave lak snow-dreef come on Lac
    Wayagamack
I tak' de place w'ere long ago we use to sit, us
    two,
An' wait until de lightning bring de leetle red
    canoe.

Two Hundred Years Ago

TWO honder year ago, de worl' is purty slow
    Even folk upon dis contree 's not so
    smart,
Den who is travel roun' an' look out de
    pleasan' groun'
    For geev' de Yankee peop' a leetle start?

I 'll tole you who dey were! de beeg rough
 voyageurs,
W'it deir cousin w'at you call coureurs de bois,
Dat 's fightin' all de tam, an' never care a dam,
An' ev'ry wan dem feller he 's come from
 Canadaw
 Baptême!
He 's comin' all de way from Canadaw.

But He watch dem, le bon Dieu, for He 's got
 some work to do,
 An He won't trus' ev'ry body, no siree!
Only full blood Canadien, lak Marquette an'
 Hennepin,
 An' w'at you t'ink of Louis Verandrye?
On church of Bonsecours! makin' ready for
 de tour,
See dem down upon de knee, all prayin' dere—
Wit' de paddle on de han' ev'ry good Canad-
 ien man,
An' affer dey be finish, hooraw for anyw'ere.
 Yass, sir!
Dey 're ready now for goin' anyw'ere.

De nort' win' know dem well, an' de prairie
 grass can tell
 How offen it is trample by de ole tam botte
 sauvage—

An' grey wolf on hees den kip very quiet, w'en
   He hear dem boy a' singin' upon de long
      portage.
An' de night would fin' dem lie wit' deir faces
   on de sky,
An' de breeze would come an' w'isper on deir
   ear
'Bout de wife an' sweetheart dere on Sorel an'
   Trois Rivieres
Dey may never leev' to see anoder year,
         Dat 's true,
Dey may never leev' to kiss anoder year.

An' you 'll know de place dey go, from de
   canyon down below,
  Or de mountain wit' hees nose above de cloud,
De lake among de hill, w'ere de grizzly drink
   hees fill
  Or de rapid on de reever roarin' loud;
Ax de wil' deer if de flash of · de ole Tree
   Reever sash
He don't see it on de woods of Illinois
An' de musk ox as he go, w'ere de camp fire
   melt de snow,
De smell he still remember of tabac Canadien
       Ha! Ha!
It 's hard forgettin' smell of tabac Canadien!

So, ma frien', de Yankee man, he mus' try an'
      understan'
  W'en he holler for dat flag de Star an'
      Stripe,
If he 's leetle win' still lef', an' no danger hurt
      hese'f,
  Den he better geev' anoder cheer, ba cripe!
For de flag of la belle France, dat show de way
      across
From Louisbourg to Florida an' back;
So raise it ev'ryw'ere, lak' de ole tam voy-
      ageurs,
W'en you hear of de la Salle an' Cadillac—
        Hooraw!
For de flag of de la Salle an' Cadillac.

The Voyageur

DERE 's somet'ing stirrin' ma blood to-
    night,
  On de night of de young new year,
W'ile de camp is warm an' de fire is bright,
  An' de bottle is close at han'—
Out on de reever de nort' win' blow,
Down on de valley is pile de snow,
But w'at do we care so long we know
  We 're safe on de log cabane?

Drink to de healt' of your wife an' girl,
   Anoder wan for your frien',
Den geev' me a chance, for on all de worl'
   I 've not many frien' to spare—
I 'm born, w'ere de mountain scrape de sky,
An' bone of ma fader an' moder lie,
So I fill de glass an' I raise it high
   An' drink to de Voyageur.

For dis is de night of de jour de l'an,*
   W'en de man of de Grand Nor' Wes'
T'ink of hees home on de St. Laurent,
   An' frien' he may never see—
Gone he is now, an' de beeg canoe
No more you 'll see wit' de red-shirt crew,
But long as he leev' he was alway true,
   So we 'll drink to hees memory.

Ax' heem de nort' win' w'at he see
   Of de Voyageur long ago,
An' he 'll say to you w'at he say to me,
   So lissen hees story well—
"I see de track of hees botte sau-vage†
On many a hill an' long portage
Far, far away from hees own vill-age
   An' soun' of de parish bell—

  * New Year's Day.   † Indian boot.

THE VOYAGEUR

"I never can play on de Hudson Bay
  Or mountain dat lie between
But I meet heem singin' hees lonely way
  De happies' man I know—
I cool hees face as he 's sleepin' dere
Under de star of de Red Rivière,
  An' off on de home of de great w'ite bear,
    I 'm seein' hees dog traineau.*

"De woman an' chil'ren 's runnin' out
  On de wigwam of de Cree—
De leetle papoose dey laugh an' shout
  W'en de soun' of hees voice dey hear—
De oldes' warrior of de Sioux
Kill hese'f dancin' de w'ole night t'roo,
An de Blackfoot girl remember too
  . De ole tam Voyageur.

"De blaze of hees camp on de snow I see,
  An' I lissen hees 'En Roulant'
On de lan' w'ere de reindeer travel free,
  Ringin' out strong an' clear—
Offen de grey wolf sit before
De light is come from hees open door,
An' caribou foller along de shore
  De song of de Voyageur.

* Dog-sleigh.

261

"If he only kip goin', de red ceinture,*
    I 'd see it upon de Pole
Some mornin' I 'm startin' upon de tour
    For blowin' de worl' aroun'—
But w'erever he sail an' w'erever he ride,
De trail is long an' de trail is wide,
An' city an' town on ev'ry side
    Can tell of hees campin' groun'."

So dat 's de reason I drink to-night
    To de man of de Grand Nor' Wes',
For hees heart was young, an' hees heart was
        light
    So long as he 's leevin' dere—
I 'm proud of de sam' blood in my vein
I 'm a son of de Nort' Win ' wance again—
So we 'll fill her up till de bottle 's drain
    An' drink to de Voyageur.

Bruno the Hunter

YOU never hear tell, Marie, ma femme,
    Of Bruno de hunter man,
Wit' hees wild dogs chasin' de moose an' deer,
Every day on de long, long year,
Off on de hillside far an' near,
    An' down on de beeg savane?

* Canadian sash.

Not'ing can leev' on de woods, Marie,
  W'en Bruno is on de track,
An' young caribou, an' leetle red doe
Wit' baby to come on de spring, dey know
De pity dey get w'en hees bugle blow
  An' de black dogs answer back.

No bird on de branch can finish hees song,
  De squirrel no longer play—
De leaf on de maple don't need to wait
Till fros' of October is at de gate
'Fore de blood drops comè: an' de fox sleeps late
  W'en Bruno is pass dat way.

So de devil ketch heem of course at las'
  Dat 's w'at de ole folk say,
An' spik to heem, "Bruno, w'at for you kill
De moose an' caribou of de hill
An' fill de woods wit' deir blood until
  You could run a mill night an' day?

"Mebbe you lak to be moose youse'f,
  An' see how de hunter go,
So I 'll change your dogs into loup garou,*
An' wance on de year dey 'll be chasin' you—
An' res' of de tam w'en de sport is t'roo,
  You 'll pass wit' me down below."

   * Were wolf.

An' dis is de night of de year, Marie,
   Bruno de hunter wake:
Soon as de great beeg tonder cloud
Up on de mountain 's roarin' loud—
He 'll come from hees grave w'ere de pine tree
      crowd
   De shore of de leetle lake.

You see de lightning zig, zig, Marie,
   Spittin' lak' loup cervier,*
Ketch on de trap? Oh! it won't be long
Till mebbe you lissen anoder song,
For de sky is dark an' de win' is strong,
   An' de chase is n't far away.

W'y shiver so moche, Marie, ma femme,
   For de log is burnin' bright?
Ah! dere she 's goin', "Hulloo! Hulloo!"
   An' oh! how de tonder is roarin' too!
But it can't drown de cry of de loup garou
   On Bruno de hunter's night.

Over de mountain an' t'roo de swamp,
   Don't matter how far or near,
Every place hees moccasin know
Bruno de hunter he 's got to go
'Fore de grave on de leetle lake below
   Close up for anoder year.

   * Lynx.

264

But dey say de ole feller watch all night,
    So you need n't be scare, Marie,
For he 'll never stir from de rocky cave
W'ere door only open beneat' de wave,
Till Bruno come back to hees lonely grave—
    An' de devil he turn de key.

Dat 's way for punish de hunter man
    W'en murder is on hees min'—
So he better stop w'ile de work is new,
Or mebbe de devil will ketch heem too,
An' chase heem aroun' wit' de loup garou
    Gallopin' close behin'.

Pride

MA fader he spik to me long ago,
    "Alphonse, it is better go leetle slow
Don't put on de style if you can't afford,
But satisfy be wit' your bed an' board.
De bear wit' hees head too high alway,
    Know not'ing at all till de trap go smash.
An' mooshrat dat 's swimmin' so proud to-day
    Very offen to-morrow is on de hash."*

* Old proverb of Ste. Flore.

Edouard de Seven of Angleterre,
　　An' few oder place beside,
He 's got de horse an' de carriage dere
　　W'enever he want to ride.
Wit' sojer in front to clear de way,
Sojer behin' all dress so gay,
Ev'rywan makin' de grand salaam,
An' plaintee o' ban' playin' all de tam.

Edouard de Seven of Angleterre,
　　All he has got to do,
W'en he 's crossin' de sea, don't matter w'ere,
　.Is call for de ship an' crew.
Den hois' de anchor from down below,
Vive le Roi! an' away she go,
An' flag overhead, w'en dey see dat sight
W'ere is de nation don't be polite?

An' dere 's de boss of United State,
　　An' w'at dey call Philippine—
De Yankee t'ink he was somet'ing great,
　　An' beeg as de king or queen—
So dey geev' heem a house near touch de sky,
An' paint it so w'ite it was blin' de eye
An' long as he 's dere beginnin' to en',
Don't cos' heem not'ing for treat hees frien'.

PRIDE

So dere 's two feller, Edouard de King
  An' Teddy Roos-vel' also,
No wonder dey 're proud, for dey got few t'ing
  Was helpin' dem mak' de show—
But oh! ma Gosh! w'en you talk of pride
An' w'at dey call style, an' puttin' on side,
W'ere is de man can go before
De pig-sticker champion of Ste. Flore?

Use to be nice man too, dey say,
  Jeremie Bonami,
Talk wit' hees frien' in a frien'ly way
  Sam' as you' se'f an' me—
Of course it 's purty beeg job he got,
An' no wan expec' heem talk a lot,
But still would n't hurt very moche, I 'm sure,
If wance in a w'ile he 'd say, "Bonjour."

Yi! Yi! to see heem come down de hill
  Some mornin' upon de fall,
W'en de pig is fat an' ready to kill,
  He don't know hees frien' at all—
Look at hees face an' it seem to say,
"Important duty I got to-day,
Killin' de pig on de contree side,—
Is n't dat some reason for leetle pride?"

PRIDE

Lissen de small boy how dey shout
 W'en Jeremie 's marchin' t'roo
De market place wit' hees cane feex out
 Wit' ribbon red, w'ite, an' blue—
An' den he jomp on de butcher's block,
An' affer de crowd is stop deir talk,
An' leetle boy holler no more "Hooray,"
Dis is de word Jeremie he say—

"I 'm de only man on de w'ole Ste. Flore
 Can kill heem de pig jus' right,
Please t'ink of dat, an' furdermore
 Don't matter it 's day or night,
Can do it less tam, five dollar I bet,
Dan any pig-sticker you can get
From de w'ole of de worl' to w'ere I leev'—
Will somebody help to roll up ma sleeve?

"Some feller challenge jus' here an' dere,
 An' more on deir own contree,
But me—I challenge dem ev'ryw'ere
 All over de worl'—sapree!
To geev' dem a chance, for dere might be some
 Beeg feller, for all I know,
But if dey 're ready, wall! let dem come,
 An' me—I 'm geevin' dem plaintee show."

Challenge lak dat twenty year or more
   He 's makin' it ev'ry fall,
But never a pig-sticker come Ste. Flore
   'Cos Jeremie scare dem all—
No wonder it 's makin' heem feel so proud,
   Even Emperor Germanie
Can't put on de style or talk more loud
   Dan Jeremie Bonami.

But Jeremie's day can't las' alway,
   An' so he commence to go
W'en he jomp on de block again an' say
   To de crowd stannin' dere below,
"Lissen, ma frien', to de word I spik,
For I 'm tire of de challenge until I 'm sick,
Can't say, but mebbe I 'll talk no more
For glory an' honor of ole Ste. Flore.

"I got some trouble aroun' ma place
   Wit' ma nice leetle girl Rosine,
An' I see w'en I 'm lookin' on all de face,
   You 're knowin' jus' w'at I mean—
Very easy to talk, but w'en dey come
For seein' her twenty young man ba Gum!
I tole you ma' frien', it was purty tough,
'Sides wan chance in twenty is not enough—

PRIDE

"Now lissen to me, all you young man
   Is wantin' ma girl Rosine—
I offer a chance an' you 'll understan'
   It 's bes' you was never seen—
T 'ree minute start I 'll geev'—no more—
An' if any young feller upon Ste. Flore
Can beat me stickin' de pig nex' fall,
Let heem marry ma girl Rosine—dat 's all."

All right—an' very nex' week he start,
   De smartes' boy of de lot—
An' he 's lovin' Rosine wit' all hees heart,
   De young Adelard Marcotte—
Don't say very moche about w 'ere he go,
But I t 'ink mese'f it was Buffalo—
An' plaintee more place on de State dat 's beeg
W 'ere he don't do not 'ing but stick de pig.

So of course he 's pickin' de fancy trick
   An' ev'ryt'ing else dey got—
Work over tam—but he got homesick
   De young Adelard Marcotte
Jus' about tam' w 'en de fall come along—
So den he wissle hees leetle song
An' buy tiquette for de ole Ste. Flore,
An' back on de village he come some more.

PRIDE

Ho! Ho! ma Jeremie Bonami,
   Get ready you' se'f to-day,
For you got beeg job you was never see
   Will tak' all your breat' away—
"Come on! come on!" dey be shoutin' loud,
De Bishop hese'f could n't draw de crowd
Of folk on de parish for mile aroun',
Till dey could n't fin' place upon de groun'.

Hi! Hi! Jeremie, you may sweat an' swear,
   Your tam is arrive at las'—
Dere 's no use pullin' out all your hair
   Or drinkin' de w'isky glass—
Spit on your han' or hitch de pants—
You 'll never have anyt'ing lak a chance,
Hooraw! Hooraw! let her go wance more,
An' Adelard 's champion of all Ste. Flore!

"Away on de pump!" de crowd is yell,
   "No use for heem goin' die."
Dey nearly drown Jeremie on de well
   But he 's comin' roun' bimeby
Rosine dat 's laughin' away all day
Is startin' to cry, an' den she say—
"O fader dear, won't you geev' me kiss
For I never s'pose it would come to dis?

"Don't blame de boy over dere, 't was me
    Dat sen' away Adelard—
He 's sorry for beat you, I 'm sure, bâ oui,
    An' dat 's w'at I 'm crying for—
'Cos it 's all ma fault you was lick to-day,
Don't care w'at anywan else can say—
But remember too, an' you 'll not forget
De championship 's still on de familee yet."
             An' de ole man smile.

Dieudonné (God-Given)

IF I sole ma ole blind trotter for fifty dollar
    cash
    Or win de beeges' prize on lotterie,
If some good frien' die an' lef' me fines' house
    on St. Eustache,
    You t'ink I feel more happy dan I be?

No, sir! An' I can tole you, if you never know
    before,
    W'y de kettle on de stove mak' such a fuss,
W'y de robin stop hees singin' an' come peekin'
    t'roo de door
    For learn about de nice t'ing 's come to us—

An' w'en he see de baby lyin' dere upon de bed
  Lak leetle Son of Mary on de ole tam long
     ago—
Wit' de sunshine an' de shadder makin' ring
     aroun' hees head,
  No wonder M'sieu Robin wissle low.

An' we can't help feelin' glad too, so we call
     heem Dieudonné;
  An' he never cry, dat baby, w'en he's
     chrissen by de pries'
All de sam' I bet you dollar he'll waken up
     some day,
  An' be as bad as leetle boy Bateese.

The Devil

A LONG de road from Bord à Plouffe
    To Kaz-a-baz-u-a
W'ere poplar trees lak sojers stan',
An' all de lan' is pleasan' lan',
In off de road dere leev's a man
  Call Louis Desjardins.

An' Louis, w'en he firse begin
  To work hees leetle place,
He work so hard de neighbors say,
"Unless he tak's de easy way
Dat feller's sure to die some day,
  We see it on hees face."

'T was lak a swamp, de farm he got,
   De water ev'ryw'ere—
Might drain her off as tight as a drum.
An' back dat water is boun' to come
In less 'n a day or two—ba Gum!
   'T would mak' de angel swear.

So Louis t'ink of de bimeby,
   If he leev' so long as dat,
W'en he 's ole an' blin' an' mebbe deaf,
All alone on de house hese'f,
No frien', no money, no not'ing lef',
   An' poor—can't kip a cat.

So wan of de night on winter tam,
   W'en Louis is on hees bed,
He say out loud lak a crazy man,
"I 'm sick of tryin' to clear dis lan',
Work any harder I can't stan',
   Or it will kill me dead.

"Now if de devil would show hese'f
   An' say to me, 'Tiens! Louis!
Hard tam an' work she 's at an' en',
You 'll leev' lak a Grand Seigneur ma frien',
If only you 'll be ready w'en
   I want you to come wit'me.'

THE DEVIL

"I 'd say, 'Yass, yass— 'maudit! w'at 's dat?''
  An' he see de devil dere—
Brimstone, ev'ryt'ing bad dat smell,
You know right away he 's come from—well,
De place I never was care to tell—
  An' wearin' hees long black hair,

Lak election man, de kin' I mean
  You see aroun' church door,
Spreadin' hese'f on great beeg speech
'Bout poor man 's goin' some day be reech,
But dat 's w'ere it alway come de heetch,
  For poor man 's alway poor.

De only diff'rence—me—I see
  'T ween devil an' long-hair man
It 's hard to say, but I know it 's true,
W'en devil promise a t'ing to do
Dere 's no mistak', he kip it too—
  I hope you understan'.

So de devil spik, "You 're not content,
  An' want to be reech, Louis—
All right, you 'll have plaintee, never fear
No wan can beat you far an' near,
An' I 'll leave you alone for t'orty year,
  An' den you will come wit' me.

"Be careful now— it 's beeg contrac',
   So mebbe it 's bes' go slow;
For me—de promise I mak' to you
Is good as de bank Rivière du Loup
For you—w'enever de tam is due,
   Ba tonder! you got to go."

Louis try hard to tak' hees tam
   But w'en he see de fall
Comin' along in a week or so,
All aroun' heem de rain an' snow
An' pork on de bar'l runnin' low,
   He don't feel good at all.

An' w'en he t'ink of de swampy farm
   An' gettin' up winter night,
Watchin' de stove if de win' get higher
For fear de chimley go on fire,
It 's makin' poor Louis feel so tire
   He tell de devil, "All right."

"Correct," dat feller say right away,
   "I 'll only say, Au revoir,"
An' out of de winder he 's goin' pouf!
Beeg nose, long hair, short tail, an' hoof
Off on de road to Bord à Plouffe
   Crossin' de reever dere.

W'en Louis get up nex' day, ma frien',
   Dere 's lot of devil sign—
Bar'l o' pork an' keg o' rye,
Bag o' potato ten foot high,
Pile o' wood nearly touch de sky,
   Was some o' de t'ing he fin'.

Suit o' clothes would have cos' a lot
   An' ev'ryt'ing I dunno,
Trotter horse w'en he want to ride
Eatin' away on de barn outside,
Stan' all day if he 's never tied,
   An' watch an' chain also.

An' swamp dat 's bodder heem many tam,
   W'ere is dat swamp to-day?
Don't care if you 're huntin' up an' down
You won't fin' not'ing but medder groun',
An' affer de summer come aroun'
   W'ere can you see such hay?

Wall! de year go by, an' Louis leev'
   Widout no work to do,
Rise w'en he lak on winter day,
Fin' all de snow is clear away,
No fuss, no not'ing, dere 's de sleigh
   An' trotter waitin' too.

W'en t'orty year is nearly t'roo
   An' devil 's not come back
'Course Louis say, "Wall! he forget
Or t'ink de tam 's not finish yet;
I 'll tak' ma chance an' never fret,"
   But dat 's w'ere he mak' mistak'.

For on a dark an' stormy night
   W'en Louis is sittin' dere,
Affer he fassen up de door
De devil come as he come before,
Lookin' de sam' only leetle more,
   For takin' heem—you know w'ere.

"Asseyez vous, sit down, ma frien',
   Bad night be on de road;
You come long way an' should be tire—
Jus' wait an' mebbe I feex de fire—
Tak' off your clothes for mak' dem drier,
   Dey mus' be heavy load."

Dat 's how poor Louis Desjardins
   Talk to de devil, sir—
Den say, "Try leetle w'isky blanc,
Dey 're makin' it back on St. Laurent—
It 's good for night dat 's cole an' raw,"
   But devil never stir,

THE DEVIL

Until he smell de smell dat come
    W'en Louis mak' it hot
Wit' sugar, spice, an' ev'ryt'ing,
Enough to mak' a man's head sing—
For winter, summer, fall an' spring—
    It 's very bes' t'ing we got.

An' so de devil can't refuse
    To try de w'isky blanc,
An' say, "I 'm tryin, many drink,
An' dis is de fines' I don't t'ink,
De firse, ba tonder! mak' me wink—
    Hooraw, pour Canadaw!"

"Merci—non, non—I tak' no more,"
    De devil say at las',
"For tam is up wit' you, Louis,
So come along, ma frien', wit' me,
So many star I 'm sure I see,
    De storm she mus' be pas'."

"No hurry—wait a minute, please,"
    Say Louis Desjardins,
"We 'll have a smoke before we 're t'roo,
'T will never hurt mese'f or you
To try a pipe, or mebbe two,
    Of tabac Canayen."*

* Canadian tobacco.

279

THE DEVIL

"Wan pipe is all I want for me—
  We 'll finish our smoke downstair,"
De devil say, an' it was enough,
For w'en he tak' de very firse puff
He holler out, "Maudit! w'at stuff!
  Fresh air! fresh air!! fresh air!!!"

An' oh! he was never sick before
  Till he smoke tabac Bruneau—
Can't walk or fly, but he want fresh air,
So Louis put heem on rockin' chair
An' t'row heem off on de road out dere—
  An' tole heem go below.

An' he shut de door an' fill de place
  Wit' tabac Canayen,
An' never come out, an' dat 's a fac'—
But smoke away till hees face is black—
So dat 's w'y de devil don't come back
  For Louis Desjardins.

An' dere he 's yet, an' dere he 'll stay—
  So weech of de two 'll win
Can't say for dat—it 's kin' of a doubt,
For Louis, de pipe never leave hees mout',
An' night or day can't ketch heem out,
  An' devil's too scare go in.

The Family Laramie

HSSH! look at ba-bee on de leetle blue
  chair,
  W'at you t'ink he 's tryin' to do?
Wit' pole on de han' lak de lumberman,
  A-shovin' along canoe.
Dere 's purty strong current behin' de stove,
  W'ere it 's passin' de chimley-stone,
But he 'll come roun' yet, if he don't upset,
  So long he was lef' alone.

Dat 's way ev'ry boy on de house begin
  No sooner he 's twelve mont' ole;
He 'll play canoe up an' down de Soo
  An' paddle an' push de pole,
Den haul de log all about de place,
  Till dey 're fillin' up mos' de room,
An' say it 's all right, for de storm las' night
  Was carry away de boom.

Mebbe you see heem, de young loon bird,
  Wit' half of de shell hangin' on,
Tak' hees firse slide to de water side,
  An' off on de lake he 's gone.
Out of de cradle dey 're goin' sam' way
  On reever an' lake an' sea;
For born to de trade, dat 's how dey 're made,
  De familee Laramie.

An' de reever she 's lyin' so handy dere
   On foot of de hill below,
Dancin' along an' singin' de song
   As away to de sea she go,
No wonder I never can lak dat song,
   For soon it is comin' w'en
Dey 'll lissen de call, leetle Pierre an' Paul,
   An' w'ere will de moder be den?

She 'll sit by de shore w'en de evenin's come,
   An' spik to de reever too:
"O reever, you know how dey love you so,
   Since ever dey 're seein' you,
For sake of dat love bring de leetle boy home
   Once more to de moder's knee."
An' mebbe de prayer I be makin' dere
   Will help bring dem back to me.

Yankee Families

YOU s'pose God love de Yankee
   An' de Yankee woman too,
Lak he love de folk at home on Canadaw?
   I dunno—'cos if he do,
W'at 's de reason he don't geev' dem familee
Is dere anybody hangin' roun' can answer me
W'ile I wait an' smoke dis pipe of good tabac?

An' now I 'll tole you somet'ing
   Mebbe help you bimeby,
An' dere 's no mistak' it 's w'at dey call sure
      sign—
   W'en you miss de baby's cry
As you 're goin' mak' some visit on de State
Dat 's enough—you need n't ax if de train 's
      on tam or late,
You can bet you 're on de Yankee side de line.

Unless dere 's oder folk dere,
   Mebbe wan or two or t'ree,
Canayen is comin' workin' on de State—
   Den you see petite Marie
Leetle Joe an' Angelique, Hormisdas an'
      Dieudonné,
But you can't tole half de nam'—it don't mat-
      ter any way—
'Sides de fader he don't t'ink it 's not'ing great.

De moder, you can see her
   An' she got de basket dere
Wit' de fine t'ing for de chil'ren nice an' slick—
   For dey can't get fat on air—
Cucumber, milk, an' onion, some leetle cake also
De ole gran'moder 's makin' on de farm few
      days ago—
W'at 's use buy dollar dinner mak' dem sick?

YANKEE FAMILIES

But look de Yankee woman
  Wit' de book upon her han',
Readin', readin', an' her husban', he can't get
  Any chance at all, poor man,
For sit down, de way de seat 's all pile up wit'
        magazine—
De t'ing lak dat on Canadaw is never, never seen.
Would n't she be better wit' some chil'ren?
        Wall! you bet!

No wonder dey was bringin'
  For helpin' dem along
So many kin' of feller I dunno—
  Chinee washee from Hong Kong
An' w'at dey call Da-go, was work for dollar a
        day,
But w'en dey mak' some money, off dey 're
        goin', right away—
Dat 's de reason dey was get de nam' Da-go.

Of course so long dey 're comin'
  From ev'ry place dey can,
Not knowin' moche, dere 's not'ing fuss about
  Only boss de stranger man—
But now dem gang of feller dat 's come across
        de sea—
He 's gettin' leetle smarter, an' he got de
        familee—
So Uncle Sam mus' purty soon look out.

I wonder he don't know it—
  It 's funny he don't see
Dere 's somet'ing else dan money day an'
      night—
  Non—he 'll work hese'f cra-zee,
Den travel roun' de worl', an' use de money
      too—
De King hese'f can't spen' lak de Yankee man
      is do—
But w'ere 's de leetle chil'ren? dat 's not right!

W'at 's use of all de money
  If dere ain't some boy an' girl
Mak' it pleasan' for de Yankee an' hees wife
  W'en dey travel on de worl'?
For me an' Eugenie dere 's not'ing we lak bes'
Dan gader up de chil'ren an' get dem nicely
      dress—
W'y it 's more dan half de pleasure of our life.

I love de Yankee woman
  An' de Yankee man also,
An' mebbe dey 'll be wiser bimeby—
  But I lak dem all to know
If dey want to kip deir own, let dem raise de
      familee—
An' den dey 'll boss de contree from de moun-
      tain to de sea,
For dey 're smart enough to do it if dey try.

The Last Portage

I 'M sleepin' las' night w'en I dream a dream
   An' a wonderful wan it seem—
For I 'm off on de road I was never see,
Too long an' hard for a man lak me,
So ole he can only wait de call
Is sooner or later come to all.

De night is dark an de portage dere
Got plaintee o' log lyin' ev'ryw'ere,
Black bush aroun' on de right an' lef',
A step from de road an' you los' you' se'f
De moon an' de star above is gone,
Yet somet'ing tell me I mus' go on.

An' off in front of me as I go,
Light as a dreef of de fallin' snow—
Who is dat leetle boy dancin' dere
Can see hees w'ite dress an' curly hair,
An' almos' touch heem, so near to me
In an' out dere among de tree?

An' den I 'm hearin' a voice is say,
"Come along, fader, don't min' de way,
De boss on de camp he sen' for you,
So your leetle boy 's going to guide you t'roo
It 's easy for me, for de road I know,
'Cos I travel it many long year ago."

THE LAST PORTAGE

An' oh! mon Dieu! w'en he turn hees head
I 'm seein' de face of ma boy is dead—
Dead wit' de young blood in hees vein—
An' dere he 's comin' wance more again
Wit' de curly hair, an' dark-blue eye,
So lak de blue of de summer sky—

An' now no more for de road I care,
An' slippery log lyin' ev'ryw'ere—
De swamp on de valley, de mountain too,
But climb it jus' as I use to do—
Don't stop on de road, for I need no res'
So long as I see de leetle w'ite dress.

An' I foller it on, an' wance in a w'ile
He turn again wit' de baby smile,
An' say, "Dear fader, I 'm here you see—
We 're bote togeder, jus' you an' me—
Very dark to you, but to me it 's light,
De road we travel so far to-night.

"De boss on de camp w'ere I alway stay
Since ever de tam I was go away,
He welcome de poores' man dat call,
But love de leetle wan bes' of all,
So dat 's de reason I spik for you
An' come to-night for to bring you t'roo."

Lak de young Jesu w'en he 's here below
De face of ma leetle son look jus' so—
Den off beyon', on de bush I see
De w'ite dress fadin' among de tree—
Was it a dream I dream las' night
Is goin' away on de morning light?

Getting On

I KNOW I 'm not too young, an' ma back is
    not as straight
  As it use to be some feefty year ago;
Don't care to go aroun' if de rain is fallin'
    down
  'Less de rheumateez is ketch me on de toe—
But dat is ma beez-nesse, an' no matter how I
    feel—
  Oder folk dey might look out deir own affair
'Stead o' w'isperin', "Wall! ba Gosh! lissen
        poor Maxime Meloche,
  How dat leetle drop o' rain is mak' heem
        swear!
                De ole man 's gettin' on!"

Smart folk lak dat, of course, mebbe never hear
    de news
  Of de tam he 's comin' sick Guillaume La-
    roche,

Who 's tak' heem home to die w'en de rap-
    ide 's runnin' high,
  An' carry heem on hees shoulder t'roo de
    bush?
Oh! no, it was n't me, only wan of dem young
    man
  Hardly got de baby moustache on de
    mout',
Dat 's de reason w'y I say to mese'f mos' ev'ry
    day,
  "Purty hard dere 's not'ing else dan talk
    about
          'De ole man 's gettin' on.'"

W'at 's mak' me feelin' mad is becos dey don't
    spik out,
  Non! dey 'll sneak aroun' for watch me as
    I go,
An' if I mebbe spill leetle water on de hill,
  W'en I 'm comin' from de well down dere
    below,
No use for tellin' me—I know too moche mese'f,
  Dat 's de tam I 'm very sure dey alway say,
"See heem now, how slow he go—don't I
    offen tole you so?
  We 're sorry, but Maxime is have hees
    day,
        De ole man 's gettin' on."

It 's foolish t'ing to do, for dere 's alway hang
 aroun'
 Some crazy feller almos' ev'ry day—
So I might a' stay at home 'stead o' tryin' feex
 de boom,
 Dough I 'm sure de win' is blow de oder way;
For I never hear dem shout w'en dey let de
 water out,
 An' de log dey come a-bangin' down de chute,
But leetle Joe Leblanc ketch me on de pant,
 hooraw!
 Den spile de job by w'isperin', "I 'm afraid
 I spik de trut',
   De ole man 's gettin' on."

Only yesterday de pig get loose an' run away,
 An' de nex' t'ing he was goin' on de corn—
So I run an' fetch de stick, an' affer heem so
 quick
 Jus' to mak' heem feelin' sorry he was born;
An' dat pig he laugh at me, an' he fill hees
 belly full
 'Fore he 's makin' up his min' for come
 along—
I 'm sure I see heem wink—should n't wonder
 if he t'ink,
 "Very easy see dere 's somet'ing goin'
 wrong—
   De ole man 's gettin' on."

If only I can get some doctor feex me up,
   Mak' me feel a leetle looser on de knee—
On de shoulder, ev'ryw'ere—ba tonder! I
     don't care,
   I 'll spen' a couple o' dollar, mebbe t'ree—
Jus' to larn dem feller dere how to skip an'
     how to jomp,
   On de way I beat deir fader long ago—
Yass siree! an' purty soon dey 'll sing anoder
     tune,
   An' wonder w'at de devil 's dere to show
           De ole man 's gettin' on.

Oh! dat maudit rheumateez! now she 's ketchin'
     me again
   On de back becos I 'm leetle bit excite,
An' put ma finger down, widout stoopin' on
     de groun'—
   But I 'll do dat trick to-morrow, not to-
     night—
All de sam' I offen t'ink ev'ry dog is got hees
     day,
   Dat 's de lesson I was learnin' on de school;
So I can't help feelin' blue w'en I wonder if
     it 's true
   W'at dey 're sayin—dough o' course dey 're
     only fool—
           De ole man 's gettin' on.

Pioneers

IF dey 're walkin' on de road side, an' dey 're
    bote in love togeder,
  An' de star of spring is shinin' wit' de young
    moon in between,
It was purty easy guessin' dey 're not talkin'
    of de wedder,
  W'en de boy is comin' twenty, an' de girl is
    jus' eighteen.

It 's a sign de winter 's over, an' it 's pleasan'
    hear de talkin'
  Of de bull-frog on de swamp dere wit' all
    ·hees familee—
But it 's lonesome doin' not'ing, an' dere 's
    not moche fun in walkin',
  So we fin' some fence dat 's handy for mese'f
    an' Rosalie.

An' I dunno how it happen, w'en her head
    come on ma shoulder,
  An' her black eye on de moonlight, lak de
    star shine—dat 's de way.
(Mebbe it 's becos de springtam) so I ketch her
    han' an' tole her
  Of how moche I 'd lak to tak' her on some
    contree far away.

Den she say, I 'll mak' an offer, if you 're sure
      you want to tak' me
  On de place I dunno w'ere—me—you mus'
      pay beeg price, Jo-seph.
You can carry me off to-morrow, so I 'm never
      comin' back—me—
  But you 'll lose upon de bargain, for de price
      I want 's you' se'f."

I was purty good for tradin', mebbe tak' it
      from ma fader,
  For de ole man 's alway tryin' show me
      somet'ing dat was new—
But de trade I mak' dat evenin' wit' poor
      Rosalie, I rader
  Not say not'ing moche about it, dough it 's
      bes' I never do.

So we settle on de reever wit' de bush for miles
      behin' us—
  Here we buil' de firse log shaintee, only me
      an' Rosalie—
Dat 's de woman help her husban'! an' w'en
      winter come an' fin' us
  We was ready waitin' for heem jus' as happy
      as could be.

Bar'l o' pork an' good potato, wan or two oder
 t'ing too
  Leetle w'isky, plaintee flour, an' wood-pile
   stannin' near—
Don't min' de hardes' winter, an' fat enough
  in spring too—
  De folk dat 's comin' handy w'en you want
   de contree clear!

Rosalie, you see her outside on de porch dere
  wit' her knittin'—
  Yass, of course I know she 's changin' since
   de day she marry me—
An' she 'll never sit no more dere on de fence
  lak leetle kitten—
  She 'd be safer on a stone wall, but she 's
   still ma Rosalie.

All alone: de neares' shaintee, over ten mile
  down de reever—
  An' might be only yesterday, I 'member it
   so well—
W'en I 'm comin' home wan morning affer
  trappin' on de beaver,
  An' ma wife is sayin', "Hurry, go an' fetch
   Ma-dame Labelle."

If you 're stan'in' on de bank dere, you mus'
    t 'ink I 'm crazy feller
  By de way I work de paddle, an' de way
    canoe she go—
But Ma-dame know all about it, an' I never
    need to tell her,
  An' we jus' get back in tam' dere for wel-
    come leetle Joe.

Dat 's de way dem woman 's doin' for help
    along each oder,
  For Pierre Labelle he 's comin' now an' den
    for Rosalie—
Of course dere 's many tam too, dey got to
    be godmoder—
  An' w'en dey want godfader, w'y dere 's
    only Pierre an' me.

Twenty year so hard we 're workin', twenty
    year reapin', sowin',
  Choppin' tree an' makin' portage, an' de
    chil'ren help us too—
But it 's never feelin' lonesome w'ile de fami-
    lee is growin',
  An' de cradle seldom empty, an' we got so
    moche to do.

Den w'en all de work is finish, w'at dey 're
    callin' de surveyor
  He 's comin' here an' fin' us, an' of course
    so well he might—
For it 's easy job to foller, w'en de road is
    lyin' dere,
  So blin' man he can walk it wit' hees eyes
    closed, darkes' night.

An' de nex' t'ing dere 's a township, an' de
    township bring de taxes,
  An' it 's leetle hard on us too, dat 's way it
    seem to me—
An' de Gover'ment, I s'pose dey 'll never t'ink
    at all to ax us
  For de small account dey 're owin' mese'f
    an' Rosalie.

So we 'll see de beeg procession very soon
    come up de reever—
  Some will settle on de roadside, some will
    stay upon de shore—
But de ole place we be clearin', I don't t'ink
    we 'll never leave her,
  Dough we 're all surroun' by stranger an'
    we 're in de worl' wance more.

Natural Philosophy

VERY offen I be t'inkin' of de queer folk
  goin' roun',
  And way dey kip a-talkin' of de hard tam
  get along—
May have plaintee money too, an' de healt'
  be good an' soun'—
  But you'll fin' dere's alway somet'ing goin'
  wrong—
'Course dere may be many reason w'y some
  feller ought to fret—
  But me, I'm alway singin' de only song I
  know—
'T isn't long enough for music, an' so short
  you can't forget,
  But it drive away de lonesome, an' dis is
  how she go,
    "Jus' tak' your chance, an' try your
    luck."

Funny feller's w'at dey call me—"so diff'ren'
  from de res',"
  But ev'rybody got hees fault, as far as I can
  see—
An' all de t'ing I'm doin', I do it for de bes',
  Dough w'en I'm bettin' on a race, dat's
  offen loss for me—

"Oho!" I say, "Alphonse ma frien', to-day
    is not your day,
  For more you got your money up, de less
    your trotter go—
But never min' an' don't lie down," dat's
    w'at I alway say,
  An' sing de sam' ole song some more, mebbe
    a leetle slow—
    "Jus' tak' your chance, an' try your luck."

S'pose ma uncle die an' lef' me honder dollar,
    mebbe two—
  An' I don't tak' hees advice—me—for put
    heem on de bank—
'Stead o' dat, some lot'rie ticket, to see w'at
    I can do,
  An' purty soon I'm findin' out dey're w'at
    you call de blank—
  Wall! de bank she might bus' up dere—
    somet'ing might go wrong—
Dem feller, w'en dey get it, mebbe skip before
    de night—
  Can't tell—den w'ere's your money? So I
    sing ma leetle song
An I don't boder wit' de w'isky, an' again I
    feel all right,
    "Jus' tak' your chance, an' try your luck."

If you 're goin' to mak' de marry, kip a look
     out on de eye,
  But no matter how you 're careful, it was
     risky anyhow—
An' if you 're too unlucky, jus' remember
     how you try
  For gettin' dat poor woman, dough she may
     have got you now—
All de sam', it sometam happen dat your wife
     will pass away—
  No use cryin', you can't help it—dere 's
     your duty to you' se'f—
You don't need to ax de neighbor, dey will tell
     you ev'ry day
  Start again lak hones' feller, for dere 's plain-
     tee woman lef'—
    "Jus' tak' your chance, an' try your luck."

Poor man lak me, I 'm not'ing: only w'en
     election 's dere,
  An' ev'rybody 's waitin' to ketch you by de
     t'roat—
De money I be makin' den, wall! dat was mon
     affaire—
  An' affer all w'at diff'rence how de poor man
     mak' de vote?
So I do ma very bes'—me—wit' de wife an'
     familee—

On de church door Sunday morning, you
    can see us all parade—
Len' a frien' a half a dollar, an' never go on
    spree—
So w'en I 'm comin' die—me—no use to be
    afraid—
    "Jus' tak' your chance, an' try your luck."

Champlain

"W'ERE 'll we go?" says Pierre de Monts,*
    To hese'f as he walk de forwar' deck,
"For I got ma share of Trois Rivieres
    An' I never can lak Kebeck—
Too moche Nort' Pole—maudit! it 's cole
    Oh! la! la! de win' blow too.
An' I 'm sure w'at I say, M'sieu Pontgravé
    He know very well it 's true.

"But here 's de boat, an' we 're all afloat
    A honder an' fifty ton—
An' look at de lot of man we got,
    No better beneat' de sun—
Provision, too, for all de crew
    An' pries' for to say de prayer,
So mes chers amis, dey can easy see
    De vessel mus' pass somew'ere.

    * De-mo.

CHAMPLAIN

"If I only know de way to go
    For findin' some new an' pleasan' lan',"
But jus' as he spik, he turn roun' quick,
    An' dere on de front, sir, stan' de Man.
"You was callin' me, I believe," says he,
    As brave as a lion—"Tiens!
W'en we reach de sea, an' de ship is free,
    You can talk wit' Samuel de Champlain."*

Wan look on hees eye an' he know for w'y
    Young Samuel spik no more,
So he shake hees han', an' say, "Young man,
    Too bad you don't come before;
But now you are here, we 'll geev' t'ree cheer,
    An' away w'erever you want to go—
For I lak your look an' swear on de Book
    You 'll fin' de good frien' on Pierre de Monts."

So de sail 's set tight, an' de win' is right,
    For it 's blowin' dem to de wes'—
An' dey say deir prayer, for God knows w'ere
    De anchor will come to res'—
Adieu to de shore dey may see no more—
    Good-bye to de song an' dance—
De girl dey love, an' de star above
    Kipin' watch on de lan' of France.

* Shaum-pla.

301

Den it's "Come below, M'sieu Pierre de
      Monts,"
  Champlain he say to de capitaine—
"An' I'll tell to you, w'at I t'ink is true
  Dough purty hard, too, for understan'—
I dream a dream an' it alway seem
  Dat God hese'f he was say to me—
'Rise up, young man, de quick you can
  An' sail your ship on de western sea.

"'De way may be long, an' de win' be strong,
  An' wave sweep over de leetle boat—
But never you min', an' you're sure to fin',
  If you trus' in me, you will kip afloat.'
An' I tak' dat ship, an' I mak' de trip
  All on de dream I was tellin' you—
An' oh! if you see w'at appear to me,
  I wonder w'at you was a-t'inkin' too?

"I come on de lan' w'ere dere's no w'ite man—
  I come on de shore w'ere de grass is green—
An' de air is clear as de new-born year,
  An' of all I was see, dis lan's de Queen—
So I'm satisfy if we only try
  An' fin' if dere's anyt'ing on ma dream,
An' I'll show de way," Champlain is say—
  Den Pierre de Monts he is answer heem,

CHAMPLAIN

"All right, young man, do de bes' you can—
    So long you don't bring me near Kebeck—
Or Trois Rivieres, not moche I care,
    An' I hope your dream 's comin' out correc'."
So de brave Champlain he was say, "Trés
        bien,"
An' soon he was boss of de ship an' crew
An' pile on de sail, wedder calm or gale—
    Oh! dat is de feller know w'at to do.

Don't I see heem dere wit' hees long black hair
    On de win' blowin' out behin'—
Watchin' de ship as she rise an' dip,
    An' always follerin' out de Sign?
An' day affer day I can hear heem say
    To de sailor man lonesome for home an'
        frien',
"Cheer up, mes amis, for soon you will see
    De lan' risin' up on de oder en'."

Wall! de tam go by, an' still dey cry
    "Oh! bring us back for de familee's sake."
Even Pierre de Monts fin' it leetle slow
    An' t'ink mebbe somebody mak' mistake—
But he don't geev' in for he 's boun' to win'—
    De young Champlain—an' hees heart grow
        strong
W'en de voice he hear say, "Never fear;
    You won't have to suffer for very long."

Alone on de bow I can see heem now
    Wan mornin' in May w'en de sun was rise—
Smellin' de air lak a bloodhoun', dere—
    An' de light of de Heaven shine on hees
        eyes.
A minute or more he is wait before
    He tak' off de hat an' raise hees han'—
Den down on de knee, sayin', "Dieu merci!"
    He cross hese'f dere, an' I understan'—

"Ho! Ho! De Monts! are you down below,
    Sleepin' so soun' on de bed somew'ere?
If you 're feelin well, come up an' tell
    W'at kin' of a cloud you be seein' dere."
Den every wan shout w'en de voice ring out
    Of de young Champlain on dat summer day,
"Lan'! it is lan'!" cry de sailor man—
    You can hear dem holler ten mile away.

Port Rossignol is de place dey call
    (I 'm sorry dat nam' it was disappear);
An' mos' ev'ry tree dem Frenchman see
    Got nice leetle bird singin', "Welcome here."
An' happy dey were, dem voyageurs
    An' de laugh come out on de sailors' face—
No wonder, too, w'en de shore dey view,
    For w'ere can you see it de better place?
  .   .   .   .   .   .

If you want to fin' w'at is lef' behin'
   Of de story I try very hard tell you,
Don't bodder me now or raise de row,
   But study de book de sam' I do.

Pro Patria

WAS leevin' across on de State Vermont
      W'ere mountain so high you see—
Got plaintee to do, so all I want
   Is jus' to be quiet—me—
No bodder, no fuss, only work aroun'
   On job I don't lak refuse—
But affer de familee settle down
   It 's come w'at dey call war-news.

De Spanish da-go he was gettin' mad,
   An' he 's dangerous l'Espagnol!
An' ev'ry wan say it was lookin' bad,
   Not safe on de State at all—
So Yankee he 's tryin' for sell hees farm,
   An' town 's very moche excite,
Feexin' de gun an' de fire-alarm,
   An' ban' playin' ev'ry night.

An' soon dere 's comin', all dress to kill,
   Beeg feller from far away,
Shoutin' lak devil on top de hill,
   An' dis is de t'ing he say—

"Strike for your home an' your own contree!
Strike for your native lan'!
Kip workin' away wit' de spade an' hoe,
Den jump w'en you hear de bugle blow,
For danger 's aroun', above, below,
But de bugle will tell if it 's tam to go."

An' he tak' de flag wit' de star an' stripe,
    An' holler out—"Look at me!
If any wan touch dat flag, bâ cripe!
    He 's dead about wan—two—t'ree."
Den he pull it aroun' heem few more tam,
    An' sit on de rockin' chair,
Till somebody cheer for hees Uncle Sam,
    Dough I don't see de ole man dere.

I got a long story for tell dat night
    On poor leetle Rose Elmire,
An' she say she 's sorry about de fight
    We 're doin' so well down here—
But it 's not our fault an' we can't help dat,
    De law she is made for all,
So our duty is wait for de rat-tat-tat
    Of drum an' de bugle call.

An' it 's busy week for Elmire an' me,
    I 'm sure you 'd pity us too—
Workin' so hard lak you never see,
    For dere 's plaintee o' job to do—

Den half o' de night packin' up de stuff
　　We got on de small cabane—
An' buyin' a horse, dough he cos' enough,
　　For Yankee 's a hard trade man.

An' how can I sleep if ma wife yell out—
　　"Gédéon, dere she goes!"
An' bang an' tear all de house about,
　　W'en Johnnie is blow hees nose?
Poor leetle chil'ren dey suffer too,
　　Lyin' upon de floor,
Wit' de bed made up, for dey never go
　　On de worl' lak dat before.

We got to be ready, of course, an' wait—
　　De chil'ren, de wife, an' me,
For show de Yankee upon de State,
　　Ba Golly! how smart we be.
You know de game dey call checker-boar'?
　　Wall! me an' ma wife Elmire,
We 're playin' dat game on de outside door
　　Wit' leetle wan gader near;

Jus' as de sun on de sky go down
　　An' mountain dey seem so fine,
Ev'ryt'ing quiet, don't hear a soun',
　　So I 'm lookin' across de line.

An' I t'ink of de tam I be leevin' dere
  On county of Yamachiche,
De swamp on de bush w'ere I ketch de hare
  De reever I use to feesh.

An' ma wife Elmire w'en she see de tear,
  She cry leetle bit herse'f—
Put her han' on ma neck, an' say, "Ma dear,
  I 'm sorry we never lef';
But money 's good t'ing, an' dere 's nice folk
      too,
  Leevin' upon Vermont—
Got plaintee o' work for me an' you—
  Is dere anyt'ing more we want?

"Dere 's w'at dey 're callin' de war beez-nesse—
  It 's troublesome t'ing, of course,
But no gettin' off—mus' strike wit' de res',
  No matter—it might be worse—
We 're savin' along—never lose a day,
  An' ready w'en bugle blow—"
But dat was de very las' word she say,
  For dere it commence to go,

Blowin' away on de mountain dere,
  W'ere snow very seldom melts,
Down by de reever an' ev'ryw'ere,
  We could n't hear not'ing else—

PRO PATRIA

Nobody stop to fin' out de place,
    Too busy for dat to-day—
But we never forget de law in de case
    W'en feller he spik dis way—

"Strike for your home an' your own contree!
Strike for your native lan'!
Kip workin' away wit' de spade an' hoe,
Den jump w'en you hear de bugle blow,
For danger 's aroun', above, below,
But de bugle will tell if it 's tam to go."

An' de chil'ren yell, an' de checker-boar'
    Don't do her no good at all—
An' nobody never jump before
    Lak de crowd w'en dey hear de call,
Dat was de familee,—bet your life
    I 'm prouder, ba Gosh! to-day
Mese'f, de leetle wan, an' de wife,
    Dan anyt'ing I can say—

'Cos nobody strike on de way we do—
    For home an' deir own contree—
Wit' fedder bed, stove, de cradle too,
    An' ev'ryt'ing else we see—
Pilin' de wagon up ten foot high
    Goin' along de road—
An' de Yankee say as we 're passin' by
    Dey never see such a load—

So dat 's how we 're comin' to Yamachiche—
   An' dat 's w'y we 're stayin' here—
Jus' to be quiet an' hunt an' feesh,
   Not'ing at all to fear—
An' if ever you lissen de Yankee folk
   Brag an' kick up de fuss—
An' say we 're lak cattle upon de yoke,
   An' away dey can trot from us—

Jus' tell dem de news of Gédéon Plouffe—
   How he jump wit' de familee
An' strike w'en de bugle is raise de roof
   For home an' hees own contree.

Getting Stout

EIGHTEEN, an' face lak de—w'at 's de
   good?
   Dere 's no use tryin' explain
De way she 's lookin', dat girl Marie—
   But affer it pass, de rain,
An' sun come out of de cloud behin',
   An' laugh on de sky wance more—
Wall! dat is de way her eye it shine
   W'en she see me upon de door.

GETTING STOUT

An' dere she 's workin' de ole-tam sash,
    De fines' wan, too, for sure.
"Who is it for, ma belle Marie—
    You 're makin' de nice ceinture?
Come out an' sit on de shore below,
    For watchin' dem draw de net,
Ketchin' de feesh," an' she answer, "No,
    De job is n't finish yet;

"Stan' up, Narcisse, an' we 'll see de fit.
    Dat sash it was mak' for you,
For de ole wan 's gettin' on, you know,
    An' o' course it 'll never do
If de boy I marry can't go an spen'
    W'at dey 're callin' de weddin' tour
Wit' me, for visitin' all hees frien',
    An' not have a nice ceinture."

An' den she measure dat sash on me,
    An' I fin' it so long an' wide
I pass it aroun' her, an' dere we stan',
    De two of us bote inside—
"Could n't be better, ma chère Marie,
    Dat sash it is fit so well—
It jus' suit you, an' it jus' suit me,
    An' bote togeder, ma belle."

So I wear it off on de weddin' tour
    An' long affer dat also,
An' never a minute I 'm carin' how
    De win' of de winter blow—
Don't matter de cole an' frosty night—
    Don't matter de stormy day,
So long as I 'm feex up close an' tight
    Wit' de ole ceinture fleché.

An' w'ere 's de woman can beat her now,
    Ma own leetle girl Marie?
For we 're marry to-day jus' feefty year
    An' never a change I see—
But wan t'ing strange, dough I try ma bes'
    For measure dat girl wance more,
She say—"Go off wit' de foolishness,
    Or pass on de outside door.

"You know well enough dat sash get tight
    Out on de snow an' wet
Drivin' along on ev'ry place,
    Den how can it fit me yet?
Shows w'at a fool you be, Narcisse,
    W'enever you go to town;
Better look out, or I call de pries'
    For makin' you stan' aroun'."

But me, I 'm sure it was never change,
  Dat sash on de feefty year—
An' I can't understan' to-day at all,
  W'at 's makin' it seem so queer—
De sash is de sam', an' woman too,
  Can't fool me, I know too well—
But woman, of course dey offen do
  Some funny t'ing—you can't tell!

Doctor Hilaire

A STRANGER might say if he see heem
    drink till he almos' fall,
"Doctor lak dat for sick folk, he 's never no
    use at all,"
But wait till you hear de story dey 're tellin'
    about heem yet,
An' see if you don't hear somet'ing, mebbe
    you won't forget.

Twenty odd year she 's marry, Belzemire La-
    freniere,
An' oh! but she 's feelin' lonesome 'cos never
    a sign is dere—
Purty long tam for waitin', but poor leetle
    Belzemire
She 's bad enough now for pay up all of dem
    twenty year.

Call heem de oldes' doctor, call heem de
    younges' wan,
Bring dem along, no matter if ev'ry dollar 's
    gone—
T'ree of dem can't do not'ing, workin' for two
    days dere,
She was a very sick woman, Belzemire La-
    freniere.

Pierre he was cryin', cryin' out on de barn
    behin',
Neighbors tryin' to kip heem goin' right off
    hees min',
W'en somebody say, "Las' winter, ma wife she
    is nearly go,
An' who do you t'ink is save her? ev'ry wan
    surely know.

"Drink? does he drink de w'isky? don't care
    I 'm hees only frien',
Dere 's only wan answer comin', Wall! leetle
    bit now an' den
Doctor Hilaire he tak' it, but if it was me or
    you
Leevin' on Beausejour dere, w'at are you goin'
    to do?

"An' so you may t'ank de w'isky, 'cos
    w'ere 'll he be to-day
If he never is drinkin' not'ing? Many a mile
    away
Off on de great beeg city, makin' de money
    quick,
W'ere ev'ry wan want de doctor w'enever he 's
    leetle sick.

"Remember de way to get heem is tell heem
    it's bad, bad case,
Or Doctor Hilaire you 'll never see heem upon
    dis place!
Tell heem dere 's two life waitin', an' sure to
    be comin' die
Unless he is hurry quicker dan ever de bird can
    fly.

"T'orty mile crick is runnin' over de road, I 'm
    sure,
But if you can fin' de crossin' you 'll ketch
    heem at Beausejour.
Sober or drunk, no matter, bring heem along
    you mus',
For Doctor Hilaire 's de only man of de lot for
    us."

Out wit' de quickes' horse den, Ste. Genevieve
    has got,
An' if ever you show your paces, now is de tam
    to trot—
Johnnie Dufresne is drivin', w'at! never hear
    tell of heem,
Off on de Yankee circus, an' han'le a ten-horse
    team?

Dat was de lonesome journey over de moun-
    tain high,
Down w'ere de w'ite fog risin' show w'ere de
    swamp is lie,
An' drive as he can de faster, an' furder away
    he get
Johnnie can hear dat woman closer an' closer
    yet.

Offen he tell about it, not'ing he never do
Geev' heem de funny feelin' Johnnie is goin'
    t'roo,
But he is sure of wan t'ing, if Belzemire's
    comin' die,
Poor woman, she 'd never foller affer heem wit'
    her cry.

Dat is de t'ing is cheer heem, knowin' she
    is n't gone,
So he answer de voice a-callin', tellin' her to
    hol' on,
Till he bring her de help she 's needin' if only
    she wait a w'ile
Dat is de way he 's doin' all of dem t'orty
    mile—

Lucky he was to-night, too, for place on de
    crick he got,
Search on de light of day-tam, he could n't
    fin' better spot,
But jus' as it happen', mebbe acre or two
    below,
Is place w'ere de ole mail-driver 's drownin'
    a year ago.

W'ere is de road? he got it, an' very soon
    Beausejour
Off on de hillside lyin', dere she is, small an'
    poor,
Lookin' so lak starvation might a' been t'roo
    de war,
An' dere, on de bar-room sleepin', de man he is
    lookin' for.

Drunk? he is worse dan ever—poor leetle man!
    too bad!
Lissen to not'ing neider, but Johnnie is feel so
    glad
Ketchin' heem dere so easy, 'fore he can
    answer, "No"—
He 's tyin' heem on de buggy, an' off on de
    road he go—

Half o' de journey 's over, half o' de night is
    pass,
W'en Doctor Hilaire stop swearin', an start to
    get quiet at las'—
Don't do any good ax Johnnie lettin' heem
    loose again,
For if any man tak' de chances, would n't be
    Johnnie Dufresne.

Hooraw for de black horse trotter! hooraw for
    de feller drive!
An' wan leetle cheer for Belzemire dat 's kipin'
    herse'f alive
Till Johnnie is bring de doctor, an' carry heem
    on de door
An' loosen heem out as sober as never he was
    before.

Quiet inside de house now, quiet de outside
  too,
Look at each oder smokin', dat's about all we
  do;
An' jus' as we feel, ba tonder! no use, we mus'
  talk or die,
Dere on de house we're hearin' poor leetle
  baby's cry.

Dat's all, but enough for makin' tear comin'
  down de face,
An' Pierre, if you only see heem jumpin' aroun'
  de place
You'd t'ink of a colt in spring-tam—den off
  on de barn we go
W'ere somebody got de bottle for drinkin' de
  healt', you know.

Takin' it too moche w'isky, is purty hard job
  to cure,
But only for poor ole w'isky, village of Beausejour
Can never have such a doctor, an' dat's w'y it
  ain't no tam
Talk very moche agin it, but fill her up jus' de
  sam'.

An' drink to de baby's moder, here's to de
  baby too,
An' Doctor Hilaire, anoder, beeger dan all, for
  you.
For sober or drunk, no matter, so long as he
  understan'
It's very bad case is waitin', Doctor Hilaire's
  de man.

Barbotte (*Bull-pout*)

DERE's some lak dory, an' some lak bass,
    An' plaintee dey mus' have trout—
An' w'ite feesh too, dere's quite a few
    Not satisfy do widout—
Very fon' of sucker some folk is, too,
    But for me, you can go an' cut
De w'ole of dem t'roo w'at you call menu,
    So long as I get barbotte—
        Ho! Ho! for me it's de nice barbotte.

No fuss to ketch heem—no row at all,
    De sam' as you have wit' bass—
Never can tell if you hook heem well,
    An' mebbe he's gone at las'!
An' trout, wall! any wan's ketchin' trout
    Dey got to be purty smart—
But leetle bull-pout, don't have to look out,
    For dem feller got no heart—
        Good t'ing, dey ain't got no heart.

BARBOTTE (BULL-POUT)

Dat 's wan of de reason I lak heem too—
  For all you have got to do
Is takin' your pole on de feeshin' hole
  An' anchor de ole canoe—
Den spit on de worm for luck, an' pass
  De leetle hook up de gut,
An' drop it down slow, jus' a minute or so,
  An' pull up de nice barbotte,
        Ha! Ha! de fine leetle fat barbotte.

Pleasan' to lissen upon de spring
  De leetle bird sing hees song,
W'ile you watch de line an' look out for sign
  Of mooshrat swimmin' along;
Den tak' it easy an' smoke de pipe,
  An' w'ere is de man has got
More fun dan you on de ole canoe
  W'en dey 're bitin', de nice barbotte—
        De nice leetle fat barbotte.

No runnin' aroun' on de crick for heem,
  No jompin' upon de air,
Makin' you sweat till your shirt is wet
  An' sorry you 're comin' dere—
Foolin' away wit' de rod an' line
  Mebbe de affernoon—
For sure as he bite he 's dere all right,
  An' you 're ketchin' heem very soon—
        Yass sir! you 're gettin' heem purty soon.

Den tak' heem off home wit' a dozen more
   An' skin heem so quick you can.
Fry heem wit' lard, an' you 'll fin' it hard
   To say if dere 's on de pan
Such feesh as dat on de worl' before
   Since Adam, you know, is shut
Out of de gate w'en he 's comin' home late,
   As de nice leetle fat barbotte—
      Dat 's true, de nice leetle sweet barbotte.

The Rossignol

Air—" Sur la Montagne "

JUS' as de sun is tryin'
   Climb on de summer sky
Two leetle bird come flyin'
   Over de mountain high—
Over de mountain, over de mountain,
Hear dem call,
Hear dem call—poor leetle rossignol!

Out of de nes' togeder,
   Broder an' sister too,
Out on de summer wedder
   W'en de w'ole worl' is new—
Over de mountain, over de mountain,
Hear dem call,
Hear dem call—poor leetle rossignol!

THE ROSSIGNOL

No leetle heart was lighter,
  No leetle bird so gay,
Never de sun look brighter
  Dan he is look to-day—
Over de mountain, over de mountain,
Hear dem call,
Hear dem call—poor leetle rossignol!

W'y are dey leave de nes' dere
  W'ere dey was still belong?
Better to stay an' res' dere
  Until de wing is strong.
Over de mountain, over de mountain,
Hear dem call,
Hear dem call—poor leetle rossignol.

W'at is dat watchin' dere now
  Up on de maple tall,
Better look out, tak' care now,
  Poor leetle rossignol,
Over de mountain, over de mountain,
Hear dem call,
Hear dem call—poor leetle rossignol!

Here dey are comin' near heem
  Singin' deir way along—
How can dey know to fear heem
  Poor leetle bird so young—

323

Over de mountain, over de mountain,
Hear dem call,
Hear dem call—poor leetle rossignol!

Moder won't hear you cryin',
  W'at is de use to call,
W'en he is comin' flyin'
  Quick as de star is fall?
Over de mountain, over de mountain,
Hear dem call,
Hear dem call—poor leetle rossignol!

.   .   .   .

Up w'ere de nes' is lyin',
  High on de cedar bough,
W'ere de young hawk was cryin'
  Soon will be quiet now.
Over de mountain, over de mountain,
Hear heem call,
Hear heem call—poor leetle rossignol!

If he had only kissed her,
  Poor leetle rossignol!
But he was los' hees sister,
  An' it 's alone he call—
Over de mountain, over de mountain,
Hear heem call,
Hear heem call—poor leetle rossignol!

Only a day of gladness,
  Only a day of song,
Only a night of sadness
  Lastin' de w'ole life long.
Over de mountain, over de mountain,
Hear heem call,
Hear heem call—poor leetle rossignol!

Meb-be

A QUIET boy was Joe Bedotte,
    An' no sign anw'ere
Of anyt'ing at all he got
    Is up to ordinaire—
An' w'en de teacher tell heem go
    An' tak' a holiday,
For wake heem up, becos' he 's slow,
    Poor Joe would only say,
                    "Wall! meb-be."

Don't bodder no wan on de school
    Unless dey bodder heem,
But all de scholar t'ink he 's fool
    Or walkin' on a dream—
So w'en dey re closin' on de spring
    Of course dey 're moche surprise
Dat Joe is takin' ev'ryt'ing
    Of w'at you call de prize.

An' den de teacher say, "Jo-seph,
  I know you 're workin' hard—
Becos' w'en I am pass mese'f
  I see you on de yard
A-splittin' wood—no doubt you stay
  An' study half de night?"
An' Joe he spik de sam' ole way
  So quiet an' polite,
               "Wall! meb-be."

Hees fader an' hees moder die
  An' lef' heem dere alone
Wit' chil'ren small enough to cry,
  An' farm all rock an' stone—
But Joe is fader, moder too,
  An' work bote day an' night
An' clear de place—dat 's w'at he do,
  An' bring dem up all right.

De Curé say, "Jo-seph, you know
  Le bon Dieu 's very good—
He feed de small bird on de snow,
  De caribou on de wood—
But you deserve some credit too—
  I spik of dis before."
So Joe he dunno w'at to do
  An' only say wance more,
               "Wall! meb-be."

An' Joe he leev' for many year
   An' helpin' ev'ry wan
Upon de parish far an' near
   Till all hees money 's gone—
An' den de Curé come again
   Wit' tear-drop on hees eye—
He know for sure poor Joe, hees frien',
   Is well prepare to die.

"Wall! Joe, de work you done will tell
   W'en you get up above—
De good God he will treat you well
   An' geev' you all hees love.
De poor an' sick down here below,
   I 'm sure dey 'll not forget,"
An' w'at you t'ink he say, poor Joe,
   Drawin' hees only breat'?
                "Wall! meb-be."

Snubbing (*Tying-up*) *the Raft*

L AS' night dey 're passin', de golden plover,
   Dis mornin' I 'm seein' de bluebird's
     wing,
So if not'ing go wrong, de winter 's over,
  An' not very long till we got de spring.

An' nex' t'ing de reever she 'll start a-hummin',
   An' den you 'll hear it, de song an' laugh,
Is tellin' de news, de boys are comin'
   Home again on de saw-log raf'.

All very well for see dem swingin'
   Roun' de beeg islan' dere on de bay,
Nice t'ing too, for to hear dem singin',
   'Cos it mak' me t'ink of de good ole day.

An' me—I could lissen dem song forever,
   But it is n't so pleasan' w'en evenin' fall,
An' dey 're lookin' for place to stay, an' never
   Snub de raf' on ma place at all—

Dat 's de fine cove if dey only know it—
   Hard to fin' better on St. Maurice,
Up de reever or down below it,
   An' house on de hill only leetle piece.

W'at is de reason den, w'en dey fin' dem
   Raf' comin' near me, dey all get scare,
An' pull lak de devil was close behin' dem,
   An' way down de reever to Joe Belair?

Two mile more, wit' de rock an' stone dere,
   An' water so shallow can't float canoe,
But ev'ry boy of de gang, he 's goin' dere,
   Even de cook, an' de captain too—

SNUBBING THE RAFT

W'at is de reason, I lak to know—me—
  Ma own leetle cove 's lyin empty dere,
An' nobody stop till dey go below me,
  Snubbin' de raf' on Joe Belair?

Not'ing lak dat twenty year ago, sir,
  W'en voyageurs' comin' from up above,
Dere 's only wan place us feller know, sir,
  W'en dey 're goin' ashore, an' dat 's de cove.

An' dere on door of de house she 's stannin'
  To welcome us back, Madame Baribeau,
An' Pierre hese'f, he was on de lannin',
  Ready for ketchin' de rope we t'row.

An' oh! de girl use to mak' us crazy—
  For many a fine girl Pierre has got—
Right on de jomp too—never lazy,
  But Sophie 's de fines' wan of de lot.

Me—I was only a common feller,
  An' love—wall! jus' lak de leetle calf,
An it 's true, I 'm sure, w'at dey often tell her,
  I 'm de uglies' man on boar' de raf'.

But Sophie 's so nice an' good shese'f too,
  De uglies' man upon all de worl'
Forget hees face an' forget hese'f too,
  T'ree minute affer he see dat girl—

An' dat's de reason de chance is better,
  For you must n't be t'ink of you' se'f at all,
But t'ink of de girl if you want to get her
    An' so we're marry upon de fall.

An' purty soon den dey all get started,
  For marryin' fever come so strong
W'en de firse wan go, dat dey're broken-
      hearted
    An' tak' mos' anyt'ing come along.

So Joe Belair, w'en hees house is buil' dere,
  He go down de reever wit' Eugenie,
An' place I settle on top de hill dere,
  De ole man geev' it to Sophie an' me.

An' along dey come, wan foller de oder,
  Dozen o' girl—not a boy at all—
Never a girl tak' affer de moder,
  But all lak de fader, beeg an' small—

A dozen o' girl, of course, no wonder
  A few of dem look lak me—sapree!
But w'en dey're comin' dat way, ba tonder!
  She's jus' a leetle too moche for me.

An' Joe Belair, he was down below me,
  Funny t'ing too, he is ketch also,
Ev'ryt'ing girl—how it come dunno—me—
  But dey're all lak de familee Baribeau—

330

SNUBBING THE RAFT

Growin' up purty de sam' de moder—
  An' soon as dey know it along de shore
De boys stop comin' an' never bodder
  For snub de raf' on ma place no more—

So w'at is de chance ma girl she's gettin',
  Don't care w'ere I look, none at all I see,
No use, I s'pose, kipin' on a-frettin',
  Dough it's very hard case poor man lak me.

W'at 'll I do for bring dem here,—me?
  Can't be blowin' dem to de moon—
Or buil' a dam on de reever near me
  For fear we're sure to be drownin' soon.

To-night I can hear hees darn ole fiddle,
  Playin' away on Joe Belair—
Can hear heem holler, "Pass down de middle
  An' dance on your partner over dere."

Pleasan' t'ing too, for to smell de w'isky
  Off on de leetle back room—bâ oui—
Helpin' de ole folk mak' dem frisky,
  Very pleasan' for dem, but not for me—

Oh! it mak' me mad, an' I'm tire tryin'
  To show how I feel, an' it's hard to tell—
So I'll geev' it up, for dere's no good cryin';
  'Sides w'at is de use of a two-mile smell?

Non!—I don't go dere if dey all invite me,
  Or de worl' itse'f—she come to an' en'.
De Bishop hese'f, ba Gosh! can write me,
  But Jo-seph Belair, he 's no more ma frien'.

Can't fin' me dere if de sky come down, sir,
  I rader ma girl she would never dance—
But far away, off on de Yankee town, sir,
  I 'll tak' dem w'ere mebbe dey have a chance.

An' reever an' cove, dough I 'll not forget
    dem,
  An' voyageurs too, an' Joe Belair,
Can do w'at dey lak, an' me—I 'll let dem
  Go w'ere dey want to, for I don't care.

A Rainy Day in Camp

A RAINY day in camp! how you draw the
    blankets closer,
  As the big drops patter, patter on the
    shingles overhead,
How you shudder when recalling your wife's
      "You ought to know, sir,
  That it 's dangerous and improper to smoke
    a pipe in bed."

A rainy day in camp! is it possible to find
   better?
   Tho' the lake is like a caldron, and aloft the
   thunder rolls;
Yet the old canoe is safely on the shore where
   you can let her
   Stay as long as Jupiter Pluvius in the clouds
   is punching holes.

A rainy day in camp! and the latest publication
   That the mice have left unnibbled, tells you
   all about "Eclipse,"
How the Derby fell before him, how he beat
   equine creation,
   But the story yields to slumber with the pipe
   between your lips.

Wake again and turn the pages, where they
   speak of Lester Wallack
   And the heroes of the buskin over thirty
   years ago—
Then in case the damp surroundings cause an
   inconvenient colic,
   What's the matter with the treatment neu-
   tralizing H_2O?

A RAINY DAY IN CAMP

A rainy day in camp! what an interesting col-
lection,
In this magazine so ancient, of items small
and great—
The History of the Negro, illustrating every
section,
So different from the present White House
Colored Fashion Plate!

A rainy day in camp! and you wonder how the
C. P.
And the G. T. competition will affect the
Golden West—
But these problematic matters only tend to
make you sleepy,
And again beneath the blankets, like a babe
you sink to rest.

Cometh now the giant moose heads, that no
eye of man can number—
Every rain-drop on the roof-tree is a plung-
ing three-pound trout—
Till a musk ox in a snow-drift turns and butts
you out of slumber,
And you wake to hear Bateese say, "Dat 's
too bad, de fire 's gone out."

A rainy night in camp! with the blazing logs
      before us,
  Let the wolf howl in the forest and the loon
      scream on the lake,
Turn them loose, the wild performers of Na-
      ture's Opera Chorus
  And ask if Civilization can sweeter music
      make.

Josette

I SEE Josette on de car to-day,
  Leetle Josette Couture,
An' it 's easy tellin' she 's been away
  On market of Bonsecour—
'Cos dere 's de blueberry on de pail
  Wit' more t'ing lyin' about—
An' dere 's de basket wit' de tail
  Of de chicken stickin' out.

Ev'ry conductor along de road
  Help her de bes' he can,
An' I see dem sweat wit' de heavy load,
  Many a beeg, strong man—
But it 's differen' t'ing w'en she tak' hol',
  Leavin' dem watchin' dere—
For wedder de win' blow hot or cole
  Josette never turn a hair.

Wonderful woman for seexty-five—
   Smart leetle woman sure!
An' if he 's wantin' to kip alive
   On church of de Bonsecour
De pries' he mus' rise 'fore de rooster crow,
   Or mebbe he 'll be too late
For seein' dere on de street below,
   Josette comin' in de gate.

An' half of de mornin' she don't spen' dere
   Hangin' aroun' de pew—
Bodderin' God wid de long, long prayer—
   For bote of dem got to do
Plaintee work 'fore de day 's gone by,
   An' well she know—Josette—
No matter how busy an' hard she try,
   De work 's never finish yet.

An' well he know it, de habitant,
   Who is it ketch heem, w'en
He 's drivin' along from St. Laurent—
   For it 's easier bargain den—
'Cos if de habitant only sole
   De whole of hees load dat way—
Of course he 's savin' de market toll
   An' not'ing at all to pay.

Dey call her ole maid, but I can't tell—me—
  De chil'ren she has got:
No fader, no moder, dat 's way dey be—
  You never see such a lot—
An' if you ax how she fin' de clothes
  An' food for de young wan dere—
She say: "Wit' de help of God, I s'pose
  An' de leetle shop down stair."

Comin' an' goin' mos' all de tam,
  Helpin' dem all along,
Jus' lak de ole sheep watch de lamb
  Till dey are beeg an' strong—
Not'ing lak dat I be seein' yet,
  An' it 's hard to beat for sure—
So dat 's de reason dey call Josette
  Leetle Sister of de poor.

Joe Boucher

Air—"Car si mon moine."

JOE BOUCHER was a frien' of mine,
  Joe Boucher was a happy man,
Till he tell a young girl he 'd lak to fin'
  Some nice leetle wife for hees new cabane.
Now he 's los' hees life too,
All on account of de wife too,
An' I know you 'll be sorry 'bout dat poor feller,
I know you 'll be sorry for Joe Boucher.

De nam' dat girl she 's Azeel-daw,
    An' purty good worker, too, dey say—
She don't lose chance for a brave garçon,
    An' so she marry Joe Boucher.
Now he 's los' hees life too,
All on account of de wife too,
An' I know you 'll be sorry 'bout dat poor feller,
I know you 'll be sorry for Joe Boucher.

Den off on de wood poor Joe he lef',
    An' w'en he 's home wit' de bird in spring,
An' fin' leetle feller jus' lak hese'f.
    Mebbe Joe don't dance an' Joe don't sing!
Now he 's los' hees life too,
All on account of hees wife too,
An' I know you 'll be sorry 'bout dat poor feller,
I know you 'll be sorry for Joe Boucher.

Dat 's all very well till de fall come along,
    An' Joe got to go on de bush encore,
But w'en he come back he sing no song,
    For dere was two leetle baby more.
Now he 's los' hees life too,
All on account of de wife too,
An I know you 'll be sorry 'bout dat poor
        feller,
I know you 'll be sorry for Joe Boucher.

JOE BOUCHER

He don't say not'ing, but he t'ink beeg lot,
   An' won't tak' a drink for two, t'ree day,
But not moche money poor Joe he got,
   So off on de reever he's goin' away.
Now he's los' hees life too,
All on account of de wife too,
An' I know you'll be sorry 'bout dat poor
      feller,
I know you'll be sorry for Joe Boucher.

W'en May come along dat beau garçon
   He's only gettin' anoder scare—
For he know by de smile on Azeel-daw
   She got t'ree fine new baby dere.
Now he's los' hees life too,
All on account of de wife too,
An' I know you'll be sorry 'bout dat poor
      feller,
I know you'll be sorry for Joe Boucher.

So he kill hese'f dead, dat beau garçon
   He work so hard for de familee,
An' he say, "Too bad, but Azeel-daw,
   I'm sorry she marry poor man lak me."
Now he's los' hees life too,
All on account of hees wife too,
An' I know you'll be sorry 'bout dat poor
      feller,
I know you'll be sorry for Joe Boucher.

CHARMETTE

Now I know very well dat all poor man
  He tak' some chance w'en he get marié,
So he better look out all de bes' he can,
  Or he 'll be ketch lak Joe Boucher—
Now he 's los' hees life too,
All on account of de wife too,
An' I know you 'll be sorry 'bout dat poor
    feller,
I know you 'll be sorry for Joe Boucher.

Charmette

AWAY off back on de mountain-side,
    Not easy t'ing fin' de spot,
W'ere de lake below is long an' wide,
  A nice leetle place I got,
Mebbe ten foot deep by twenty-two,
  An' if you see it, I bet
You 'll not be surprise w'en I tole to you
  I chrissen dat place Charmette.

Dat 's purty beeg word, Charmette, for go
  On poor leetle house so small,
Wit' only wan chimley, a winder or so,
  An' no galerie at all—
But I want beeg word, so de worl' will know
  W'at dat place it was mean to me,
An' dere on de book of Jean Jacques Rousseau,
  Charmette is de nam' I see.

CHARMETTE

O ma dear Charmette! an' de stove is dere,
  (Good stove) an' de wood-pile too.
An' stretch out your finger mos' anyw'ere,
  Dere 's plaintee for comfort you—
You 're hongry? wall! you got pork an' bean
  Mak' you feel lak Edouard de King—
You 're torsty? Jus' look dere behin' de
    screen,
  An' mebbe you fin' somet'ing—

Ha! Ha! you got it. Ma dear Charmette.
  Dere 's many fine place, dat 's true,
If you travel aroun' de worl', but yet
  W'ere is de place lak you?
Open de door, don't kip it close—
  W'at 's air of de mornin' for?
Would you fassen de door on de win' dat blows
  Over God's own boulevard?

You see dat lake? Wall! I alway hate
  To brag—but she 's full of trout,
So full dey can't jump togeder, but wait
  An' tak' deir chance, turn about—
An' if you be campin' up dere above,
  De mountain would be so high,
Very offen de camp you 'd have to move,
  Or how can de moon pass by?

It 's wonderful place for sure, Charmette,
    An' ev'ry wan say to me—
I got all de pleasure de man can get
    'Cept de wife an' de familee—
But somebody else can marry ma wife,
    Have de familee too also,
W'at more do I want, so long ma life
    Was spare to me here below?

For we can't be happier dan we been
    Over twenty year, no siree!
An' if ever de stranger come between
    De leetle Charmette an' me,
Den all I can say is, kip out de way,
    For dynamite sure I 'll get,
An' affer dat you can hunt all day
    For me an' ma dear Charmette.

Lac Souci

TALK about lakes! dere 's none dat lies in
    Laurentide mountain or near de sea,
W'en de star 's gone off an' de sun is risin',
    Can touch w'at dey call it Lac Souci,
Restin' dere wit' de woods behin' her,
    Sleepin' dere t'roo de summer night—
But watch her affer de mornin' 's fin' her,
    An' over de hill-top shine de light.

LAC SOUCI

See w'ere de shadder sweep de water,
  Pine tree an' cloud, how dey come an' go;
Careful now, an' you 'll see de otter
  Slidin' into de pool below—
Look at de loon w'en de breeze is ketch heem
  Shakin' hese'f as he cock de eye!
Takes a nice leetle win' to fetch heem,
  So he 's gettin' a chance to fly.

Every bird dey mus' kip behin' heem
  W'en he 's only jus' flap de wing,
Ah! dere he 's goin'—but never min' heem,
  For lissen de robin begin to sing—
Trout 's comin' up too!—dat 's beeg rise dere,
  Four of dem!   Golly! it 's purty hard case,
No rod here, an' dey 're all good size dere!
  Don't ax me not'ing about de place.

No use nobody goin' murder
  T'ree an' four pounder lak dat, siree!
Wall! if you promise it won't go furder
  I 'll tole you nex' summer—bimeby—
      mebbe—
W'at is dat movin' among de spruce dere?
  Sure as I 'm livin' dere 's 'noder wan too—
Offen enough I 'm gettin' a moose dere,
  Non!—It 's only a couple of caribou.

343

LAC SOUCI

Black duck so early?   See how dey all come,
   Wan leetle family roun' de ben'—
Let dem enjoy it, wait till de fall come,
   Dey won't be feelin' so happy den!
Smoke on de mountain?   Yass, I can smell her—
   Who is it now, Jean Bateese Boucher?
Geev' me some tam, an' I 'll feex dat feller
   Shootin' de moose on de summer day.

W'at do you t'ink of a sapree beaver
   Hittin' hees tail on de lake dat way?
Ought to be home wit' hees wife—not leave
      her
   Workin' away on de house all day—
Funny t'ing, too, how he alway fin' me
   Sailin' along on de ole canoe,
Lookin' for sign—den bang! behin' me
   An' down on de water—dat 's w'at he do.

Otter feeshin' an' bob cat cryin'—
   Up on de sky de beeg black hawk—
Down on de swamp w'ere a dead log 's lyin',
   Pa'tridge doin' hees own cake-walk!
If you never was seen dem, hear dem—
   Tak' leetle tour on de Lac Souci,
An' w'enever you 're comin' near dem,
   You 're goin' crazy de sam' as me.

Talk about lakes of every nation,
   Talk about water of any kin',
Don't matter you go over all creation—
   De Lac Souci she can beat dem blin'.
Happy to leev an' happy to die dere—
   But Heaven itself won't satisfy me,
Till I fin' leetle hole off on de sky dere
   W'ere I can be lookin' on Lac Souci!

Poirier's Rooster

"W'AT 's dat? de ole man gone, you say
     Wall! Wall! he mus' be sick,
For w'en he pass de oder day,
   He walk along widout de stick,
Lak twenty year or so—
Fine healt'y man, ole Telesphore,
I never see heem sick before,
Some rheumateez, but not'ing more—
     Please tell me how he go."

You 're right, no common t'ing for sure
   Is kill heem lak de res';
No sir! de man was voyageur
   Upon de Grande Nor' Wes'
Until he settle here
Is not de feller 's goin' die
Before he 's ready by an' bye,
So if you want de reason w'y
     I 'll tell you, never fear.

You know how moche he lak to spik
   An' tole us ev'ryt'ing about
De way de French can alway lick
   An' pull de w'ole worl' inside out,
Poor Telesphore Cadotte!
He 's knowin' all de victory,
An' braves' t'ing was never be.
To hear heem talk it 's easy see
      He 's firse-class patriot.

Hees leetle shoe store ev'ry night
   Can hardly hol' de crowd of folk
Dat come to lissen on de fight,
   An' w'en you see de pile of smoke
An' hear ole Telesphore
Hammer de boot upon hees knee,
You t'ink of course of Chateauguay,
An' feel dat 's two, t'ree enemy
      Don't bodder us no more.

But oh! dat evening w'en he sen'
   De call aroun' for come en masse,
An' den he say, "Ma dear ole frien',
   Dere 's someting funny come to pass,
I lak you all to hear—
You know dat Waterloo affair?
H-s-s-h! don't get excite, you was n't dere—
All quiet? Wall! I 'll mak' it square,
      So lissen on your ear.

POIRIER'S ROOSTER

"I 'm readin' on de book to-day
    Some book, dey say, was guarantee),
An' half a dollar too I pay,
    But cheap, because it 's tellin' me
De t'ing I 'm glad to know—
Of course de w'ole worl' understan'
Napoléon fight de bes' he can,
But he 's not French at all, dat man,
        But leetle small Da-go.

"Anoder t'ing was mak' it show
Dere 's not'ing new below de sun,
Is w'en I 'm findin' as I go—
Dat feller dey call Welling-ton,
He 's English?   No siree!
But only maudit Irlandais!
(Dat 's right! dey 're alway in de way,
Dem Irish folk), an' so I say
        I 'm satisfy for me.

"It 's not our fault, dat 's all explain—
Dere 's no use talk of Waterloo,
Not our affair—" an' off again
He hammer, hammer on de shoe,
An' don't say not'ing more,
But w'issle "*Madame Isabeau*,"
Good news lak dat is cheer heem so—
Den tak' a drink before we go,
        De poor ole Telesphore!

An' now he 's gone! Wall! I dunno,
Can't say—he 's better off meb-be,
Don't work so hard on w'ere he go—
Dat 's wan t'ing sure I 'm t'inkin'—me—
Unless he los' hees track.
But w'en dat boy come runnin' in
De leetle shop, an' start begin
On Poirier's rooster, how he win—
      I lak to break hees back.

Poor Telesphore was tellin' how
   Joe Monferrand can't go to sleep,
Until he 's kickin' up de row,
   Den pile dem nearly ten foot deep,
Dem English sojer man—
Can't blame de crowd dey all hooraw,
For bes' man on de Ottawaw,
An' geev' t'ree cheer for Canadaw,
     De very bes' dey can.

An' Telesphore again he start
   For tell de story leetle more,
Anoder wan before we part,
   W'en bang! a small boy t'roo de door
On w'at you call "full pelt,"
Is yellin' till it reach de skies,
"Poirier's rooster got de prize,
Poirier's rooster got de prize,
     An' win de Champion belt!"

An' sure enough, he beat dem all,
    Joe Poirier's leetle red game bird,
On beeges' show dey have dis fall,—
    De Yankee rooster only t'ird
An' Irish number two—
We hear a jump, an' Telesphore—
I never see de lak before—
He flap hees wing upon de floor
        An' cock a doodle doo!

Dat 's finish heem, he 's gone at las',
    An' never come aroun' again—
We 'll miss heem w'en we 're goin' pas',
    An' see no light upon de pane—
But pleasure we have got,
We 'll kip it on de memory yet,
An' dough of course we 'll offen fret,
Dere 's wan t'ing sure, we 'll not forget
Poor Telesphore Cadotte!

Dominique

YOU dunno ma leetle boy Dominique?
    Never see heem runnin' roun' about de
        place?
'Cos I want to get advice how to kip heem
        lookin' nice,
    So he won't be alway dirty on de face—

349

Now dat leetle boy of mine, Dominique,
    If you wash heem an' you sen' heem off to
        school,
But instead of goin' dere, he was playin' fox
        an' hare—
    Can you tell me how to stop de leetle fool?

"I 'd tak' dat leetle feller Dominique,
    An' I 'd put heem on de cellar ev'ry day,
An' for workin' out a cure, bread an' water 's
        very sure,
    You can bet he mak' de promise not to
        play!"

Dat 's very well to say, but ma leetle Domi-
        nique
    W'en de jacket we put on heem 's only new,
An' he 's goin' travel roun' on de medder up
        an' down,
    Wit' de strawberry on hees pocket runnin'
        t'roo,
An' w'en he climb de fence, see de hole upon
        hees pant,
    No wonder hees poor moder 's feelin' mad!
So if you ketch heem den, w'at you want to
        do, ma frien'?
    Tell me quickly an' before he get too bad.

"I 'd lick your leetle boy Dominique,
   I 'd lick heem till he 's cryin' purty hard,
An' for fear he 's gettin' spile, I 'd geev' heem
      castor ile,
     An' I would n't let heem play outside de
      yard."

If you see ma leetle boy Dominique
   Hangin' on to poor ole "Billy" by de tail,
W'en dat horse is feelin' gay, lak I see heem
      yesterday,
     I s'pose you t'ink he 's safer on de jail?
W'en I 'm lightin' up de pipe on de evenin'
      affer work,
     An' de powder dat young rascal 's puttin' in,
It was makin' such a pouf, nearly blow me
      t'roo de roof—
     W'at 's de way you got of showin' 't was a sin?

"Wall! I put heem on de jail right away,
   You may bet de wan is got de beeges' wall!
A honder foot or so, w'ere dey never let heem go,
   Non! I would n't kip a boy lak dat at all."

Dat 's good advice for sure, very good,
   On de cellar, bread an' water—it 'll do,
De nice sweet castor ile geev' heem ev'ry leetle
     w'ile,
    An' de jail to finish up wit' w'en he 's t'roo!

Ah! ma frien', you never see Dominique,
  W'en he's lyin' dere asleep upon de bed,
If you do, you say to me, "W'at an angel he
    mus' be,
  An' dere can't be not'ing bad upon hees head."

Many t'ank for your advice, an' it may be
    good for some,
  But de reason you was geev' it is n't very
    hard to seek—
Yass! it's easy seein' now w'en de talk is
    over, how
  You dunno ma leetle boy Dominique.

Home

"OH! Mother the bells are ringing as never
    they rang before,
And banners aloft are flying, and open is every
    door,
While down in the streets are thousands of
    men I have never seen—
But friendly are all the faces—oh! Mother,
    what can it mean?"

"My little one," said the mother, "for many
    long, weary years—
Thro' days that the sunshine mocked at, and
    nights that were wet with tears, .

HOME

I have waited and watched in silence, too
    proud to speak, and now
The pulse of my heart is leaping, for the
    children have kept the vow.

"And there they are coming, coming, the
    brothers you never knew,
But, sightless, my ears would know them, so
    steady and firm and true
Is the tramp of men whose fathers trod where
    the wind blows free,
Over the heights of Queenston, and willows of
    Chateaugay.

"For whether it be a thousand, or whether a
    single man—
In the calm of peace, or battle, since ever the
    race began,
No human eye has seen it—'t is an undis-
    covered clime,
Where the feet of my children's fathers have
    not stepped and beaten time.

"The enemy at my threshold had boasted and
    jeered and cried—
'The pledge of your offsprings' birthright your
    children have swept aside—

They cumber the land of strangers, they dwell
  in the alien's tent
Till "home" is a word forgotten, and "love"
  but a bow unbent.

"Planners and builders of cities (were ever
  such men as these?),
Counsellors, guides, and moulders of the
  strangers' destinies—
Conquerors, yet are they conquered, and this
  is the word and sign,
You boast of their wise seed-sowing, but the
  harvest they reap is *mine*.'

"Ah! little the stranger knew me—this mock-
  ing but friendly foe,
The youngest mother of nations! how could
  the stranger know
The faith of the old grey mother,—her sorrows
  and hopes and fears?
Let her speak when her sons are tested, like
  mine, for a thousand years!

"Afar in the dim savanna when the dawn of
  the spring is near,
What is it wakes the wild goose, calling him
  loud and clear?

What is it brings him homeward, battered and
    tempest-torn?
Are they weaker than birds of passage, the
    children whom I have borne?

"Nay! the streets of the city tremble with the
    tread that shakes the world,
When the sons of the blood foregather, and
    the mother flag flies unfurled—
Brothers are welcoming brothers, and the
    voices that pierce the blue
Answer the enemy's taunting—and the chil-
    dren of York are true!

"Wanderers maybe, traitors never! By the
    scroll of their fathers' lives!
The faith of the land that bore them, and the
    honor of their wives!
We may lose them, our own strong children,
    blossom and root and stem—
But the cradle will be remembered, and home
    is aye home to them!"

Canadian Forever

WHEN our fathers crossed the ocean
    In the glorious days gone by,
They breathed their deep emotion
    In many a tear and sigh—

CANADIAN FOREVER

Tho' a brighter lay before them
Than the old, old land that bore them
And all the wide world knows now
   That land was Canada.

So line up and try us,
Whoever would deny us
The freedom of our birthright
   And they 'll find us like a wall—
For we are Canadian—Canadian forever
   Canadian forever—Canadian over all.

Our fathers came to win us
   This land beyond recall—
And the same blood flows within us
   Of Briton, Celt, and Gaul—
Keep alive each glowing ember
Of our sireland, but remember
Our country is Canadian
   Whatever may befall.

So line up and try us,
Whoever would deny us
The freedom of our birthright
   And they 'll find us like a wall—
For we are Canadian, Canadian forever,
   Canadian forever—Canadian over all.

Who can blame them, who can blame **us**
   If we tell ourselves with pride
How a thousand years to tame us
   The foe has often tried—
And should e'er the Empire need us,
She 'll require no chains to lead us,
For we are Empire's children—
   But Canadian over all.

Then line up and try us,
Whoever would deny us
The freedom of our birthright
   And they 'll find us like a wall—
For we are Canadian, Canadian forever,
   Canadian forever—Canadian over all!

Twins

I CONGRATULATE ye, Francis,
   And more power to yer wife—
An' from Montreal to Kansas,
   I could safely bet my life
Ye wor proud enough, I hould ye—
   Runnin' with the safety pins
Whin ould Mrs. Dolan tould ye,
   "Milia murther! she has twins!"

TWINS

Ye might kill me without warnin'—
    Lay me out there on the shelf—
For a sight of ye that mornin',
    Throwin' bookays at yerself!
Faix! ye thought ye had a cinch there,
    An' begob! so well ye might,
For not even with the Frinch there,
    Twins like thim come every night!

Francis, aisy now an' listen
    To yer mother's brother James—
Whin the twins ye go to christen,
    Don't ye give thim fancy names—
Irene—Edith—Gladys—Mavis—
    Cecil Rhodes an' Percival—
If it 's names like that, Lord save us!
    Don't live close to the canal!

Michael Whalen of St. Lambert
    Had a boy some years ago—
Called him Clarence Montizambert—
    Where he got it I dunno—
Monty used to have a brother
    (*He* was Marmaduke Fitzjames)
Killed himself some way or other
    Thryin' to pronounce his names!

Bet was three times in a minute,
    An' he thrained hard for the same,
But the lad was never in it—
    Tho' they tell me he died game!
Well, sir!—Monty grew the height of
    Fin McCool or Brian Boru—
Truth I 'm tellin', but in spite of
    Ev'rything poor Mike could do—

Divil a dacint situation
    Monty got, but dhrive a hack,
At the Bonaventure station—
    'T was the name that kept him back—
Till his friend, John Reilly, tould him,
    "Change the haythen name for Pat—"

Pathrick Joseph—now behould him
    Walkin' dillygate! think o' that!
So be careful, Master Francis,
    An' ye 'll bless yer uncle James—
Don't be takin' any chances
    With thim God-forsaken names!

Keep Out of the Weeds

NO smarter man you can never know
    W'en I was a boy, dan Pierre Nadeau,
An' quiet he 's too, very seldom talk,
But got an eye lak de mountain hawk,
See all aroun' heem mos' ev'ryw'ere,
An' not many folk is foolin' Pierre.

KEEP OUT OF THE WEEDS

Offen I use to be t'inkin'—me—
How on de worl' it was come to be
He know so moche, w'en he never go
On college or school, ole Pierre Nadeau,
Feesh on de reever de summer t'roo,
An' trap on de winter—dat 's all he do.

"Hi! boy—Hi! put your book away,
An' come wit' your uncle Pierre to-day,
Ketch hol' of de line an' hang on tight,
An' see if your moder won't cook to-night
Some nice fresh feesh for de familee,"
Many a tam he was say to me—

An' den I 'm quiet, too scare to spik,
W'ile Pierre he paddle me down de crick,
Easy an' nice he mak' her go
Close to de shore w'ere de bulrush grow,
W'ere de pike an' de beeg feesh lak to feed,
Deir nose stickin' out w'ere you see de weed—

"Lissen, ma boy," say Pierre Nadeau,
"To some of de t'ing you ought to know:
Kip a lookout on de hook an' line,
In case dey 're gettin' too far behin';
For it 's purty hard job know w'at to do,
If de reever weed 's ketchin' hol' of you.

"But if you want feesh, you mus' kip leetl**
  close,
For dat 's w'ere de beeg feller come de mos',
Not on de middle w'ere water 's bare,
But near to de rushes over dere.
'Cos dat was de spot dey alway feed—
All de sam' you got to look out for weed.

"Ho! Ho! a strike! let heem have it now—
Gosh! ain't he a-kickin' heem up de row,
Pullin' so hard, never min', ma son,
W'en he go lak dat he was nearly done,
But he 's all right now, so don't be afraid,
Jus' hit heem again wit' de paddle blade.

"Yass! over an' over, it 's good advice,
An' me, I know, for I pay de price
On w'at you call compoun' interes' too,
For larnin' de lesson I geev' to you,
Close as you lak, but, ma boy, tak' heed
You don't run into de beeg long weed.

"An' by an' by w'en you 're growin' up,
An' mebbe drink of de black, black cup
Of trouble an' bodder an' dunno w'at,
You 'll say to you' se'f, 'Wall! I forgot
De lesson ole Pierre he know I need,'
W'en he say to me, 'Boy, look out for weed'—

"For de worl 's de sam' as de reever dere,
Plaintee of weed lyin' ev'ryw'ere,
But work aroun' or your life is gone,
An' tak' some chance or you won't get on,
For if you don't feesh w'ere de weed is grow,
You 'll only ketch small leetle wan or so—

"Dere 's no use sayin', 'I 'll wait an' see
If some of dem feesh don't come to me,
I 'll stay outside, for it 's pleasan' here,
W'ere de water 's lookin' so nice an' clear,'
Dat 's way you 'll never get w'at you need—
Keep feeshin' away, but look out for weed."

   .   .   .   .

Dat was de lesson ole Pierre Nadeau
Tell to me offen, so long ago—
Poor ole Pierre! an' I 'm tryin' too,
Tak' hees advice, for I know it 's true,
But far as it goes we 're all de same breed,
An' it 's not so easy kip out de weed.

The Holy Island

DEY call it de Holy Islan'
    W'ere de lighthouse stan' alone,
Lookin' across w'ere de breaker toss,
    Over de beeg grey stone;

Dey call it de Holy Islan,'
   For wance, on de day gone by,
A holy man from a far-off lan'
   Is leevin' dere, till he die.

Down from de ole, ole people,
   Scatter upon de shore,
De story come of Fader Jerome,
   De pries' of Salvador
Makin' hees leetle house dere,
   Wit' only hees own two han',
Workin' along, an' singin' de song
   Nobody understan'.

"All for de ship an' sailor
   Out on de stormy sea,
I mak' ma home," say Fader Jerome,
   "W'ere de rock an' de beeg wave be.
De good God up on de Heaven
   Is answer me on de prayer,
An' bring me here, so I 'll never fear,
   But foller heem ev'ryw'ere!"

Lonely it was, dat islan',
   Seven league from de coas',
An' only de cry, so loud an' high,
   Of de poor drown sailors' ghos'

You hear, wit' de screamin' sea gull;
   But de man of God he go
An' anchor dere, an' say hees prayer
   For ev'rywan here below.

.   .   .   .   .   .   o

Night on de ocean 's fallin',
   Deep is de fog, an' black,
As on dey come, to deir islan' home,
   De sea-bird hurryin' back;
W'at is it mak' dem double
   An' stop for a minute dere,
As if in fear of a soun' dey hear,
   Meetin' dem on de air?

Sweeter dey never lissen,
   Magic it seem to be,
Hangin' aroun' dat wonderful soun',
   Callin' across de sea;
Music of bell 's widin it,
   An' foller it on dey go
High on de air, till de islan' dere
   Of Salvador lie below.

Dat 's w'ere de bell 's a-ringin'
   Over de ocean track,
Troo fog an' rain an' hurricane,
   An' w'enever de night is black;

THE HOLY ISLAND

Kipin' de vow he 's makin',
  Dat 's w'at he 's workin' for,
Ringin' de bell, an' he do it well,
  De Fader of Salvador!

An' de years go by, an' quickly,
  An' many a sailor's wife
She 's prayin' long, an' she 's prayin' strong
  Dat God he will spare de life
Of de good, de holy Fader,
  Off w'ere de breakers roar,
Only de sea for hees companie,
  Alone on Salvador.

.   .   .   .

Summer upon de islan',
  Quiet de sea an' air,
But no bell ring, an' de small bird sing,
  For summer is ev'ryw'ere;
A ship comin' in, an' on it
  De wickedes' capitaine
Was never sail on de storm, or gale,
  From here to de worl's en'!

"Geev' me dat bell a-ringin
  For not'ing at all, mon père;
Can't sleep at night, w'en de moon is bright,
  For noise she was makin' dere.

I 'm sure she was never chrissen,
    An' we want no heretic bell;
W'ere is de book?   For you mus' look
    An' see if I chrissen it well!"

Leevin' heem broken-hearted,
    For Fader Jerome is done,
He sail away wit' de bell dat day,
    Capitaine Malcouronne;
An' down w'ere dead man 's lyin',
    Down on de ocean deep,
He sink it dere, w'ile he curse an' swear,
    An' tole it to go to sleep.

An' t'ree more year is passin',
    An' now it 's a winter night:
Poor Salvador, so bles' before,
    Is sittin' among de fight
Of breaker, an' sea-bird yellin',
    An' noise of a tousan' gun,
W'en troo de fog, lak a dreefin' log,
    Come Capitaine Malcouronne!

Gropin' along de sea dere,
    Wonderin' w'ere he be,
Prayin' out loud, before all de crowd
    Of sailor man on hees knee;

Callin' upon de devil,
  "Help! or I 'm gone!" he shout;
"Dat bell it go to you down below,
  So now you can ring me out.

"To de open sea, an' affer
  I promise you w'at I do.
Yass, ev'ry day I 'll alway pray
  To you, an' to only you—
Kip me in here no longer,
  Or de shore I won't see again!"
T'ink of de prayer he 's makin' dere,
  Dat wicked ole capitaine!

An' bell it commence a-ringin',
  Quiet at firse, an' den
Lak tonder crash, de ship go smash,
  An' w'ere is de capitaine?
An' de bell kip ringin,' ringin',
  Drownin' de breakers' roar,
An' dere she lie, w'ile de sea-birds cry,
  On de rock of Salvador.

The Rivière des Prairies

I SEE de many reever on de State an' ev'ry-
    w'ere,
  From Maine to California, New York to
    Michigan,

An' wan way an' de oder, I tell you I don't
    care;
  I travel far upon dem as moche as any man—
But all de t'ousan' reever I was never pass
    along,
    For w'at dey call de beauty, from de moun-
      tain to de sea,
Dere's wan dat I be t'inkin', de wan w'ere I
    belong,
    Can beat dem all, an' easy, too, de Rivière
      des Prairies!

Jus' tak' de Hudson Reever, an' de Mississippi
    too,
  Missouri, an' de res' of dem, an' oders I can't
    t'ink,
Dey're all beeg, dirty places, wit' de steam-
    boat gruntin' troo,
  An' de water runnin' in dem is black as any
    ink,
An' de noises of dem reever never stoppin'
    night or day,
  An' de row along de shore, too, enough to
    mak' you scare;
Not a feesh is wort' de eatin', 'less you're
    starvin' by de way,
  An' you're feeling purty t'orsty if you
    drink de water dere!

So ketch de han' I geev' you w'ile I 'm on de
      humor now,
  An' I bet you won't be sorry w'en you go
      along wit' me,
For I show you all aroun' dere, until you 're
      knowin' how
  I come so moche to brag—me—on de
      Rivèire des Prairies.
It 's a cole October mornin', an' de maple leaf
      is change
  Ev'ry color you can t'ink of, from de purple
      to de green;
On de shore de crowd of blackbird, an' de
      crow begin' arrange
  For de journey dey be takin' w'en de nort'
      win's blowin' keen.

Quick! down among de bushes!—don't you
      hear de wil' goose cry
  An' de honk de great beeg gander he was
      makin' up above?
On de lake dey call Two Mountain is de place
      dey 're goin' fly,
  But only spen' de night-tam, for dey 're
      alway on de move;
Jus' see de shadder dancin' up an' down, up
      an' down,
  You t'ink dem geese was passin' in an' out
      between de tree

W'en de branch is bendin' over on de water all
    aroun'
  Now you see de place I 'm talkin', dat 's de
    Rivière des Prairies!

Missouri! Mississippi! better wait till you go
    back—
  No tam for talk about dem w'en dis reever
    you can see,
But watch de cloud a-sailin' lak a racer on de
    track,
  An' lissen to de music of de Rivière des
    Prairies—
An' up along de shore dere, don't you envy
    Bord à Plouffe?
  Oh! dat's de place is lucky, have de reever
    come so near—
I 'm knowin' all de people, ev'ry chimley,
    ev'ry roof,
For Bord à Plouffe she never change on over
    feefty year!

St. Martin's bell is ringin', can't you hear it
    easy now?
  Dey 're marryin' or buryin' some good ole
    frien' of me,

I wonder who it can be, don't matter anyhow,
  So long as we 're a-lookin' on de Rivière des
    Prairies.
Only notice how de sun shine w'en he 's comin'
    out to peep,
  I 'm sure he 's leetle brighter dan anyw'ere
    you see,
An' w'en de fall is over, an' de reever 's gone
    to sleep,
  De w'ites' snow is fallin' on de Rivière des
    Prairies!

I love you, dear ole reever, more dan ev'ry
    Yankee wan;
  An' if I get de money, you will see me on
    de train,
Wit' couple o' t'ousan' dollar, den hooraw! it 's
    good-bye, John!
  You can kill me if you ketch me leavin' Bord
    à Plouffe again.
But sometam it 'll happen dat a feller 's gettin'
    stop
  Because he 's comin' busy wit' de wife an'
    familee—
No matter, if de good God he won't forget to
    drop,
  Ev'ry day an' night, hees blessin' on de
    Rivière des Prairies!

371

The Wind that Lifts the Fog

OVER de sea de schooner boat
    Star of de Sout' is all afloat,
Many a fine brave feesherman
Sailin' away for Newfunlan';
Ev'ry feller from St. Malo,
Dem is de boy can mak' her go!
Tearin' along t'roo storm or gale,
Never sparin' an inch of sail—

Down below w'en de night is come,
Out wit' de bottle an' t'ink of home,
Push it aroun' till bottle 's drain,
An' drink no more till we 're home again,
"Here 's to de win' dat lif' de fog,
No matter how she 's blowin',
Nort' or sout', eas' or wes',
Dat is de win' we love de bes',
Ev'ry sailor an' young sea dog,
Here 's to de win' dat lif' de fog
An' set de ship a-goin'."

Flyin' over de wave she go,
Star of de Sout' from St. Malo,
Never a tack, before she ran
Out on de bank of Newfunlan'—

Drop de anchor, an' let her down,
Plaintee of comrade all aroun',
Feeshin' away till night is fall,
Singin' away wit' ev'ry haul,
"Here's to de win' dat lif' de fog,
No matter how she's blowin'
Nort' or sout', eas' or wes',
Dat is de win' we love de bes',
Ev'ry sailor an' young sea dog,
Here's to de win' dat lif' de fog
An' set de ship a-goin'."

. . . .

Star of de Sout'—did you see de light
Steamin' along dat foggy night?
Poor leetle bird! anoder star
Shinin' above so high an' far
Dazzle you den, an' blin' de eye,
W'ile down below on de sea you lie
Anchor dere—wit' your broken wing
How could you fly w'en de sailor sing
"Here's to de win' dat lif' de fog
No matter how she's blowin',
Nort' or sout', eas' or wes',
Dat is de win' we love de bes',
Ev'ry sailor an' young sea dog,
Here's to de win' dat lif' de fog
An' set de ship a-goin'"?

THE FOX HUNT

The Fox Hunt

I 'M all bus' up, for a mont' or two,
  On account of de wife I got,
Wit' de fuss an' troublesome t'ing she do,
  She 's makin' me sick a lot;
An' I 'm sorry dat woman was go to school
  For larnin' de way to read,
Her fader an' moder is great beeg fool
  For geevin' her more she need!

'Cos now it 's a paper ev'ry week,
  Dollar a year, no less—
Plaintee o' talkin' about musique,
  An' tell you de way to dress;
Of course dat 's makin' her try to sing
  An' dress, till it 's easy see
She 's goin' crazy about de t'ing
  Dey 're callin'—Societee.

Las' week, no sooner I come along
  From market of Bonsecour,
Dan I 'm seein' right off, dere 's somet'ing
      wrong,
  For she 's stannin' outside de door
Smilin' so sweetly upon de face,
  Lookin' so nice an' gay—
Anywan t'ink it 's purty sure case
  She marry me yesterday.

374

Can't wait a minute till supper's t'roo
    Before she commence to go—
"Oh! Johnnie, dere's somet'ing I mus' tole
        you—
    Somet'ing you lak to know—
To-morrow we're goin' for drive aroun'
    An' it won't be de heavy load,
Jus' me an' you, for to see dem houn'
    T'row off on de Bord à Plouffe road."

"Denise, if dat was de grande affaire
    On w'at you call à la mode—
Lookin' dem fox dog stannin' dere
    T'row off on de Bord à Plouffe road,
You can count me out!" An' she start to cry—
    "You know very well," she say,
"I don't mean dat—may I never die
    But you're a beeg fool to-day!

"Johnnie, to-morrow you'll come wit' me
    Watchin' dem run de race,
Ketchin' de fox—if you don't, you see
    We're bote on de beeg disgrace.
Dey're all comin' out from de reever side,
    An' over from Beaurepaire,
Seein' de folk from de city ride,
    An' ev'rywan's sure be dere."

All right—an' to-morrow dere 's two new shoe,
  So de leetle horse mak' de show,
Out wit' de buggy: de new wan too,
  Only get her ten year ago—
An' dere on de road, you should see de gang
  Of folk from aroun' de place,
Billy Dufresne, an' ole Champagne,
  Comin' to see de race,

Wit' plaintee of stranger I never see,
  An' some of dem from Pointe Claire,
All of dem bringin' de familee,
  W'enever dere 's room to spare.
Wonderful sight—I 'm sure you say—
  To see how Societee
(W'atever dat mean?) she got de way
  Of foolin' de w'ole contree.

Den I 'm heetchin' de horse on de fence, for
    fear
  Somebody run away.
So man wit' de bugle he 's comin' near,
  An' dis is de t'ing he say—
"You see any fox to-day, ma frien',
  Runnin' aroun' at all,
You know any place he got hees den?
  For we lak it to mak' de call."

376

An' me—I tell heem, "You mus' be wrong,
  An' surely don't want to kill
De leetle red fox, about two foot long,
  Dat 's leevin' below de hill;
Jompin' de horse till he break hees knee,
  W'ile spotty dog mak' de row,
For a five-dollar fox?   You can't fool me—
  I know w'at you 're wantin' now!

"You hear de story of ole Belair,
  He 's seein' de silver fox
W'enever he 's feeshin' de reever dere,
  Sneakin' along de rocks."
But ma wife get madder I never see,
  An' say, "Wall! you *mus'* be green—
Shut up right away," she 's tellin' me,
  "It 's de leetle red fox he mean!"

So me—I say not'ing, but watch de fun—
  An' spotty dog smell aroun'
Till dey start to yell, an' quick as a gun
  Ev'rywan 's yellin', "Foun'!"
An' de way dey 're goin' across de fiel',
  De lady in front, before,
Dunno, but I 'm willin' to bet good deal
  Somebody mus' be sore!

THE FOX HUNT

Over de fence dey 're jompin' now,
  Too busy for see de gate
Stannin' wide open, an' den dey plough
  Along at a terrible rate;
All for de small red fox, dey say,
  Only de leetle fox,
You 're buyin' for five dollar any day,
  An' put heem on two-foot box.

I 'm foolish enough, but not lak dat—
  Never lak dat at all,
Sam' as you see a crazy cat
  Tryin' to climb de wall;
So I say to ma wife, I 'm satisfy
  On ev'ryt'ing I was see,
But happy an' glad, until I die,
  I 'm not on Societee!

Lison' a day on de fall 's no joke,
  Dat 's w'at I 'm tellin' you,
Jus' for de pleasure of see dem folk
  Dress up on de howdy do;
So I 'm sorry you go to school,
  Larnin' de readin' dere—
Could do it mese'f an' play de fool,
  If money I got to spare.

But potatoes a dollar a bag,
   An' easy to sell de load,
Watchin' de houn' to see heem wag
   Hees tail, on de Bord à Plouffe road
Foolin' away w'en de market 's good
   For seein' Societee
Chasin' de leetle fox t'roo de wood
   Wit' crazy folk!—no siree!

The Great Fight

BAD luck to fight on New Year's night
   An' wit' your neighbor man,
But w'en you know de reason w'y
I hit heem hard on bote hees eye,
An' kick heem till he nearly die,
I t'ink you 'll understan'.

If you could see ma wife an' me
   At home on Pigeon Bay,
You 'd say, "How nice dey bote agree!
Dey mus' be firse-class familee
An' go de sam' as wan, two, tree,"
I know dat 's w'at you say.

An' New Year's Day on Pigeon Bay,
   You ought to see us den,
W'it parlor feex it up so fine,
Spruce beer an' w'isky, cake an' wine,
Cigar—an' only very bes' kin'
   For treatin' all our frien'.

But on de las' New Year is pas'
De win' begin to rise,
An' snow she dreef in such a way,
W'en mornin' come, ma wife she say,
"Dere won't be many folk to-day,
Or I 'll be moche surprise."

We never see, ma wife an' me,
So quiet New Year Day,
But very happy all de sam',
An' talk a lot about de tam'
Before she come to me, ma femme,
W'ile kettle sing away.

An' as we talk, de good ole clock
Go tick, tick on de wall,
De cat 's asleep upon de stair,
De house is quiet ev'ryw'ere,
An' Jean Bateese, hees image dere,
Is smilin' over all.

I buy dat leetle Jean Bateese
On Market Bonsecour,
Two dollar an' your money down,
He 's fines' wan for miles aroun',
Can hardly beat heem on de town,
An' so I love heem sure.

W'at 's dat I hear, but never fear,
Dere 's no wan on de door?
Yass, sure enough, Joe Beliveau,
An' nearly smoder wit' de snow.
Entrez! We 're glad to see you, Joe—
W'y don't you come before?

"Bonjour, Ma-dame—Camille, your femme,
She 's younger ev'ry day;
I hope de New Year will be bright,
I hope de baby feel all right,
Don't wake you up too moche at night?"
An' dat 's w'at Joe he say.

He 's so polite it 's only right
He wish heem ev'ry t'ing
Dat 's good upon de worl' at all,
An' geev heem two tree w'at you call
Dat fancy Yankee stuff, "high ball,"
An' den he start to sing.

You dunno Joe? Wall, you mus' know
He 's purty full of life,
An' w'en he 's goin' dat way—Joe,
Mus' tak' heem leetle easy, so
I don't say not'ing w'en he go
For start an' kiss ma wife.

An' up an' down dey dance aroun'
An' laugh an' mak' de fun.
For spree lak' dat, on New Year's Day,
Is not'ing moche on Pigeon Bay,
Beside he 's frien' of me alway,
An' so dere 's no harm done.

I lak' to know jus' how it go,
Dat w'en we feel secure
Not'ing at all is goin' wrong,
An' life is lak' a pleasan' song,
De devil 's boun' to come along,
An' mak' some trouble sure.

For bimeby, Joe cock hees eye,
An' see poor Jean Bateese,
An' say right off, "If I can't show
A better wan at home, I 'll go
An' drown me on de crick below,"
So dat 's de en' of peace.

Dis very day along de Bay,
Dey tell about de fight.
Never was seen such bloody war,
On Pigeon Bay before, ba gor'!
An' easy understan' it, for
De battle las' all night.

THE GREAT FIGHT

So hard we go, dat me an' Joe
Get tire soon, an' den
We bote sit down an' tak' de res'
For half a secon', mebbe less,
An' w'en de win' come on our ches',
We start her up again.

De house is shake lak' beeg eart'quake,
De way we jump aroun',
An' people living far away,
Dey lissen hard an' den dey say,
"It 's all up, sure, wit' Pigeon Bay—
She 's tumble to de groun'."

'T was bad enough, de way we puff,
But w'en de stovepipe fall,
An' all de smoke begin to tear
Right t'roo de house, an' choke de air,
An' me an' Joe can't see no w'ere,
Dat 's very wors' t'ing of all.

It 's not a joke, de maudit smoke—
Dat 's w'at I 'm tellin' you—
But sure enough it stop de fight;
It 's easy killin' Joe all right,
But w'at about de wife all right
An' mebbe baby too?

A man dat 's brave, should always save
De woman she 's hees wife;
Dat 's firse t'ing he mus' do an' w'en
I open de door, Joe 's runnin' den,
As hard as he can lick, ma frien',
So all han's save hees life.

An' since de fight, dey 're all polite,
Dey smile an' touch de hat,
An' say, "I hope you 're feelin' purty gay,
An' no more fight on Pigeon Bay,
Or else you 'll kill a man some day."
So w'at you t'ink of dat?

Victoria Square—An Idyll

OH! we are a band of bummers, and for
many joyous summers
On the Square that 's called "Victoria" we
have sported on the green.
"Evan's Corner" erstwhile knew us, but the
blooming coppers flew us,
So we sought the kind protection of Her
Majesty the Queen.
Her Majesty the Queen!
Lord bless the big bronze Statue of Her
Majesty the Queen.

Ah, it's there we love to linger till what time
    the rosy finger
Of Aurora paints the heavens with golden
    rays serene,
And altho' our lives are "checkered," yet
    we've always held the record
For strong unchanging fealty to the Statue
    of the Queen.
        To the Statue of the Queen!
Oh! we're the Guard of Honor to the Statue
    of the Queen.

Sitting round the sun-kissed fountain, sit-
    uate between the mountain
And the river gently flowing, oh! 't is a
    pleasant scene.
For alternately the breezes from both
    sources come to please us,
As we linger round the Statue of Her Majesty
    the Queen.
        The Statue of the Queen!
As we worship round the Statue of Her
    Majesty the Queen.

Like veterans in the trenches, we occupy
    the benches,
Where we watch the busy sparrows as they
    flutter round their nests;

And the new wild-eyed bacteria we have
    introduced, would weary a
Wyatt Johnston, for he 'd find them unre-
    sponsive to his tests.
        Unresponsive to his tests!
Oh! we think we see them smiling 'neath his
    pathologic tests.

We are born of many nations, we have rules
    and regulations
Which if any member fracture, we arise in all
    our wrath—
Then you ought to hear him holler, as we
    seize him by the collar,
For well he knows his punishment necessi-
    tates a bath.
        Necessitates a bath!
Oh! the agony inflicted by the order of the
    bath!

Oh! the scientific lacin' we applied to Billy
    Mason,
And submerged him in the basin while the
    coppers were away,
And before the coppers found him, we had
    very nearly drowned him

'Cause he wore a laundered night-shirt on
  Victoria's Natal Day!
          On Victoria's Natal Day!
Tho' he said he only donned it just in honor
  of the day.

For there's one thing we take pride in 't is
  the shadow we abide in
Of the glorious law of freedom, unchange-
  abilitee;
Then let us range unfettered, tho' we may
  be unlettered,
For we furnish picturesqueness and true
  simplicitee.
          And true simplicitee,
As we camp around the Statue of Her Glorious Majestee!

Marriage

THERE's a girl at Calabogie an' another
    at the Soo,
An' with sparkin' and colloguin', I 've been
  foolish with the two;
But I 'm foolish now for ever, an' worst of
  all it come
From a girl I thought was dacint when I
  used to live at home.

She could dance to bate the fairies that my
    gran'mother 'ud tell
Over there in Ireland ha'nted what they
    call the "holy well."
She was purty as a wood-duck whin you
    see him on a tree,
But so proud and independint that she'd
    never look at me.

So it made me feel onaisy, an' I drifted
    far away,
An' I wint to Calabogie a workin' by the
    day.
Of any kind of money the place is mighty
    bare,
But a girl that took my fancy happened to
    be livin' there.

Still the other down the river—how I'd
    dream of her at night!
Spite of all the times I'd wish her gone
    completely out o' sight,
For she used to spile the comfort with the
    new wan that I had,
An' a little consolation sure I needed purty
    bad.

Thin the times begin to slacken, an' I 'm get-
    tin' hard up too,
So good-bye to Calabogie, an' I started for
    the Soo;
An' the girl I left behind me? Lord knows,
    it 's hard to tell,
But another came between, an' she liked me
    just as well.

Whin you speak of bad luck comin', mine
    is worse nor any man's—
Think of all the good intintions an' with two
    o' thim on my han's!
One of thim at Calabogie, an' the other at
    the Soo,
An' engaged to both, it 's hard to say exactly
    what to do.

The Cobalt-silver fever was the worst that 's
    ever known,
An' it came in purty handy in cases like my
    own;
Besides of all the chances, 't was the one I
    fancied best,
So I had to go prospectin' jus' the same
    as all the rest.

An' the girls, of course they suffered, for I
    had n't time to write,
Divil a thing but pick an' shovel, an' workin'
    day an' night,—
Till a dacint wild-cat claim I sold for fifteen
    thousand too—
Now I sez, "It 's all a toss-up—Calabogie or
    the Soo?"

Calabogie won it aisy, but, the next thing
    that I heard,
She got tired o' waitin' for me whin she never
    got a word;
So she married John Mahaffy—"little John"
    that runs the farm,
An' the only thing she wished me was,
    "I 'd never come to harm."

An' the Soo girl done the same thing—took
    a brakesman on a freight;
An' in Winnipeg they 're livin', so I come a
    trifle late;
But I 'm not afeared to visit Calabogie or the
    Soo,
For I 've tried to to do my duty, an' sure
    ayther wan 'ud do!

MARRIAGE

Well, I stood it for a little an' thin home agin
    I wint,
For with fifteen thousand dollars, any man
    should be contint,
An' the girl that used to give me many a
    beautiful heartache,
Sure I was n't back a fortnight, till I seen
    her at a wake.

Quiet now! No palpitation! Watch yerself,
    my laddy buck,
Take your time—don't get excited—maybe
    you 'll have better luck.
Then she said her darlin' mother missed me
    for a year or more,
'T would have saved some trouble if her
    mother spoke like that before.

"Wan thing leadeth to another" sez the
    poet—dunno who,
But we purty soon got married, so the
    prophecy come true;
An' whinever all my fortune's settled on
    the daughter sure,
Some wan seen the mother dance a sailor's
    hornpipe on the floor.

It 's no wonder I 'm distracted whin the two
   o' thim 'll say,
"Oh! Patrick, mind the baby, sure you got
   out yesterday"—
Lord forgive me, I 'd be happy if the ould
   wan only died,
But she 's healthy as a tom-cat an' she
   could n't if she tried.

I suppose I 'm doin' pinance for the sins of
   airly youth,
Tho' I blame it on the women—they betrayed
   me—that 's the truth.
But for all I know about thim, 't would have
   been the same thing too,
With the girl from Calabogie, or the other
   at the Soo.

We 're Irish Yet

WHAT means this gathering to-night?
   What spirit moves along
The crowded hall, and, touching light
   Each heart among the throng,
Awakes, as tho' a trumpet blast
   Had sounded in their ears,
The recollections of the past,
   The memories of the years?

Oh! 't is the spirit of the West,
   The spirit of the Celt,
The breed that spurned the alien breast,
   And every wrong has felt—
And still, tho' far from fatherland,
   We never can forget
To tell ourselves, with heart and hand,
   We 're Irish yet!   We 're Irish yet!

And they outside the clan of Conn
   Would understand, but fail,
The mystic music played upon
   The heart-strings of the Gael—
His ear, and his alone, can tell
   The soul that lies within,
The music which he knows so well,
   The voice of Kith and Kin.

He hears the tales of old, old days
   Of battle fierce by ford and hill,
Of ancient Senachie's martial lays,
   And race unconquered still.
It challenges with mother's pride
   And dares him to forget
That, tho' he cross the ocean wide,
   He 's Irish yet!   He 's Irish yet!

His eye may never see the blue
    Of Ireland's April sky,
His ear may never listen to
    The song of lark on high,
But deep within his Irish heart
    Are cloisters, dark and dim,
No human hand can wrench apart,
    And the lark still sings for him.

We 've bowed beneath the chastening rod,
    We 've had our griefs and pains,
But with them all, we still thank God,
    The Blood is in our veins,
The ancient blood that knows no fear,
    The Stamp is on us set,
And so, however foes may jeer,
    We 're Irish yet! We 're Irish yet.

Chibougamou

DID you ever see an air-hole on the ice
    Wit' de smoke a risin' roun' about it
    dere?
De reever should be happy w'ere it 's feelin'
    warm an' nice,
    But she t'ink she ought to get a leetle air.

An' she want to be a lookin' on de sky,
    So of course de cole win' hit her on de
    nose—

"I 'll come up again," she say, "on de
    spring tam, bimeby,
  But I 'm better now below," and off she goes.

Dat 's de way I feel mese'f on de farm a
    year ago,
  W'ere ev'ryt'ing should be a pleasan'
    dream;
Lak de foolish reever dere, I 'm not satisfy
    below,
  So I got to let me off a leetle steam.

Den a man he come along an' he say to me,
    "Look here—
  Don't you know that place dey call
    Chibougamou
W'ere de diamon' lie aroun' like de mush-
    room on de groun',
  An' dey 're findin' all de gole an' silver too?

"W'at 's de use of stayin' here den? Did n't
    Johnnie Drutusac
  Lif' de mor'gage off hees place an' buy a cow?
Only gone a leetle w'ile—hardly miss heem
    till he 's back;
  He 's easy workin' man too, an' look at
    Johnnie now?

"Well enough, ma frien', you know I can
      never tell de lie
  W'en I say de gole is comin' t'ousan'
      ounces on de ton,
An' de solid silver mak' you feel funny on de
      eye,
  Lak de snow-blin' on de winter w'en it
      shine de morning sun.

"I s'pose you won't believe, but you know
      dat gravel walk
  Ma fader got it facin' on hees house at
      St. Bidou—
But w'at 's de use of spikin', w'at 's de use
      of talk?
  Dat 's de way you see de diamon' on dat
      place Chibougamou.

"Course you got to go an' fin' dem quickly,
      or de stranger man
  Come along wit' plaintee barrel—an'
      you 're never knowin' w'en
Couple o' Yankee off the State, he was buyin'
      all de lan';
  Affer dat an' w'ere 's your gole an' silver
      goin' den?

"So, Bateese, get up an' hurry, sell de farm,
　　mon cher ami,
　　Leave de girl an' bring provision, pork an'
　　　bean, potato too,
Leetle w'isky, an' I 'll put heem on de safe
　　place under me
　　W'ile I sit an' steer you off to dat place
　　　Chibougamou."

Oh! de day an' night we 're passin', me dat
　　never was before
　　On de bush, except w'en heifer go away
　　　an' den got los';
Oh! de pullin' an' de haulin', till I 'm feelin'
　　purty sore,
　　But of all de troub an' worry, de skeeter,
　　　he 's de boss.

Beeg? lak de leetle two-mont' robin. Sing?
　　lak a sawmill on de spring.
　　Put de blanket roun' your body an' den
　　　he bite you troo.
Me, I never tak' hees measure, but I t'ink
　　across de wing
　　He 's t'ree inch sure—dem skeeter, on dat
　　　place Chibougamou.

De man he's goin' wit' me, never paddle,
    never haul,
    Jus' smoke an' watch an' lissen for dat
        ole Chibougamou;
I s'pose he can't be bodder doin' any work
    at all,
    For de feller tak' you dere jus' have
        not'ing else to do.

T'ousan' mile we mak' de travel—t'ousan'
    mile an' mebbe more,
    An' I do de foolish prayin' lak' I never
        pray at home,
'Cos I want a chance to get it, only let me
    see de shore
    Of Chibougamou a little w'ile before de
        winter come.

No use prayin', no use climbin' on de beeg
    tree ev'ry day,
    Lookin' hard to see de diamon', an' de
        silver, an' de gole—
I can't see dem, an' de summer she begin to
    go away,
    An' de day is gettin' shorter, an' de night
        is gettin' cole.

CHIBOUGAMOU

So I kick an' raise de row den, an' I tole
ma frien' lookout—
Purty quick de winter's comin' an'
we 'll hurry up an' go;
Never min' de gole an' silver—diamon' too
we 'll go widout,
Or de only wan we 're seein', is de diamon'
on de snow.

Mebbe good place w'en you get dere, w'at
you call Chibougamou,
But if we never fin' it, w'at 's de use
dat place to me?
'Tak' de paddle, for we 're goin', an' mese'f
I 'll steer canoe,
For I 'm always firse-class pilot on de road
to St. Elie.

Oh! to see me on de mornin', an' de way I
mak' heem sweat,
You can see de water droppin' all aroun'
hees neck an' face;
"Now, Chibougamou," I tell heem, "hurry
up, an' mebbe yet
You 'll have chance again to try it w'en you
leave me on ma place."

399

So we have a beeg procession, w'en we pass
    on St. Elie,
  All de parish comin' lookin' for de gole an'
    silver too,
But Louise, she cry so moche dere, jus' becos
    she 's seein' me,
  She forget about de diamon' on dat ole
    Chibougamou.

Affer all is gone an' finish, an' you mak' a fool
    you' se'f,
  An' de worl' is go agen you, w'at 's de
    medicine is cure
Lak de love of hones' woman w'en she geev
    it all herse'f?
  So Louise an' me is happy, no matter if
    we 're poor.

So de diamon' may be plaintee, lak de gravel
    walk you see
  W'en you 're comin' near de house of ole
    Telesphore Beaulieu,
But me, I got a diamon' on ma home on
    St. Elie
  Can beat de pil is lyin' on dat place
    Chibougamou.

The First Robin

OH! it's bad to be unlucky in ev'ryt'ing
   you do,
   An' worse if you can't help it, 'cos I'm
      de torteen chile,
An' w'en you play for number wan, an' den
      you're number two,
   I wonder w'ere's de feller he don't feel a
      leetle rile?

Few mont' ago it happen dat I'm goin' walk
      aroun',
   Gettin' ready for de ploughin' is comin' on
      de spring,
An' soon I wait an' listen, for I t'ink I hear
      de song
   Of de firse, de early robin, as he jus'
      begin to sing.

It was very, very lucky w'en de firse wan
      come along—
   An' you see upon your farm dere is de
      place de robin stop,
Settle down to feex hees fedder, an' com-
      mence to mak' hees song—
   For o' course it's always makin' beeg dif-
      ference wit' de crop.

So I sneak aroun' so quiet, t'roo de orchard on
de hill,
T'roo de fence, along de crik too, w'ere
de snow is lyin' yet—
Ev'ry kin' o' luck again me as I travel dere
until
Ba de tam de job is finish, golly, I was
feelin' wet!

W'at 's de matter wit' dat robin, dat he
is n't comin' here,
'Stead o' goin' half an acre jus' to tak'
de luck away?
No Siree!—I don't forgive heem, if he leev
a honder year,
For dere 's hees singin', singin' on de farm
of Joe Lahaie.

Joe hese'f is sittin' dere too, lookin' happy
on hees face,
For de way dat bird is yellin', is enough to
scare de dead;
An' he ax me, "W'at you doin' sneakin'
all aroun' ma place?
Don't you know I own dat robin he was
singin' overhead?

"Mebbe he was work for not'ing, my leetle
      boy Louis,
   W'en he's startin' out dis mornin' for
      milkin' on de cow,
An' he fin' dat robin flyin' purty near your
      apple-tree,
   An' he shoo heem up, an' bring heem on
      de place you see heem now.

"Did n't get heem off too early, for anoder
      minute more
   An' I bet dat robin's singin' among your
      apple-tree;
But de boy's too smart to let heem, an' he
      scare heem here before
   He begin to mak' de music—so dat bird
      belong to me.

"Talk about your lucky season! Wait an' see
      de wan I got;
   Should n't wonder if I'm needin' anoder
      wagon sure.
How I wish de fall would hurry, for de crop
      your uncle get,
   It will mak' dem all go crazy on de market
      Bonsecours.

"Me—I lissen many robin, an' de fines' of
    de crowd
  Is de wan dat 's sittin' up dere, workin'
    w'at you call de charm;
Dat 's de robin for ma money, he can holler
    out so loud,
  But o' course de res' was alway on some
    oder feller's farm.

"Only sorry ma ole woman is n't comin' here
    to see,
  For she can't help feelin' happy w'en de
    firse bird of de spring
Mak' hees choice upon our tree dere, jus' so
    natural an' free,
  Non! She would n't tak' a dollar ev'ry
    tam dat feller sing."

An' he sit an' smoke away dere, Joe Lahaie,
    an' talk hees fill,
  He 's all right, an' *he* don't bodder how de
    res' de parish go;
Never hear a man so foolish, mak' me feelin'
    mad until
  I could kill dat maudit robin, an' Jo-seph
    Lahaie also.

An' den bimeby de summer come along, but
w'at 's de use
   Call it summer, for de fine day is w'at we
seldom get.
So I tak' it purty easy, for de man mus' be a
goose
   If he don't kip nice an' quiet, w'en de
wedder she 's so wet.

But Joe Lahaie, dat feller, he was t'ink so
moche, ba gum,
   About hees poor ole robin, he forget about
de rain;
Ev'ry day you see heem workin', an' w'en
de fall is come
   He got de fines' crop upon St. Polycarpe de
plaine.

An' me—Wall! I could bet you, w'en de
springtam' melt de snow,
   I 'll never go to bed unless I 'm sleepin'
on ma pants;
Den w'en I hear de robin, hoopla! off she
go,
   An' he 'll never lef' ma garden, so I 'll
have anoder chance!

Bloom—A Song of Cobalt

OH! the blooming cheek of beauty, tho'
    it's full of many a peril,
Where's the miner does n't love it? for he
    thinks he knows the girl,
While the bloomer! Oh! the bloomer! of
    emancipated She,
May it bloom and promptly wither every
    seventh century.

Oh! the early bloom of blossom on the apple
    tree in June,
Is there mortal having seen it, can forget
    the picture soon?
And the wine of red October where Falernian
    juices flow,
I have sipped the blooming beaker (in the
    ages long ago!).

Oh! the bloom along the hill-side, shining
    bright among the trees,
When the banners of the autumn are flung
    out to every breeze,
How it blazes—how it sparkles, and then
    shivers at a breath:
What is it when all is spoken but the awful
    bloom of death!

Oh! I 've watched the rose's petals, and be-
    held the summer sun
Dipping down behind Olympus, when the
    great day's work was done;
But to-day I 'm weary, weary , and the
    bloom I long to see,
Is the bloom upon the cobalt—that 's the
    only bloom for me.

The Boy from Calabogie

HE was twenty-one in April—forty inches
    round the chest,
  A soupler or a better boy we 'll never see
    again—
And the way we cheered the lad when he
    started for the West!
  The town was like a holiday, the time he
    took the train
            At Calabogie.

"Are ye ever comin' back with the fortune,
    little Dan,
  From the place they say the money 's like
    the leaves upon the tree?"
"If the minin' boss 'll let me, as sure as I 'm
    a man,
  The mother's Christmas turkey won't have
    to wait for me
            At Calabogie."

407

And the letters he was writin' to his mother
  from the West,
 Sure ev'rybody read them, and who could
  see the harm?
Tellin' how he 'd keep the promise to come
  home and have a rest;
 And the money that was in them was
  enough to buy a farm
    At Calabogie.

What is it that makes the fever leave the
  weak and kill the strong,
 And who 'd 'a' thought our Dannie would
  ever come to this?
When the Sister had to raise him, and say,
  "It won't be long
 Till it 's home, my lad, you 're goin' to
  receive a mother's kiss
    At Calabogie."

So we met our little Dannie, Christmas morn-
  ing at the train,
 And we lifted up the long-box without a
  word to say;
Och! such a boy as Dannie we 'll never see
  again
 God forgive us! 't was n't much of a Merry
  Christmas Day
    At Calabogie!

The Calcite Vein—A Tale of Cobalt

I USED to be leevin' on Bonami,
  Fines' place on de lake, you bet!
An' dough I go off only wance sapree!
  I t'ink I will leev' dere yet;
Wit' tree growin' down to de water side,
  W'ere leetle bird dance an' sing—
Only come an' see you don't shout wit' me
  Hooraw for Temiskaming!

But silver "boom" an de cobalt bloom,
  Play de devil wit' Bonami,
So off on de wood, we all mus' go,
  Leavin' de familee—
Shovel an' pick, hammer an' drill,
  We carry dem ev'ryw'ere,
For workin' away all night an' day
  Till it 's tam to be millionaire.

So it ain't very long w'en I mak' de strike,
  W'at dey 're callin' de vein cal-cite,
Quarter an inch, jus' a leetle "pinch,"
  But she is come all right
An' widen out beeg: mebbe wan sixteen,
  An' now we have got her sure;
So we jump on our hat w'en she go like dat,
  Me an' Bateese Couture!

Early in de spring we see dat vein,
   W'en de pat-ridge begin to drum,
De leaf on de bush start in wit' a rush,
   An' de skeeter commence to come—
Very nice time on de wood for sure,
   If you want to be goin' die,
Skeeter at night till it 's come daylight,
   An' affer dat, small black fly!

Couple o' gang like dat, ma frien',
   'Specially near de swamp,
An' hongry too, dey can bite an' chew,
   An' keep you upon de jomp;
But never you min', only work away
   So long as de vein is dere,
For a t'ing so small don't count at all,
   If you want to be millionaire!

"An' dis is de price," Bateese he say,
   "T'ree million or not'ing at all."
An' I say, "You 're crazy, it 's five you mean,
   An' more if you wait till fall.
An' s'pose de silver was come along,
   An' cobalt she bloom an' bloom,
We look very sick if we sole too quick,
   An' ev'ryt'ing 's on de boom."

THE CALCITE VEIN—A TALE OF COBALT

De cash we refuse w'en dey hear de news—
    W'en I t'ink of dat cash to-day,
I feel like a mouse on a great beeg house,
    W'en de familee move away:
One million, two million, no use to us,
    Me an' Bateese Couture,
So we work away ev'ry night an' day,
    De sam' we was alway poor.

An' den one morning a stranger man,
    A man wit' hees hair all w'ite,
Look very wise, an' he 's moche surprise
    W'en he 's seein' dat vein cal-cite.
An' he say, "Ma frien', for de good advice
    I hope you 'll mak' some room—
From sweetheart girl to de wide, wide worl',
    Ketch ev'ryt'ing on de bloom.

"Keep your eye on de vein, for dere 's many
      a slip
    Till you drink of de silver cup,
An' if you 're not goin' to go 'way down,
    You 're goin' to go 'way, 'way up."

"Now w'at does he mean?"   Bateese he say,
    Affer de ole man lef',
"Mebbe want to buy, but he t'ink it 's high,
    So we 'll finish de job ourse'f.

Purty quick too." An' den hooraw!
   We form it de compagnie,
An' to give dem a sight on de vein cal-cite,
   We work it on Bonami.

Can't count de money dat 's comin' in,
   Same as de lotterie;
Ev'ry wan try, till bimeby
   Dere 's not many dollar on Bonami;
An' de gang we put onto de job right off,
   Nearly twenty beside de cook,
Hammer an' drill till dey 're nearly kill,
   An' feller to watch de book.

Too many man, an' I see it now,
   An' I 'm sorry, 'cos I 'm de boss;
For walkin' aroun' all over de groun',
   Dat 's reason de vein get los',
Easy enough wit' de lantern too,
   Seein' dat vein las' night,
But to-day I 'm out lookin' all about,
   An' w'ere is dat vein cal-cite?

Very curious t'ing, but you can't blame me,
   For I try very hard, I 'm sure,
Helpin' dem all till de vein is gone,
   Me an' Bateese Couture;

So of course I wonder de way she go,
  An' twenty cent too a share,
An' I can't understan' dat stranger man
  W'at he mean w'en he 's sayin' dere:

"Keep your eye on de vein, for there 's many
      a slip
  Till you drink of de silver cup,
An' if you 're not goin' to go way down
  You 're goin' to go 'way, 'way up."

Pierre Leblanc

(Dedicated to the Hon. Peter White)

EV'RY State upon de Union, w'en dey
    write her up to-day,
Have so many kin' of story not many under-
    stan';
But if you lissen me you can very quickly
    see
How it 's easy t'ing remember de State of
    Michigan.
An' me I know it 's true, 'cos ma fader tole
    me so,
How dat voyageur dey 're callin' Père Mar-
    quette
Come a-sailin' hees canoe, wit' de Injun from
    de Soo,
On de year so long ago dat I forget.

But wan t'ing I can say, w'en Marquette is
    reach de shore
W'ere w'at you call hees statue is stickin'
    up to-day,
Dere's a leetle French boy dere say, "Com-
    ment ça va, mon père,
You been so long a-comin' I hope you're
    goin' to stay?"
An' he show heem safes' place w'ere he put
    hees birch canoe,
An' de way he talk an' boss de Injun man—
Wall, it's very easy see dat between you' se'f
    an' me,
Dat leetle feller's born to comman'.

An' Marquette he's moche surprise at de
    smart boy he has got,
W'ere he come from, w'at's hees name, an'
    ev'ryt'ing;
But de boy he go ahead feexin' up de camp
    an' bed,
For he alway treat hees frien' jus' lak de King.
Marquette he den fin' out w'at de leetle
    feller know,
An' w'at he never see, an' all de Grosse
    Point law;
How it's mixit up so moche ev'rybody's
    scare to touch,
An' de nam' he call hese'f is Pierre Leblanc.

Wall, Marquette he 's not a fool, so he 's sayin'
    "Au revoir,"
For leetle Pierre Leblanc 's too wide awake·
No chance discoveree, so far as he can see,
Less he fin' some newer place upon de lak'.
So dere he stay upon de shore, de leetle
    Pierre,
An' buil' de fines' log house he can get;
Purty soon he have a town on de place he
    settle down,
An' call it for hees frien' M'sieu Marquette.

But de folk he 's bringin' dere fin' it hard
    w'en winter come
An' ev'ry place is pilin' wit' de snow;
Den who is volunteer bring de letter 'way
    up here,
From de contree lyin' off dere down below?
Was it feller six foot high is on de job,
Carry letter all de way from Canadaw,
Wit' hees fourteen-dog-traineau, bangin' t'roo
    de ice an' snow?
No siree! It 's only leetle Pierre Leblanc.

But de way he treat hees dog dey say is very
    bad,
Many folk is talkin' all about it yet.

So of course dey 're comin' back lak de
  racer on de track,
For hees dog, dey don't get not'ing till
  dey 're passin' on Marquette.
Wall, I s'pose he 's very poor, Pierre Leblanc,
An' de pay he 's gettin' for it 's purty small,
An' he got to eat hese'f, or mebbe he was lef',
So we never get our letter affer all.

An' den he start to grow, an' de way he work,
  dey say,
For de folk on ole Marquette an' all aroun',
Mak' heem very populaire on de contree
  ev'ryw'ere,
Till he t'ink he was de beeges' man in town.
Den hees head begin to swell, 'cos ma fader
  tole me so,
An' firse t'ing he was puttin' on de beeges'
  style he can;
But he ought to be ashame for de way he
  change hees name
To Peter White, an' try to pass for only
  Yankee man.

Mebbe leetle Injun too, can't say for dat
  mese'f,
For he alway spik sauvage de sam' as Ojibway

An' w'en he want to swear it's enough to
　　raise de hair
To hear heem sayin' "Wabigoon ah—goozah
　　—goozah—gay."
An' lak' de Injun, too, very hard to tell hees
　　age,
For he mus' be over honder, dough he's
　　lookin' forty year;
An' he's alway on de rush, you can't lose
　　heem on de bush,
An' hees eye is lak de eagle, strong an' clear.

An' he's leevin' wit' us now, Pierre Leblanc
　　dit Peter White,
But we won't say not'ing more about hees
　　name;
Let heem try it if he can, makin' out he's
　　Yankee man,
But never min', for Pierre Leblanc he's
　　good man jus' de sam'.
So if you want to know de State of Mich-
　　igan,
Very easy to remember—in case you might
　　forget—
Only two man mak' her go, 'cos ma fader
　　tole me so,
An' wan is M'sieu Pierre Leblanc, de oder
　　Père Marquette.

Silver Lake Camp

THE bleak wind sighs thro' the leafless
    trees
  Like a spirit's wail, and the white snow-
      flake
Drifts silently down with the fitful breeze
  On the lonely camp at Silver Lake.

Yet the ruddy glow of our camp-fire bright,
  Not long ago, when the fall was young,
Illumined the gathering shades of night,
  And the forest rang with the songs we
    sung.

But the song is hushed, and the merry jest
  Is heard no more, when the shadows fall;
For gone is each well-remembered guest,
  And the snow like a mantle covereth all.

Full oft, while the bright September moon
  Beamed down, did the startled camp
      awake
From its slumbers deep, as the wizard loon
  Pealed its wild cry from the neighbor-
    ing lake.

418

But the loon has taken his airy flight,
    And far away neath the southern cloud
He rests his wings, while the Frost King's might,
    Has wrapped the lake in an icy shroud.

No longer our light bark ploughs the wave,
    No longer we tempt the treacherous flood,
No sentinels watch o'er the old camp, save
    The guardian genii of the wood.

The Tale of a Cocktail

DEAR MR. EDITOR,

It has always been my camping experience that the oldest among us, especially if he be a grey-haired patriarch, is invariably the greatest "alcoholic tempter" of the party. He it is who generally paralyzes the energies of his more youthful brethren with the matutinal cocktail; hence my "Tale of a Cocktail":

THE Patriarch rose at the break of day,
        Ere the mists from the mountain had
            fled away,
And loudly his merry roundelay,
        Rang over hill and vale:
"Spirit of morn, we greet thee!
Gladly we rise to meet thee, ·
Difficult 't is to beat thee,
        Matutinal Cocktail!"

A shudder ran thro' the listening throng,
For many a time we had heard that song,
And feared, alas! he was making it strong,
      This sour cocktail.
But the sage went on with his morning lay,
And no man dared to utter nay—
Ah! little recked he what we might say,
      This Patriarch hale.

Thus he spake with deep emotion:
"Trust me, 't is a soothing potion,
      For your stomach's sake;
To reject what heaven has sent us
Is to be non compos mentis—
How much aqua bullientis
      Will you take?"

We fell on our knees with despairing cry,
And prayed that for once he would pass us
    by,
For we felt that should we that cocktail try,
      'T would be our ruin.
King Canute, 't is written on history's page,
Endeavored the billows wild to cage—
'T were easier task than restrain the Sage,
      Who still kept brewin'.

While his happy gladsome singing,
Set the hills and valleys ringing,
We were kept "ingredients" bringing,
  Much against our will:
Lagavulin, Angostura,
Which he told us would ensure a
Sound digestion, also cure a
  Sudden cold, or stop a chill.

The hills re-echoed our solemn chant,
"Te morituri salutant;
Grant us some mercy, however scant,
  This awful hour!"
But sterner and colder his visage grew,
No pity, alas! the Patriarch knew;
Hope shrieking fled as we watched him brew
  His cocktail sour.

"Let none escape," was his dire command,
"For I swear to-day, by my good right hand,
That all who refuse their cocktail stand
  On death's cold brink."
The Patriarch's awful accents fell
On our frightened ears like a funeral knell,
So bidding, each other a last farewell,
  We took our drink.

. . . .

The lusty salmon in vain may "rise,"
The merry troutlets may gaily play,
But the green, green sward where our white
    tent lies
Is good enough for us to-day.
For we 're tired—so tired—and weary too,
As we sink into dreamy reverie,
And we feel that our dreams are not all true.
The world is n't just what it seems to be.

   .   .   .   .

The tides may ebb, and the tides may flow,
And the river gleam in the valley below,
But never again shall we fishing go,
      Till the Sage's hour
Has come,—and he goes to the golden shore,
Where we trust he 'll be happy for ever more,
But we fear he may meet us at the door
      With a cocktail sour!

The Land we Live in and the Land we Left

Written for the menu of the Irish Protestant Benevolent
Society's annual dinner.   March 18, 1895.

THE children of the Western Gael
    Are gathered here this Patrick's night,
To pledge the dear old Innisfail,
To drink her health in bumpers bright.

'T is true we may not see her more,
Still we 're not likely to forget,
And though we 've sought another shore,
We 're Irish yet!   We 're Irish yet!

Deer-Hunting—(*By an Expert*)

YOU see I was there on the run-way,
    Just near where it enters the lake,
Could n't get better place if I tried it,
For the deer would be certain to take
To the water the moment he saw it,
And then I could pump in the lead
At ten or a dozen yards distance,
Till I could n't help killing him dead.
      (Oh! 't was great sport!)

(And the excitement!)
There I sat watching and waiting,
For maybe an hour or two,
I could hear my poor heart go a-throbbing,
And once, when a chipmunk drew
Near to my trembling ambush,
I had almost pulled trigger, when
He ran up a silver birch tree,
And I saw 't was a chipmunk then.
      (But 't was great!)

423

I could see the bright leaves of the autumn,
Sprinkling the forest floor,
Each leaf all bespattered with crimson,
As if dipt in the blood of more
Than a thousand innocent victims.
But, pshaw! 't was the frost and rain,
So I said to myself, "Old fellow,
Brace up!   Be a man again!"
      (And I braced.)

Then suddenly, over the hill-side,
Where the hounds killed a fawn last year,
An echo kept ringing, ringing,
'T was the baying of "Chanticleer."
"He 's got him at last," I murmur,
"And the old dog will make him jump,"
So my hold on the rifle tightened,
While my heart went thumpity-thump.

(Holy murder!)
Here he comes down the pathway,
Good Lord! how he must have run!
But with "Chanty" let out on the home-
    stretch,
Don't suppose he enjoyed the fun,
Hardly able to bring his legs with him.
Well! don't get excited yet!
Just wait till he reaches the water,
Then fill him before he gets wet.

Keep still! Why! I can hear him breathing,
And now he has passed so close,
The point of the rifle could touch him,
And easily give him a dose.
Just see how he jumped when he smelt me,
And look how he struggles and pants,
But I'll wait till he gets to the water,
And give the poor devil a chance,
      (That's right, is n't it?)

And now he has entered the water,
And when he has gone ten yards or so,
I bang away, bang! with the Marlin
Till I find I've killed a doe.
But a nice little doe I can tell you,
Is better than nothing at all,
So if Providence only spares me,
I'll try it again next fall.
      (D. V.)

"*He only Wore a Shamrock*" *

HE only wore a shamrock
    On his faithful Irish breast,
Maybe a gift from his colleen oge,
The maiden whom he loved best;

---

* Heading *Montreal Gazette*, March 18, 1894.
"Private O'Grady, 87th Regt., for wearing a shamrock in his buttonhole Patrick's Day, was court-martialed."

But the emblem of dear old Ireland,
Tho' worn on a jacket of red,
Was the emblem of rank disloyalty,
And treason most foul, they said.

Had he but borne the heather,
That grows on the Scottish hills,
A rose from an English garden,
Or a leek from the Cambrian rills,
Then he might summon his comrades,
With trumpet, and fife, and drum,
And march through the breadth of England,
Till trumpet and fife were dumb.
But he only wore a shamrock,
And tho' Britain's most gracious Queen
Had pinned her cross on his bosom,
Yet the little trefoil of green
Might not nestle down beside it,
For the color, alas! was banned,
And the Celtic soldier was made to feel
That he trod an alien land.

Oh! poor little modest symbol,
Of the glorious Trinity,
Rather bloom on your native hill-side,
Than cross the dark Irish sea;

Rather rest on the loving bosom,
Of the Mother that gave you birth,
For even *your* virtues can't chasten
The ungrateful English earth.

The Godbout

OH! pilgrim from the Godbout's shore
　　Where broad Atlantic billows roll,
Speak! hast thou seen the Commodore,
Whose brave unconquerable soul,
Athirst for wilder, fiercer game
Than haunt the calm Laurentian streams,
Burned to achieve a greater fame,
And realize his fondest dreams?
Speak! hast thou seen his grizzled locks,
By ocean's vagrant breezes fanned,
Where Weymahegan's giant rocks
Keep watch and ward o'er sea and land?
Hast seen him where the currents lave
Fair Mistassini's silver shore,
On river—sea—by land or wave,
Speak! hast thou seen the Commodore?
The pilgrim spoke—while down his cheek
The salt, salt tears coursed grievously:

"Good Sir, I feeble am and weak,
Yet I my tale may tell to thee—

I saw the veteran's wasted form,
That form we used to mark with pride,
Lie prostrate mid the wrack and storm
Of Weymahegan's awful tide.
Small strength, alack! of wind or limb
Had he upon that fearful day;
But, tho' his eagle eye was dim,
He still gazed o'er the hills where lay
The Laurentides, where he had spent
So many happy, happy hours,
Safe from the storms of life, content
Amid the Pêche's tranquil bowers.
'T was thus he spoke: 'Oh! why was I
By youthful traveller's tale beguiled
To quit the pleasant Pêche and die
In this inhospitable wild?
What lured me on to cast aside
The simple pleasures of my youth,
Until I longed for Godbout's tide—
And cared no more for trout, forsooth!
Oh! rash was I to lend an ear,
To all the legends of the sea,
To bring my faithful legion here—
Does this reward their constancy?
I cannot say, but this I know,
That should I view the Pêche again,
Could I but see its waters flow,
I 'd be the humblest of the train
That worships there; no more I 'd roam

In search of other piscine fields;
Contented with my humble home,
With all that old Laurentian yields,
I 'd gladly live and cheerful die.'
But here his accents 'gan to sink;
He thought his hour had come, till I
Administered a generous drink.
The Veteran gasped, but when the flask
He saw—tho' feeble as a child—
Bravely essayed the pleasant task
Of trying to empty it, and smiled.
Yes, tho' he 'd almost passed away
In one brief moment from our ken—
Yet wondrous 't was to see that day
His rapturous look, as he smiled again.
New strength came back to the wasted
    limbs,
The roses bloomed in his cheek once more,
And the sound of our glad thanksgiving
    hymns
Rang out o'er Weymahegan's shore;
He prayed us to pardon his misdeeds,
He wept when the legion embraced his neck,
And swore by the sacred Laurentides,
He 'd never more venture below Quebec.
So gently we bore the repentant Chief,
Tenderly placed him that awful day
On board of the gallant ship " Relief"
And swiftly to westward sailed away."

The Pilgrim ceased—his mournful task
Was ended at last, and all was well—
Then raised to his lips the magic flask,
And silently bade me a last farewell.

PÆAN

Joy! Joy at the Pêche—let the cariboo
    dance,
Let the fatted oxen at last be slain,
Let the men get full, and the bull moose
    prance,
For the Commodore has come home again!

Doonside

TO me, whose paddle-blade has cleft
    The wave where great St. Lawrence
    flows—
To me, whose ears have heard the scream
Of eagle, high above the snows,
Where Fraser darts among the hills—
What is this tiny stream to me?
And what the little melody
My soul with rapture fills,
Like some old half-forgotten croon?
A cradle song of long ago—
A mother's song so sweet and low—
    Hush! It is the Doon!

The Spanish Bird*

TELL me, O bird from the land of the Cid
    Why do thy tail feathers droop so low;
Why art thou mute that was wont to bid
    Fiercest defiance to every foe?

No longer thy clarion voice rings out,
    Pealing like thunder from earth to sky,
Waking the Pêche with thy joyous shout,
    Till rival roosters were forced to fly.

The Rooster Loquacious;

"Once I was youthful and passing fair,
    Captured first prizes at many a show,
Could lick all the birds ever flew in air,
    And beat record time on the heel and toe.

" Proud was I then of my martial past,
    Vain was I too of my gay topknot,
Successful in war and skilled in court,
    Gallinaceous beauties my favors sought.

" But family cares when I settled down
    Made the gallant topknot droop day by day,
The white wings faded—my ruddy crown
    Disappeared, till those charms had all fled
      away.

* From *Songs of Old Spain*, by the author of *Hispaniola*,
or The Lay of the Last Rooster.

"Pardon these tears, by emotion stirred,
  But keenest sorrow of all to know
Is that once I was known as the 'sacred bird,
  And now they call me 'sacré oiseau!'"

Boule

WAY back on de woods I know a man,
    Was very good hunter too;
No bodder at all to understan'
    De moose an' de cariboo.
An' wedder you 're meetin' heem on de bush,
    Or trampin' de hills aroun',
You always t'ink he was sayin', "Hush!"
    For he never mak' de soun'.

De fox w'en he 's seein' dat hunter's track
    Jus' shiver hese'f an' go,
An' say, "De noise dat hunter mak'
    Is de noise of de fallin' snow—
Don't geev me a chance, an' dat 's de way
    I pity de poor ole bear,
Never hear not'ing on stormy day,
    W'en danger is ev'ry w'ere."

Is dere an otter along de creek,
    Or mink on de beeg savanne,
Don't jomp on de water purty quick
    W'en he 's hearin' dat hunter man?

Now! an' w'at 's de reason he get so cute,
   Till hees luck is de devil's own?
Wall! it 's only becos' w'en he mak' de shoot,
   He travel aroun' alone.

But ev'ry t'ing change, an' so I 'm tole,
   Affer a long, long tam,
De hunter man change, for he 's comin' ole,
   Dough he tell us he 's jus' de sam';
An' bimeby w'en he 's sittin' dere
   Wan day on a tamarac log,
He say to hese'f, "I wonder w'ere
   I can get me a leetle dog?

"Nice leetle dog wit' stan'up tail,
   Follow me t'roo de wood,
Stick to me close along de trail,
   An' me, I will treat heem good:
Train heem up right, an' dere won't be need
   Havin' heem play de fool."
So he 's buyin' a dog—I dunno de breed—
   An' de nex' t'ing he call heem "Boule."

So he train dat dog till he 's nearly dead,
   Or wishin' hese'f in jail—
W'en to lie down, never show hees head,
   W'en he can wag hees tail;

Show heem de very bes' way to smell
    On de bush, if he 's passin' t'roo,
An' out on de lake he can do so well,
    He never upset canoe.

Wonderful dog! an' now an' den,
    Affer he finish up,
He 's takin' heem off to show hees frien'
    How he was train de pup.
"Come along, Boule, kip close to me,
    Steady, an' watch de groun',
Wait till I tell you go an' see
    If anyt'ing 's lyin' aroun'."

An' to see heem walk, dat hunter man,
    An' to hear heem talk also:
"Easy, ma frien', de bes' you can,
    Easy, an nice an' slow.
Dis is de heart of de game countree,
    Partridge on ev'ry log,
Tranquillement! for de leaf, saprée,
    Was never so dry—but w'ere 's de dog?

"Boule! Boule! Boule! Boule!"
    (Den he would raise de row!)
"Boule! Boule! you ole fool—
    W'y do you leave me now?"

BOULE

'Way on de right, w'ere de bush is t'ick,
   Dere 's a rush, an' we see a tail,
Long enough too to mak' us sick,
   An' a cariboo go full sail,
Flyin' along wit' de pup behin',
   Yellin' hees head off sure—
Maudit! if dat dog he was only mine,
   I very soon work de cure!

Yass! if to-morrow will ketch nex' wick,
   Or ma gran'moder ketch de moon,
He 's gettin some chance if he travel quick
   For ketchin' heem jus' as soon.
An' affer he 's scarin' dat cariboo,
   Back he was come encore,
Lookin' so proud of de job he do,
   An' de hunter man start some more.

"Careful now—don't mak' a noise,
   Creep on your han' an' knee;
Some of you men are jus' lak boys
   Comin' from school—saprée.
Don't you see de dog? for he's gone again,
   Off to I dunno w'ere"—
An' den lak a rushin' railway train
   We 're hearin' a beeg moose dere.

435

Tearin' along across de hill,
  Up w'ere de pine tree grow,
Poor leetle Boule a' follerin' still,
  An' hollerin' as he go!
Mebbe de hunter 's not gettin' mad
  W'en he commence to say,
"Sorry I be, but dere 's somet'ing bad
  Wrong wit' de dog to-day.

"Boule! Boule! Boule! Boule!"
  (Oh, how he raise de row!)
"Boule! Boule! you ole fool—
  W'y do you leave me now?"

"Very fine way to hunt de wood!"
  Dat 's w'at we tell heem den;
"Nice leetle dog"—it 's all no good,
  An' he say: "I dunno, ma frien',
Mebbe you 're right—w'en a man he 's ole,
  Can't learn heem a trick is new,
An' jus' as soon as de dog is sole,
  I 'll hunt as I used to do."

So he 's sellin' hees dog on Joe Laflamme,
  Kip de toll on de bridge below,
Never have dog he lak de sam',
  Dat 's w'at he 's sayin', Joe.

436

Now he 's beginning for feelin' well,
  Now he can sleep on de chair all day,
For Boule 's commencin' to mak' a yell
  W'en customer 's less dan a mile away.

Dat 's all right—an' de hunter man
  Travel agen as he used to do,
All alone, an' I understan'
  Gettin' de ole tam luck also.

Cauda Morrhuae

POOR little Tommy Cod
  Took his best fishing-rod,
Cunningly fashioned of split bamboo;
Likewise his tackle,
Of red and brown hackle,
To venture down stream in his bark canoe.

Tommy had registered,
Solemnly, I have heard,
Promised and vowed, that ere evening fell
Doré and speckled trout,
Black bass and bull-pout,
Would cheerfully yield to his magic spell.

Since time immemorial,
In things piscatorial,
Tho' Magog be famed among knights of the rod;

437

Yet, making due limit
For what may be in it,
Little Tommy might know it was no *plaice*
    for *Cod*.

Now, in the buoyant sea,
There's so much buoyancy
A *Cod* if he wishes can easily float;
But in the swift Magog,
Why, even a bullfrog.
Would much *rudder perch* on the side of a boat.

I told him the dangers
That all who are strangers
Might meet with, in case they should venture
    below;
For the mill-dam's so *turbot*
No mortal can curb it,
As those who have tried it must certainly
    know.

O Tommy, take care of
Your life and beware of
The treacherous mill-dam you shortly shall
    view!
But Tommy was vain and
He quitted the mainland,
And put out to sea in his frail canoe.

CAUDA MORRHUAE

The craft like an arrow
Sped down the long, narrow,
And turbulent channel, where wild billows rave;
Then past Point MacFarlane,
Like shot from a *marlin*,
Poor Tommy swept on to his watery grave.

When Tom struck the mill-dam,
The mill-dam, the mill-dam,
When Tom struck the mill-dam, he dam'd
 the dam'd mill;
Why should he strike it,
When there's nothing like it
To test all the best of a mariner's skill?

I saw the craft *flounder*,
As fiercely around her
The hungry waves leapt on the ill-fated prey;
And each time they struck her
Poor *Cod* cried for *sucker*,
But *sucker* was scarce on that terrible day.

To throw in the river
Some oil of cod liver,
And thereby the grim foaming waters becalm,
Was Tom's next endeavor,
But he found that his lever
Was all out of order, and not worth a dam
 (mill-dam).

CAUDA MORRHUAE

At last he went under,
And, faith! 't was no wonder,
For a *Cod* should n't go where he does n't
    belong;
"Requiescat in pace"
I murmur, in case he
Should *rise* and object to this mournful song.

. . . .

We found him next morning—
A sorrowful warning;
The short line we chartered, and shipped
    him by rail
To distant Atlantic,
By way of Megantic,
And so I 've arrived at the end of my *tail*.

Index to Titles

INDEX TO TITLES

INDEX TO TITLES

INDEX TO TITLES

Index to First Lines

INDEX TO FIRST LINES

INDEX TO FIRST LINES

447

INDEX TO FIRST LINES

INDEX TO FIRST LINES

)